Advertising Design and Typography

Alex W. White

ALLWORTH PRESS

NEW YORK

12   11   10   5   4   3   2

Published by Allworth Press
An imprint of Allworth Communications
10 East 23rd Street, New York, NY 10010

Book design, typography, and composition by
Alexander W. White, New York, NY

Library of Congress Cataloging-in-Publication Data
White, Alex (Alex W.)
Advertising Design and Typography/Alex W. White.
   p. cm.
   Includes index.

ISBN-13: 978-1-58115-465-8 (hardcover)
ISBN-10: 1-58115-465-8 (hardcover)
1. Commercial art.
2. Graphic design (Typography)
i. Title.
   NC997.W493 2006
   741.609'0511-dc22
   2006028418

Printed in Thailand

Advertising Design and Typography
Alex W. White

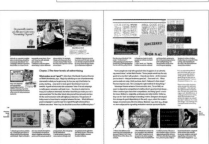

102

130

142

170

192

vii

Contents

Preface
The need for better advertising design

What makes an ad *good*? Without having a clear definition, it is enormously difficult to make your advertising *better*. This book is about making your advertising, very specifically, your advertising design and your use of type, better. The most popular way to improve advertising has been to buy advertising and design annuals, and copy or be inspired by the ideas that look best. This is based on opinion and whim, not understanding or thought about what would most effectively get a particular idea across.

The result of this me-tooism is a general sense of having seen it all before. Rarely does an ad message break through my defenses and get noticed. When I finish skimming a magazine, for example, I typically try to recall the single outstanding ad I've seen. With rare exceptions, I cannot. How can it be that *not one* of a very finite group, maybe fifty ads, has broken through with a message and presentation that made an impact? And *I'm looking for impact* where *most readers are trying to avoid* advertising's increasing noise. So, is advertising design a stupendous waste of energy and money? Is it a failing of art directors to make me recognize the importance and value of their messages? Or are good ideas being watered down by clients, account people, and dull creative directors in an era of conceptual stagnation? Whatever the cause, the cure is surely knowledge. In fact, whatever the problem, the cure is *always* knowledge.

The lifespan of an ad is brief: an issue, a program, a day, a week, a month, a season. Few ads are in use a year after their introduction. Advertising must be timely and of-the-moment to be seen and acted upon: we readers want to be current and well-informed. Advertising style changes rapidly to look current, and that's not such a bad thing: advertising must possess vitality and exuberance. Books are expected to have a slightly longer lifespan. In the time between my writing this book and your reading it, some examples in it are bound to look dated, despite my effort to choose those that will remain fresh the longest. Nevertheless, in every case, examples have been chosen for their usefulness in *illustrating an idea*.

Thanks to the art directors whose work is shown in these pages. It is among the best and reveals right thinking. But please don't copy it, *understand* it. ➤ Carol Wahler and my fellow board members of The Type Directors Club, for whom type and its inspired use are worth representing. ➤ Brian Miller. ➤ Rosinha and Isabela, whose collaboration cannot be overemphasized. ➤ P-Bob. ➤ And Lilian.

Alex W. White

New York City

A book's dedication was invented as an acknowledgment of the author's royal or church patron – literally the person who paid for the book's writing. In our era, that person is you, the reader. So this book is joyfully dedicated to every reader who is willing to engage in the struggle for quality, originality, and right thinking. Purposeful creativity is very hard work.

It is also for those in management positions who understand their job is to define a problem, lay out requirements and clear targets, then let the creative people develop their interpretation. They are the rare few who are willing to take risks for ideas that are unexpected, yet on target.

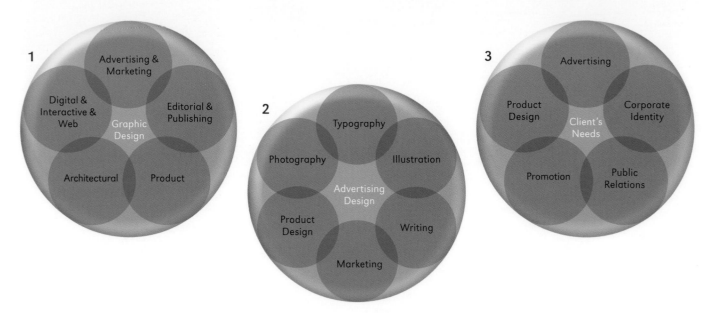

1 **Graphic design** is a family of related practices.
2 **Advertising design** encompasses six more or less equally-weighted disciplines with which an art director must be proficient, or at least familiar. Graphic design covers the same disciplines, but with a greater emphasis on typography, photography, and illustration.

3 **Client's marketing needs** include five areas of specialization. A creative director must be proficient, or at least very familiar, with each of these in order to understand and plan for their unified interaction. This will be, after all, how the client sees and plans for his company's public persona.

Where is advertising design found? In as many as 3,000 messages per person per day:

1 **At home** Newspapers and magazines; television; direct mail; the internet; branded products and packaging
2 **In public spaces** Subways and buses; billboards and banners; taxis; trucks; elevators; movie theaters; bus stops; blimps
3 **At the store/restaurant** Street level windows; tent cards; floor decals; bathroom stalls; shelf coupons; drink cups; receipts; shopping bags

Advertising
Design
and
Typography

Introduction What is advertising design? Advertising design is a specialization within the practice of graphic design, itself a term coined by W.A. Dwiggins in 1922, just as commercial art was emerging as a separate profession. Ad design is an omnium-gatherum* of several disciplines (shown above center). But ad design and graphic design differ in their degrees of emphasis on the same components: graphic design is more heavily weighted to typography and image manipulation. Ad design is more equally weighted among all six components.

A stark comparison can be made between advertising design and editorial design. The purpose of editorial design is to reveal the significance of a story to the reader and to sluice information effortlessly and memorably into the reader's mind. The purpose of advertising design is to reveal the significance of a product to a potential buyer by making a selling idea visible, and by inducing the reader to take some

* Synthesis, union, merger, combination, or collection

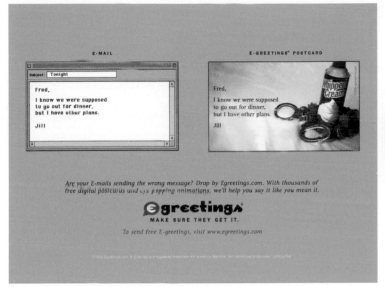

1 A half-page ad for an on line postcard company shows the improvement type and imagery give a message. But it is one thing to appreciate design's value and another to have a facility with its development. How to use image, type, and space to propel a concept off the page and into a browser's mind is tricky and takes creativity and sensitivity.

2 Marty Neumeier's pie chart shows ways of thinking: Creating, Discovering, Preserving, and Applying. Know your audience: he proposes that design appreciated by one group will be unliked by the group opposite it on the chart.

action, whether it is to buy a product, try a product, think about seeing a movie, take a test drive, make a phone call, or log onto a Web site. But the bottom line for advertising designers is that you have to sell. No sales, no more clients.

Regardless of specialization, all graphic designers must have a talent for visual presentation. There are three ingredients designers use to communicate: type, imagery, and space. Becoming familiar with all three and developing skill at using them – which is different than merely *having* them – makes the difference between just some stuff and great advertising.

Ad agencies Advertising started as verbal announcements: town criers walking the streets announcing the qualities of their wares while denigrating the quality of their competitors'. The earliest written advertisement

"If you go to an architect with a problem, the solution usually turns out to be a building. If you go to a designer, it turns out to be an ad, a brochure, or a package. If you are a designer, it's natural to want to design things."
Anonymous

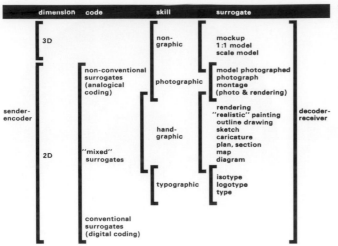

dimension	code	skill	surrogate	
		non-graphic	mockup 1:1 model scale model	
3D				
	non-conventional surrogates (analogical coding)	photographic	model photographed photograph montage (photo & rendering)	
sender-encoder		hand-graphic	rendering "realistic" painting outline drawing sketch caricature plan, section map diagram	decoder-receiver
2D	"mixed" surrogates			
		typographic	isotype logotype type	
	conventional surrogates (digital coding)			

How messages are transmitted from sender to receiver: the receiver will not be aware of the steps a message takes and the sender assumes all responsibility for the message's reception.

1

The Seven Levels of Communication
Marty Neumeier

Perception	**Contrast; Dimensionality; Color; Aesthetics** *Humans are hard-wired to respond to contrast, color, dimensionality, and motion. Perception in a design is what makes us look. Without first noticing a design, none of the other levels can be engaged. Designers must master aesthetic design.*
Sensation	**Gut reactions; Sensuality; Sexuality** *Response without thought. Sensuality and sexuality are pleasurable, so they attract viewers by being perceived as pleasant.*
Emotion	**Feelings; Desires; Needs; Interests** *Advertising has long targeted the heart rather than the mind. Positive emotions like delight, pride, and safety are equally useful tools as negative emotions like fear, envy, and guilt.*
Intellect	**Knowledge; Language; Humor; Ego; Logic** *Words are uniquely powerful at this level, which reinforces our existence as rational beings. Humor is a back door into consciousness.*
Identification	**Tribal codes; Familiarity; Need to belong** *Images and symbols are better recognized than words. Culture is dividing into smaller groups, each of which responds to its own set of signals.*
Reverberation	**History; Tradition; Nature; Truth** *When a design connects to history, tradition, or to the laws of nature, it has a richness that feels a lot like truth.*
Spirituality	**Morality; Integrity; Intuition; Beauty; Art** *Good design adheres to a code of moral and artistic values. It has integrity, completeness, and beauty. Spirituality may be more powerful than the conscious levels of communication.*

2

1 Advertising uses signals that will resonate with readers. There is a wealth of scholarly research into sign, symbol, and communication psychology and theory, like this Chart of Coding Techniques from *The Psychology of Visual Communication* (1966) by Martin Krampen. It is not the scope of this book to discuss theoretical work in depth, but it is essential that art directors who may become interested in this aspect of advertising know that it exists.

2 Neumeier's Seven Levels of Communication get more lofty as we read down. Exploring this list will lead to new ways of thinking about a project.

"Graphic design is a meta-language that can be used to magnify, obscure, dramatize, or redirect words and images. It can be powerful, elegant, banal, or irrelevant. It's not inherently anything at all, but pure potential."
J. Abbott Miller

"Advertising is the rattling of a stick inside a swill bucket."
George Orwell (1903-1950)

may be an Egyptian poster offering a gold coin for the capture of an escaped slave named Shem. Modern advertising evolved with Gutenberg's invention of movable type in Germany in 1450. That printing could be done more cheaply and far more rapidly was a boon to traders and sellers. Their announcements were hung on walls and inserted into newspapers and books. Newspapers recognized the new revenue stream in advertising, though the first regular advertising accounts weren't established until about 1650. The first separate newspaper advertising supplement didn't appear until the mid-1670s.

The first advertising agencies – by definition, an agency is an *intermediary* – were created to aid advertisers and shape their messages specifically in newspaper advertisements. The creative and planning aspects of agency work evolved, and advertising soon took more page space than the news. By paying so much into newspaper publishing,

"Let's say you're a manufacturer. Your advertising isn't working and your sales are going down. And everything depends on it. Your future depends on it, your family's future depends on it, other people's families depend on it. And you walk in this office and talk to me, and you sit in that chair. Now, what do you want out of me? Fine writing? Do you want masterpieces? Do you want glowing things that can be framed by copywriters? *Or do you want to see the goddamned sales curve stop moving down and start moving up?*" – Rosser Reeves

1

1 Advertising 101: Business exists to make money. Advertising is a service that exists to support and increase business.

Rosser Reeves, an enormously influential ad man for his pioneering and shrewd thinking on consumer motivation at New York City's Ted Bates Company in the 1950s, wrote *The Reality of Advertising* in 1961. In it, he describes the purpose of advertising, excerpted above.

advertising helped propel changes in printing technology by increasing speed and distribution. With the economic changes brought about by the Industrial Revolution in the mid-1800s, advertising helped create markets for new goods and drove the development of magazines. Radio, in the early 1900s, and television, in the 1950s, were largely funded by advertising, and these new media expanded the expertise of agencies, some of which specialized in one form or another of the growing advertising opportunities and techniques.

Agencies do three things: research and marketing planning; creative development; and production and media placement. These areas, however, aren't equally valued. From the reader's perspective, creative is the most important agency work because it can be *seen*. From the client's perspective, creative is by far the most valuable because it gets attention and persuades. Creative should be the most costly, but it has

"The demand in the field of advertising art in the past few years has been for better and better art... Intelligent visualization, good illustration, good typography – each has become a vital necessity to effective selling copy." Stanford Briggs Inc., 1925

3

1 Advertising wins readers when it simply and dramatically shows a benefit, as in this 1967 women's underwear ad that promises to "reshape you… All of a sudden, you've got a proportioned body, and your clothes fit better."

2 Magazines provide information to ad agencies and media buyers, trumpeting the magazine's readership. This reader poll shows details of ads and asks readers to identify each sponsor, demonstrating the value of a memorable visual.

"We are communicators. We should be obsessed with the details that enhance the effectiveness of our communications." Jan Conradi

historically been pegged to a percentage of media costs, which makes it seem like a mere commodity in which great, good, and poor creatives are paid equally. Be warned: this is not fair and not fun if you aim to excel.

Unless you are working in radio, sales messages have an unavoidable visual presence. Art directors have evolved from mere layout artists since the agency revolution sparked by Doyle Dane Bernbach in the early 1960s. Both copywriters and art directors must have a highly developed ability to sleuth out a potent selling idea. A copywriter must have a keen visual sense, since most of his work will be seen, not merely heard. Similarly, an art director must know how to phrase a headline for maximum impact. But, as a visually aware copywriter doesn't need to know how to actually design nor understand the principles of typography, an art director doesn't need to be able to write clear body copy. These details are what differentiate copywriters from art directors. If your interest is in

1

1 Noting some resistance to graphic design from the students in an advanced class on advertising typography, this sheet was distributed to help the students bridge their *perceived* gap between design and advertising. Whenever they encountered the word "graphic" in the text, they were to cut out and stick on "advertising," emphasizing the similarity between the two related design disciplines.

conceptualizing marketing ideas and *you have a talent and passion for design*, art direction is a good choice. If, on the other hand, your interest is in conceptualizing marketing ideas and *you lack talent and passion for design*, please, be a copywriter.

It is the art director's responsibility to translate research into potent selling ideas as powerful, thoughtful, carefully crafted image and type manipulations so they are noticeable and memorable. Often, the writer takes the lead in conceptualizing. Conceptualizers who can write but who can't design become writers (or very bad art directors, and there are plenty of them!). Conceptualizers who can't write but who can design become art directors. It takes talent, skill, and sensitivity to be an art director: at once conceptualizer, visual communicator, and typographer.

The difference between a copywriter and an art director is that some one has to *make* the ads, and that someone is always the art director.

"My advice is to learn all that stuff you can while you're young."

All but a very few advertising creatives get washed out of the business by the time they turn fifty. Is creativity a young person's game, as some have said? Or is it a business decision to hire less costly young people to replace more costly experienced people?

5

1

1 Advertising can become a cultural phenomenon, adopted even by those who don't buy the product. This mid-1990s campaign created a buzz by using Spanish (and a chihuahua) in what some thought a derogatory way. Did the art direction contribute to the adoption of this campaign by the American public? Perhaps, but only insofar as it doesn't *interfere* with the message. More likely, the timing was perfect: the goofiness of the dog's head and the easily-mastered foreign term simply struck a chord.

"You can tell the ideals of a nation by its advertisements."
Norman Douglas, 1917

Every client deserves its own unique visual personality. How does an art director manage type, image, and space to create a personality? Consider your client's direct and indirect competition: what personalities do they have? It is terribly embarrassing to accidently duplicate the competition. Learn more about the product and the competition than your client knows.

Consider yourself 100% responsible for your ads. There are no excuses for shoddy work: it is perceived to have come from a shoddy worker, whether it is you or your partner who is to blame.

Art directors vs designers There is a difference, and it isn't one of status, and it shouldn't be one of talent. Designers are skilled at an art and a craft that includes spatial organization, typography, and image manipulation. Art directors are skilled at conceptualizing, visual organization, and

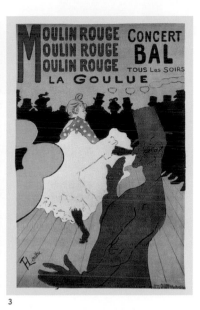

1

2

3

1 As a significant part of culture, advertising is referenced in art and can occasionally *be* art. But advertising for art's sake is very rarely the purpose of the exercise. Rather, advertising done by people with vision and the compulsion to see differently results in advertising that is eventually recognized as art. Shown are a 1934 magazine cover by John Atherton, **2** a 1986 ad by Keith Haring, and **3** Toulouse-Lautrec's first poster for the Moulin Rouge (1891), which propelled "art for clients."

managing a team of artists, who make the parts of an ad. An art director who hasn't got a gift for visual presentation, can't design, or doesn't under-understand type has very dubious value to the team. Art directors who lack design skills are a disgrace to the profession: they may or may not be good conceptualists, but they'll never make a good-looking ad.

A survey of advertising creative directors cited several weaknesses in newly hired art directors:

- *Things aren't thought out.*
- *The designs are tricky, not simple.*
- *Concepts are weak.*
- *Art directors must understand that design is the "eye candy," the lure that intrigues browsers into the message.*

- *Art directors who can't design are comparable to writers who can't write.*
- *Many young ADs are heavy on technical skills but light on thinking. An excellent presentation can't make a bad idea good.*

The birth of commercial art? Henri de Toulouse-Lautrec (1864-1901) began a series of paintings of the goings-on at Paris' Moulin de la Galette, a cabaret club in an old windmill. A year later, in 1889, he switched allegiances to the Moulin Rouge (*above left*) when it opened and became the hottest club in town. Until then, posters were elaborate and busy (*above right, Toulouse-Lautrec with Moulin Rouge's manager and a poster by Jules Chéret in 1891*). After a few starts, Toulouse-Lautrec refined his style which became an immediate hit: simplification, silhouettes, and selective use of color. His lithographic (literally, "stone-drawing") posters advertising the nightly dancing at Moulin Rouge were his high water mark as an artist. Equally important, they were the model for every poster artist in the following decades.

Business needs storytellers

Section 1
Strategies

Business needs people who can bring facts to life. Where's the story in this image? This machine is shown life size. It is one of a set of the finest model replicas ever made, housed at the American Precision Museum in Windsor, Vermont. More than a mere "toy machine," it is a study in precision; every component in this one-of-a-kind model is hand-tooled and individually fit to exact tolerances. The methods for mass production – interchangeable parts and precision machining – was pioneered in 1846 in Windsor by the Robbins and Lawrence Armory, who supplied field-repairable rifles for the Union army prior to the Civil War. Their techniques spread throughout the northeastern and the midwestern United States, where precision manufacturing was based for the following hundred years.

Advertising explains facts. It turns features, which are facts about a product, into benefits, which are reasons for someone to try the product. It does this by telling a story.

Converting facts into a story has two parts: *strategy* and *execution*. Strategy includes knowing the facts about your product; simpifying the facts – which to leave out and which to emphasize – and positioning against competitor products, typically prepared by others in a *creative brief*; and determining the *Unique Selling Proposition*, the statement that separates your product from all others.

Developing an *execution* is the realm of the creative department. We translate the message so it makes people identify with the product, recognize its status, and desire it. We also give every client an identifiable look.

Section 1 also discusses verbal and visual thinking, the *Four Levels of Advertising,* and how to be seen in an environment of noisiness.

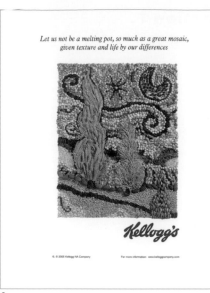

1 There are three main areas of advertising: **Consumer ads** induce a likely prospect to "try" it (see it at a store, visit its Web site, call its 800 number, test drive it, drink it, etc.).
2 Institutional advertising promotes the company rather than a particular product. The purpose of corporate advertising is to make the public think better of the company.
3 Business-to-business ads (or *trade ads*) induce sales to retailers or other businesses who use the product.

"Advertising is a game of tactics and strategy, not chance. When you bid for public response, be sure to play the trump card of effective design." Westvaco Inspiration for Printers, Number 194, 1953

"Promise, large promise, is the soul of an advertisement." Samuel Johnson (1709-1784)

Chapter 1 **Strategy vs Execution**

Hank Seiden, the author of *Advertising Pure and Simple* wrote, "A good practitioner of advertising can convince a logical prospect for a product or service to try it one time." Let's break this definition down. *Convince* means a rational appeal to another person's intelligence. *Logical prospect* means a person who is at the moment looking for such a product, has a need for it, and can afford to buy it. *Try* means a single use. *Buy*, on the other hand, indicates regular use: after having tried a product or service once, the product will be evaluated on its own merits.

Seiden concludes, "Advertising doesn't make customers. Only products make customers."

What we have here is a definition of advertising that *limits its power*. That makes the practice realistic and a lot more approachable.

Advertising
Design
and
Typography

1 An institutional ad from Coca-Cola means to increase the public's feelings of warmth and humanity toward the brand. This ad is not meant to directly affect sales of their product line. Institutional ads are often seen during a business crisis, and their messages are typically received with a large grain of salt by the public.
2 This fantastic Dutch Art Deco vehicle could stop traffic today just as well as it must have in 1928 as it announced the existence of a radio manufacturer.
3 Grey Healthcare Group's statement of goals posted in the reception area of their Manhattan headquarters.

1   2   3

1 Strategy: Apple presented their product, computers with a different operating system, by showing pictures of people

who saw or thought differently. This is Ansel Adams, who died in 1984, just as personal computers became available.

2 His ability to see and record nature more acutely than others is demonstrated in his photo (*top*) and another showing the same scene years later.

3 Self promotion for an ad agency shows, with elegant simplicity, the value they (and other agencies) add to achieve results.

Consumer, institutional, and business-to-business Advertising problems fall into three categories. Each has its own purpose and each is equally valuable to the business owner. Consumer advertising speaks to the end user of a product; institutional advertising speaks to investors, employees, and society in a public relations-style soft sell promoting good feelings about the sponsoring company; and business-to-business advertising promotes products from one business to another.

Information vs persuasion Advertising creatives convert information provided by the research and account management teams into persuasive arguments. We add value to a raw message by making it connect with an audience, by making it stand out, and by making it memorable. If we haven't added the element of persuasion, we haven't done our jobs. This is a simple yardstick to measure creative efficacy.

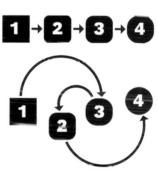

Logical thinking is linear (*top*). Creative thinking is non-linear and occurs in starts and stops in a circuitous route (*above*). Creative thought transcends the expected, so a wholly different result – represented by a perfect circle – can be realized.

1 **11**

Strategy
vs
Execution

Tax Sheltered Programs, Tax Deferred Programs, Mortgage Finance, Commercial Finance, Private Placements, Mutual Funds, Venture Capital, Variable Annuities, Computer Programming, Executive Benefit Planning, Medical Expense Reimbursement Plans, Estate Analysis, Life Insurance, Deferred Compensation, 501(C)(3) Annuities, Disability Income Insurance, Pension Plans, Profit Sharing Plans, Employee Stock Ownership Trusts, Hospitalization & Major Medical Plans, Self-Employed Retirement Plans, Individual Retirement Programs, Equity Investments, Keyman Protection, Stock Retirement Plans, Stock Redemption Plans, Section 79 Programs, Group Dental, Estate Tax Conservation and Section 303 Programs. Field Planning Corporation 41 East 42nd Street, New York, N.Y. 10017 Telephones: (212) 687-4744 (800) 223-7446 Cable: Conrafrank

Conrad Frank, C.L.U., President

1   2   3

1 Headline as label: every rule is made to be broken. The text explains that this particular vehicle (1 in 50) failed its inspection and won't be purchased

until it is made right. Now *that's* a benefit.
2 Music is shown to have a legitimate, inherent value. Hidden down by the logo is the message:

stop music piracy. The distance between the simple message and its interpretation is the value added by art directors and copywriters.

3 How do you say, "this business has many products"? This business card shows them all, making it interesting *because of* its lengthy text.

1

2

1 One idea: our beer is gritty, honest, and without pretense. To make an ad look unpolished, you have to be pretty sophisticated. This one has a no-frills headline with plenty of attitude, the photo looks like a snapshot, and the type has been damaged. The design would not look like this without careful and very conscious intervention by the art director.

2 This doesn't just *say* 20% off, it *shows* 20% off. The cheap production values reflect the frugal car rental prices.

Make a single point per ad Marty Neumeier, editor of the excellent and defunct *Critique* magazine wrote, "The Modernists, in their attempt to sweep away all irrelevancies, turned clarity into simplicity. Artist Hans Hoffman felt that to achieve clarity we must 'eliminate the unnecessary so that the necessary may speak…' Albert Einstein's formula for clarity was that 'everything should be made as simple as possible,' adding '*but no simpler…*'"

The mind resists that which is confusing and embraces that which is clear. Clarity is achieved through *predigestion of material*. Predigestion implies a thorough going-over of material in order to extract the nutritional, beneficial attributes for others. If this sounds like hard work, it is.

The speed with which we have to get a message through is increasing to almost impossible measures. As Ernie Schenck wrote in *CA* magazine, "Nothing is fast enough any more. Nothing is short enough. Everything is

1

2

3

Make a single point per ad to keep the message clear.
1 This product helps you bend your stiff, achy knees. No discussion of smell, value, or cost.

2 "The New Beetle Cabriolet" is single-minded advertising: round car with no top. Period. No discussion of color, engine size, stereo add-ons, or mileage.

3 An award-winning photo gets a minimal, though sophisticated, design treatment (*bottom right*) to identify the product. The only visual hint in the image is the distinctive shape of a BMW grille as windows. The design does not clarify the message with a caption, but it does give a Web address.

The definition of creativity is
The synthesis of
combination, unification of parts

seemingly disparate ideas
on the surface, apparently — dissimilar, unlike — thought, image

into a new and useful whole.
fresh, original — advantageous, appropriate — unity, totality

1

1 Creativity must reflect a new-ness, a freshness, an unexpect-edness, *as well as a usefulness* to solving a particular adver-tising problem. The defintion of creativity is from James L. Adams' book *Conceptual Block-busting: A Guide to Better Ideas.*

too long… We've got maybe three seconds to get our hooks into some-body's very resistant and not exactly advertising-friendly brain… A bril-liant concept, if it's anything, is a fast concept. In a heartbeat, a fast concept drives its hook into your cerebellum and that's that. The problem now is that the heartbeat has become something closer to that of a hum-mingbird on amphetamines than a person… It's almost impossible to describe how fast an idea has to be now."

With the speed necessary in today's environment, there simply isn't time for more than one idea per ad. But having a single idea itself isn't enough without a design that stops the reader.

Having a single focal point is essential to breaking through readers' barriers. The focal point is most frequently an image with the headline and subhead acting as secondary elements.

Good design is not about addition, but subtraction.

"By eliminating details, I achieve impact. By using fewer colors, I attain more contrast. By simplifying the shapes, I make them bolder." George Giusti

"Muddiness is the cloak of confused thinking. Clarity does not require the ab-sence of impurities, only that the impurities contribute to understanding." Critique magazine editors, 2000

Advertising The use of paid media to sell products or services or to communicate concepts and informa-tion by a sponsor or advertiser. *Sales, marketing, promotion, notice, message, testimonial.*

Publicity So-called "free advertising," though com-paratively uncontrolled in that the publicity source does not purchase time or space from the media. *Exposure, awareness, advocacy, notice, announce-ment, familiarization, alert, dispatch.*

Design A process of organization in which less im-portant material yields and more important material dominates through contrast; organization is made visible through similarity; and value is added to raw information on behalf of the reader or user. *v plan, intend, mean, arrange, compose; n purpose, strategy, composition, layout, motif, pattern.*

Art Treatment that causes the viewer to see or think differently. *Abstraction, invention, style.*

1

2

3

1 How do you reach designers in *Communications Arts* magazine? Show them Paul Rand, an icon of advertising and design innovation. George Lois said,

"Every art director and designer should kiss – as they say in Paul Rand's native Brooklyn – his ass."
2 A calendar cover for a printing company uses collage in this

1942 sample. Photocollage was used in Europe for a decade or more, but had not made the jump to the U.S. until Rand introduced it.

3 A 1942 special-edition gift decanter shows Rand's design abilities extended to product design. Though it is 65 years old, it is utterly contemporary.

On focus groups:
"If I had asked people what they wanted, they would have said faster horses."
Henry Ford

On research:
"As usual, your information stinks." Frank Sinatra in a telegram to *Time* magazine

On knowing your audience:
"If you want to catch a trout, don't fish in a herring barrel."
Ann Landers on singles bars

Research + communication = knowing your client and audience

Being given research is not nearly as valuable as doing your own research. You will see things others have missed. Your creativity will pick out an anomaly and be able to work it into an idea that no one else would have noticed.

A few thoughts on clients: Make the product the star. ☛ Get to know your client. Learn his language, answer his questions, and make his message your own. ☛ Can you tell the client she owns the idea? If not, get another idea. ☛ Turn a product similarity into a unique point. ☛ Turn a product disadvantage into an advantage. ☛ The guy who came up with "Lather. Rinse. Repeat." doubled shampoo sales instantly. Don't charge by time spent on a project: charge by the idea.

A few thoughts on audiences: People don't buy if they feel they are being sold to. ☛ Direct mail is called "junk mail," e-mail pitches are called

Advertising
Design
and
Typography

CLIENT

AUDIENCE

YOU
and your
copywriter

1

2

1 Post-War European advertising tended toward the witty, as in this 1954 poster by Savignac. It was not necessary – or had not yet become necessary – to say much more than that a product existed.
2 *"Keener competition in the market and shrinking purchasing power have driven (British post-War) advertisers to two extremes: pleasing so-called public taste or presenting the public with a surprise."* Charles Rosner, co-editor of *Graphis Annual.* This sounds a lot like entertainment: neither of these directions includes product benefits or reasons to try a product.

"spam," guerilla ads are called "grafitti." ➤ Ads don't work if they chase, harangue, or interrupt people. Advertising should seduce, it should attract. ➤ Be controversial. ➤ Your ads are like free samples of the product or service: entice! ➤ If you make them care first, people *will* read body copy. ➤ Be dramatic: people are in rush to see the news/Ferrari/naked lady/sports.

   A few thoughts on satisfying both clients and audiences: It is your job to interpret: take the product, digest it, and spew out its good points. ➤ If you don't add creativity and freshness, it won't get added by anyone else. Be outrageous in the face of sameness. ➤ Don't stop digging for the idea too soon. ➤ A creative trick is not a trick if it is more than a thought from left field, if it has something strongly to do with the product. ➤ If a part of an ad isn't fun, replace it – it's a sign of difficulty. ➤ Observe ads and commercials: did those creative teams have fun?

"The manufacturer is more often right than wrong when he says, 'My business is different.' Often it is exactly that difference which is fairly crying out for expression." The Blackman Company, Advertising, 1925

"A designer is duty bound to push the client as far as they will go." Mark Farrow

"Do it big or stay in bed." Larry Kelly, opera producer

Bob Beleson is an advertising and liquor branding consultant. His rules for effective advertising: Have a specific marketing objective in mind. ➤ Segment the market and identify new user groups that your brand can own. ➤ Consider the competition. What are they saying? ➤ Have a relevant message and be sure your target audience cares about your angle. ➤ Use tactical advertising where ads are placed in specific media. For example, people who sail like rum. Rum makers know this so they place their ads in sailing magazines more than other publications. As a further consequence, rum ads, wherever they appear, often show sailing or sailboats. ➤ Be single minded in your message. ➤ Develop a unique personality. ➤ Production values count. ➤ As the art director, you are 100% responsible for the ad. Allow yourself to drive everybody else nuts to get the best possible results.

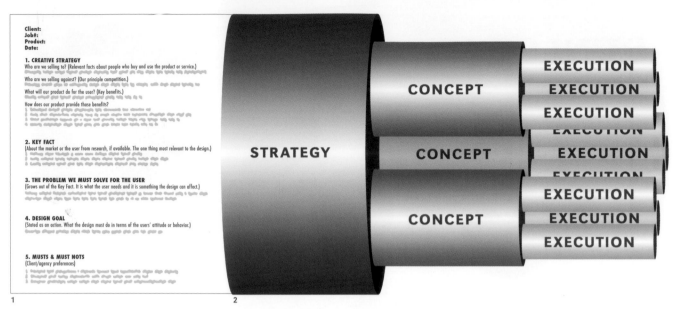

1   2

1 This is the initial document one New York ad agency uses in its creative department. It covers all the essential starting points for a new assignment.

2 The creative brief is given to the creative department in a face-to-face meeting and the strategy is carefully reviewed. These are the issues that the client will expect to see addressed. Now the creative machine chews up the brief and mulls it over and develops a few concepts – best kept simple by avoiding details by drawing with a fat marker on a pad of white paper – and each approved concept receives a few interpretations, or executions.

Roger Von Oech, a creativity consultant, suggests
1 Never state a problem the same way it was given to you.
2 Anything that is surprising is useful.
3 Play in your work: it will show in your results.
4 Be sure you have recognized the obvious.
5 Inspiration comes from regularly scheduled work sessions.
6 New ideas are resisted because no one likes change: expect that resistance and be prepared for it.

The creative brief: problem as strategy Creatives are usually given a creative brief, one or two pages of very specific information that the marketing and account people have prepared. A typical brief has one-sentence descriptions of *audience, situation, opportunity, key customer insight, key customer benefit (positioning), promise, reasons to believe, brand character, core brand insight*, and *mandatories* like colors, naming requirements, and the deadline for creative development. The brief takes weeks for the account people to prepare. But the creative process often takes unexpected twists and turns – and minds are changed as studies begin to appear. We should consider a creative brief as a somewhat fluid document while "delivering the goodies" that it calls for. Your work will be evaluated by how well you have addressed the particulars in the brief. Having produced ads that respond to the brief's specifics, persuasive arguments can be made for *additional, alternative* directions.

1 **16**

1   2   3

1 The newspaper wants to sell more classified advertising. Bob Gill simply and elegantly shows the *positive results* of small space listings.

2 How do you say "tattoos last forever"? The black and white images on the left fade away after a rain or a few weeks in the sun. The red type remains.

3 No words necessary to show bright whiteness underfoot. **Right** Marlboros were positioned as a woman's cigarette in the early 1950s.

1

2

1 How do you show the importance of sound effects in print? Did the German recording studio client really ask for this treatment?
2 What is *fart* in German? You can bet the creative brief did not mention cartoon panels or goofy comic book visual sound effects. This is the creative department's contribution as it added its storytelling skills.

We transform the problem defined in the brief into words and pictures that will resonate with consumers. One of the best ways to generate ideas is by *brainstorming*, a technique in which the goal is to discover as many solutions as possible. There are distinct rules to this process, which was invented by Alex Osborn of BBDO. Charles H. Clark, a creativity consultant in Kent, Ohio, codified the process as follows: **1** Select the problem and state it as an action, "How can we...," "How to..." **2** Set a target number of solutions, with a minimum of 35, and a time limit, typically five minutes. **3** Suspend judgment or criticism of any kind during the brainstorming session. Judgment is negative and kills creativity. There will be time later to sift through the ideas and rank them. **4** Encourage and build off each others' more unusual, peculiar ideas. Join two ideas together to make a new one. **5** Quality grows from quantity. Be an idea-generating machine.

Brainstorming judgment phrases that should never be used: That's a terrible idea. ☛ We don't know that. ☛ Be sensible. ☛ We tried that. ☛ The client isn't ready for that. ☛ That's too risky. ☛ The boss won't like it. ☛ I thought of that before and we didn't use it then. ☛ It will cost too much. ☛ You've got to be kidding. ☛ Sure, but... ☛ We'll never get it approved. ☛ It isn't possible. ☛ The public will laugh at us. ☛ It's not a new concept. ☛ What for? ☛ Your ideas stink.

On getting ideas (Dom Marino and Deana Cohen, influential teachers at SVA): Love the product. ☛ Trust your gut reactions. ☛ Use "what if..." It's your most important friend. ☛ Be crazy: go too far and be brought back by someone else. ☛ Discovering a fact is not an ad. You must dramatize, interpret, and illustrate the fact to make it an ad. To test an idea, ask "Could an account executive have done this ad?" ☛ Don't use tricks, copy-quirks, or jokes: they don't sell because they primarily throw light on the creative team rather than the product by saying, "This ad was made by a clever person." ☛ It's got to sound like normal conversation: would I say it this way on the phone to a friend? ☛ Would you want to go to the shoot: is the visual interesting enough? ☛ "Walk on snow that's never been walked on before." ☛ Take a chance. ☛ Ads are answers, not questions.

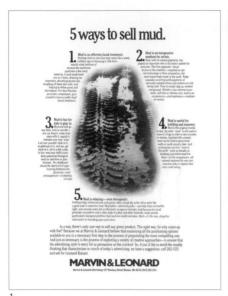

1

2

3

1 A self-promotion campaign by a Boston agency in the mid-1980s showed their skill at selling things thought to be without value. Mud is "an effective facial cleaner; an inexpensive medium for artists; fun for kids to play in; a useful construction material; and relaxing and therapeutic."

2 Water is "essential to overall good health; the world's most popular drink; the perfect drink for any occasion; calorie-free; and a cavity fighter."

3 Garbage is "a renewable energy source; an inexpensive fertilizer; a useful building material; a landscaping aid; and found art."

Jay Wolff's Ideas

1 Clearly identify the basic function of the product.

2 Identify other possible functions: cost, value, design's size/softness/smell, USP, intangibles, quality, consumers' product awareness.

3 Develop a good line of thinking in one or more directions and execute each clearly and persuasively. Draw from your own experience at all times – from what you *know* and have *experienced*. Make it believable.

4 When you get down to it, nobody *knows* what will work, so follow your own experience honestly.

Features and benefits One of the fundamental communication assumptions behind successful advertising states that the "features" of a product or service can be expressed as "benefits." Chris Zenowich, a copywriter and professor of advertising at Syracuse University, has used the following description of features and benefits in his classes: "What is a feature? A feature is an attribute, usually physical, of a product or service, e.g. 'contains retsin,' or 'overnight delivery.'

"You *create* the benefit for any given feature by expressing – either verbally or visually or both – how or why that feature fulfills a need basic to the roles of the audience you're addressing.

"Sound simple? It is, assuming you approach the project having fully familiarized yourself with the product, and with a clear definition of who your audience is. *A well-informed creative person with limited talent can produce acceptable advertising.* To be truly successful, you must select

Radioactive words that should never be used. This is an incomplete list:

Hey (your city here)...

For people who... AMERICAS FAVORITE...

NEW Finally... Introducing...

How to...

Improved!

Questions to uncover relevant features	**Charles Whittier's questions to uncover product benefits**
Try to describe the product as if no one had ever used it.	*Will the product:*
☛ What is it made of?	☛ Make the purchaser feel more important?
☛ How well is it made?	☛ Make the purchaser happier?
☛ What does it do?	☛ Make the purchaser more comfortable?
☛ How can it be identified?	☛ Make the purchaser more prosperous?
☛ What does/doesn't work about it?	☛ Make work easier for the purchaser?
☛ What movements are necessary to use it?	☛ Give the purchaser greater security?
☛ What does it cost?	☛ Make the purchaser more attractive? Better liked?
☛ How does it compare with the competition?	☛ Give the purchaser some distinction?
	☛ Improve, protect, or maintain the purchaser's health?
	☛ Appeal to the purchaser as a bargain?

1 Seeing accurately is part of the process of defining features. Have childlike eyes and see freshly. Nothing is insignificant and nothing should be overlooked.

2 Converting and reinterpreting features into benefits takes both intellectual and emotional sensitivity. You need to understand their demographic and you have to project yourself into the target users' lives to feel their needs and wants.

the features of your product or service which offer the strongest benefits to your target audience.

"When you are lucky, the features of your product or service will be unique and offer benefits that are compelling and relevant. But more often you must cope with a 'parity product' – one with essentially the same features as the others in its category. You must then seek out 'advantages,' and state those advantages uniquely and memorably.

"Charles Whittier, longtime Creative Director at J. Walter Thompson/ Chicago, suggested that there are ten basic questions you can ask to uncover the benefits suggested by the features for a product or service (*see above right*). Each of these questions directly or indirectly addresses one of our basic needs: food, shelter, health, love, and acceptance. But notice how dull advertising is when these questions are translated directly into advertising benefits, merely saying, 'You will be happy when you use this!'"

Benefit shown Only one car has a single set of footprints and the ability to have been started and driven away in the cold.

The working process Feel guilty if you're not having fun. ☛ Have enthusiasm. ☛ Dig deeper. Expose yourself. Don't play safe. ☛ Keep climbing out on a limb, even if you fall off again and again. At least you'll be remembered. ☛ Have emotion and use it. Channel anger, frustration, exhaustion, or happiness into ideas. ☛ The ad must be more than an observation about the product. The truth is not enough to make a good ad. ☛ The ad should reveal its creator as an exciting person. ☛ The idea must be big enough to campaign. What's the second ad? What's the twenty-fifth? ☛ Be prepared and able to defend the ad's idea. ☛ Don't make your ad sound important: that's advertising-ese. Make ads that are personal, human, and accessible. ☛ All's fair en route to getting a hot ad. Do whatever is necessary to get the best results: moonlight with a friend if necessary. ☛ Make a decision and stick to it. Don't compromise. Keep it pure.

1 Mix together the following ingredients and you get seasoned salt: salt, sugar, spices, pepper, onion, garlic, celery seed, oregano, paprika. They are recommended for "use on beef, chicken, pork, potatoes, popcorn, eggs, beans, rice, pasta, salads, vegetables, soups, and sauces." They are direct competitors, though each has its own mixture ratio and, more importantly, unique positioning. One is for seafood, one for steak, one for Dominicans, one for Cajun cooking, and one for everything and everyone.

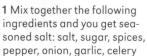

"What if your product really is just like the other guy's? Simple: invent a difference. In marketing, perception is as important as reality."
Anonymous

Parity products *Parity 1) Equality, as in amount, status, or value. 2) Equivalence, or resemblance.* Parity products are products that have no real, substantive differences. For example, Tide powder detergent is identical to Cheer and half a dozen other brands. In order to make a particular brand stand out – for it to have a USP (*see page 22*) – the advertising agency often suggests changes in the product. Adding blue speckles and calling them "ZX2" is one. Packaging in a new spouted box is another. Even claiming that "this is the detergent for cold water" will work. What is important is recognizing that there are no inherent differences in your product, researching what your competitors are saying, and carving out a niche by developing something you can claim makes your product desirable. Say, by positioning it as the detergent for really old clothes, or for 100% cotton fabric, or for toddler's clothes, or for loving spouses, or for a particular ethnic group, or for...

Advertising
Design
and
Typography

"Don't ask someone if they love you if you don't know they'll say yes," or How to win Make sure you get something *from* your work. ◆ Drop boring people from your life. ◆ Take a different route to work every day. ◆ Lighten up. ◆ Be a sponge. ◆ You are always working for yourself. ◆ Ask "what's in it for me?" The "me" is the client, the consumer, and yourself. A good ad must benefit all three. ◆ Don't show an ad that is being developed. It is too young and vulnerable. ◆ Present your ideas to your boss when she's in the best mood. ◆ When presenting an ad, introduce it with a setup line. Pose the question the ad answers. It makes the ad look better than it is. ◆ Look at ads to see what's been done. Then never settle for "it's been done." ◆ A portfolio is what you want to do, not what you've done. ◆ Your book must show you are an interesting person. ◆ When in doubt, leave it out. ◆ Win where you are before moving on.

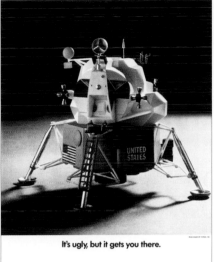

It's ugly, but it gets you there.

ugly can be beautiful

crocs

crocs.com

1 What if a radio is a car? The AM mono radio was standard until the late 1960s, so this was a significant improvement.

2 What if a car is a spaceship? Man landed on the moon in 1969, the year of this ad. VW had been mining the "ugly but reliable" position for a decade, so this was a natural, if not obvious, interpretation.

3 What if a shoe is a dog? A 2006 variation of the VW ad promoting a shoe rather than a car.

Positioning *Positioning* is the creation of a distinct identity in the marketplace so a product appeals to a defined segment of the public. No one is "everybody": ads for everybody tend to be ignored for that very reason. So pick a segment of "everybody" and sell to them. Each of us is looking for a reflection of ourselves in ads, so the better you reveal your selected part of "everybody," the better you show me to myself, the better I will respond.

The product: timeshares of a private jet. The image: a man resting on a remote beach. The positioning: a service to get the hardworking away faster *so they can slow down sooner*. The headline says: *"It's not just a card. It's a choice. A choice to speed up your life. A choice to slow it down."*

A few thoughts on positioning: ☛ Research and define enemies: Who is our competition? What are they doing? ☛ Use positioning to eliminate as much of the competition as you can. ☛ Select a position *only you can own.* ☛ Try on different roles. Be a mirror.

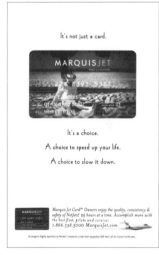

Position begets **attitude** begets **campaign**.

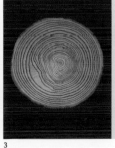

Seit 1995 senkt ESP® die Unfallzahlen.

"Since 1995 ESP® is decreasing accidents. Year after year it becomes clearer... the number of accidents of our cars has been reduced by 15%... Mercedes Benz. The future of the automobile."

1 Contrasting positions are shown in two 1962 automotive ads. Mercedes uses understated elegance with the headline, "Coupe d'Etat," a French pun joining *a violent change in government* with a style of car body. Ford uses contemporary cold war drama with text reading "The only missile you can inspect without a security clearance... waiting for your countdown."

2 Outrageous visuals were common during the dot.com boom in the late 1990s. It was thought that merely getting eyeballs on a Web site would lead to financial success.

3 Mercedes again selling more than a mere hunk of metal.

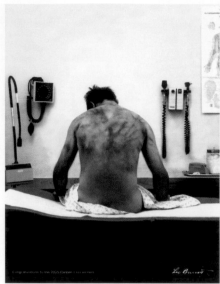

1 Three ads from one edition of an advertising trade magazine show three ways to say the same thing: *Congratulations to ourselves and our competitors for winning a desirable award for creative excellence in advertising.* There are always alternative ways of breathing life into a project brief. Which solution you choose begins with your creativity, but also depends on the taste and courage of your colleagues and clients. In these examples, those groups are one and the same.

Rosser Reeves defined good advertising as that which sells the most, not that which pleases us the most.

The Unique Selling Proposition (USP) A product or service will probably have several features worth talking about. But its advertising must select a *single one* that will separate it from its competitors in the minds of prospective buyers. This is known as the Unique Selling Proposition, a term that Rosser Reeves, of Ted Bates & Company, coined. The USP creates the *brand image, brand personality, position*, or *promise*. It is used repeatedly to make the one point: this brand is different (and beneficial) from all others. Repetition is key: back in the day, callers to Reeves' agency were greeted with, "Good morning. Ted Bates, Ted Bates, Ted Bates."

It is essential to understand that the benefit does not need to actually *be* unique, just that *it is the only brand to be claiming the benefit* in its advertising. It must be the only one *talking about that benefit*.

It is up to the creative team and the marketing planners to decide which of the advantages a product offers should be given priority. It may be a

Advertising
Design
and
Typography

1 Here are six ads from different sponsors and art directors. They appeared in a single issue of a magazine for a minority audience. Each ad has the same message: our company honors diversity, so you should consider working for us. Because they appeared all at once in one magazine, it is impossible not to perceive them in direct competition. Which of these ads goes beyond the message and stands out? Which is most persuasive, most creative, most effective? Another consideration is which of these ads has a Unique Selling Proposition, offering a promise none of the others is making?

1

2

3

Market research defines segments of the audience and what kinds of messages and symbols they respond to.

1 What if this lipstick makes you look good *without looking like you are wearing makeup*? What if this is the "un-makeup"?

2 What if this car is *naughty*? Who would buy a car that is doing pranks? The same who might "grab life by the horns"?

3 Even a country can be positioned: What if Brasil is for people who are enthusiastic and joyful about nature?

color, an ingredient, or a social standing. Everything in the ad, in the campaign, and in every branding effort should promote that single objective.

Hank Seiden, writing in *Advertising Pure and Simple*, describes the USP: "Every successful product has *got* to have a Unique Advantage. Without it, the advertiser is wasting his money (unless he can overwhelm competition simply by outspending everyone, which in itself becomes the product's Unique Advantage). But before you can promote the Unique Advantage, you've got to isolate and recognize it in your product. Here are several ways to do so: **1** First and easiest is when the Unique Advantage is inherent in the product itself. It's either visible or otherwise readily identifiable. The advertising must then point out why this unique feature will be to their benefit. **2** The Unique Advantage may be difficult to find, and once found, may not be an advantage at all, or may not even be uni-

"Art is I, science is we." Claude Bernard (1813-1878), French physiologist
Art in advertising is a truly rare commodity: "art direction" is often "layout management." When art becomes "we," when decisions are made by committee, the art that is being fooled with will almost certainly no longer be art.

1 **23**

Happy marriages, or How to work as a team Have one ad. ✒ Two people as a team are one. Work to build an idea together. ✒ Both members of the team must be 100% responsible for 100% of the ad. ✒ A design-savvy writer is as valuable as a verbally adept art director. ✒ Brainstorming is a game in which there are only two rules: 1] *criticism is not allowed* and 2] *don't be the one who lets an idea stop.* ✒ For ideas you don't like from your partner: look at it from a different point of view and "return it over the net." ✒ Phrases to keep creativity flowing: "what if...," "let's let that cook...," and "these are not the words, but..." ✒ Be willing to abandon a toyed-with ad to protect its integrity. ✒ It is a question of perspective between being thought of as a prima donna and being a strong defender of your ideas. ✒ Recognize unwinnable situations – in clients, products, account executives – and get reassigned.

A Technique for Producing Ideas has just 62 pages. These are the key points it makes, but the context is missing, making this a bit tough to absorb. Go to the original and see why it's a classic.

◆ Ideas are prepared as if on an assembly line. Their creation follows a formula.

◆ People may be divided into two groups: those who accept the way things are but don't challenge it (chumps), and those who are "preoccupied with the possibilities of new combinations." Those interested in advertising are inherently in this second group.

◆ There are two parts to ideation: Principles and Methods.

◆ Facts by themselves are not significant.

◆ **Principle 1** An idea is the combination of old materials.

◆ **Principle 2** One must be able to perceive relationships to make combinations.

◆ **Method, Step 1** Gather raw material, which is in two forms, specific (about the product, category, and consumer) and

A Technique for Producing Ideas is a small, invaluable book written in 1960 by James Webb Young. It is a concise process of digestion and recombination that anyone who is willing to put in the necessary work can follow. Relevant and dramatic ideas are the soul of advertising, and this process is as likely to produce them as anything ever devised. Reading the book is essential to understanding the technique. These are the points distilled in the briefest language.

"You must be an extensive browser of all sorts of information. For it is with the advertising person as with the cow: no browsing, no milk."
James Webb Young (1886-1973)

que at all... In a majority of cases, something will eventually be found in the appearance, ingredients, use, manufacturing process, packaging, or distribution of a product that offers prospects a compelling reason to try it. It may or may not be truly unique. So long as no one else is talking about it, it becomes unique to your product by reason of preemption. **3** Sometimes the Unique Advantage is in reality a unique disadvantage which can be turned around... At one time all tuna fish sold was pink. A new company came on the scene with a white tuna – a tremendous *dis*advantage – in a market used to pink tuna. The white tuna people didn't think so, and advertised their tuna as guaranteed not to turn pink, thereby implying that something was wrong with pink tuna... They did it so well that all tuna marketed since then is white. **4** Occasionally, no matter how hard you try, nothing unique can be found about a product. It is then the agency's responsibility to recommend the addition of a par-

1

"Advertising expresses the life of the era from which it stems."
Westvaco Inspiration for Printers, Number 200, 1955

1 Do you see distinction among matchbooks, or do you see a quaint advertising medium and kitschy art? These matchbook covers were designed a couple of generations ago. They are obviously a reflection of the times: people smoked, there were no disposable lighters, so matchbooks were carried by many and used often. Today's advertising media is different, but it is similarly awash in content. How does your advertising stand out?

general (about life, history, and events). An advertising idea comes from the combination of specific information about the product with general knowledge about life. For this, you must have an appetite for information for its own sake and have an eagerness to learn about any subject.

📖 **Method, Step 2** Chew on the material. Turn it over. Inspect it. Define it. Write down ideas until you can't get any more.

📖 **Method, Step 3** Digest the material. Set the problem aside. Arrange for the subconscious to take over. Take a brief period, an afternoon, maybe a day, to let your mind do its work. Provide emotional or intellectual stimulation on another subject entirely.

📖 **Method, Step 4** The idea will appear on its own. Ideas come after you stop straining for them – if you have genuinely prepared the mind in Steps 1 through 3.

📖 **Method, Step 5** Refine the young, fragile idea so it is useful and truly satisfies the problem. Adapt it to the practical and specific conditions in which it must exist.

Having spent his career at J. Walter Thompson, Young was asked to deliver a presentation on developing creativity to graduate students at the University of Chicago's School of Business. He prepared his notes the day before and subsequently edited them for publication. Young was a person who absorbed, condensed, then regurgitated facts in simplified form with truth revealed. It is little wonder that he had the capacity to succinctly describe the process of ideation.

ticular feature to a manufacturer. Or the agency must create a Unique Advantage for the product by repositioning it… In my experience, there are very few products for which an exclusive claim cannot be made or a new position found. Usually the agency that fails to do this is at fault; it is rarely the fault of the product. There are far more parity agencies than there are parity products."

So it is up to the creatives to play with a product, to feel it, to know it, and to recognize – or invent – what makes it special, which may be either a positive or a negative that is turned into a positive. A friend tells of buying a luxe Briggs umbrella in London. Pointing at a nearly invisible scar on the underside of the beautifully carved burled walnut handle, the salesman said, "I regret this small flaw, sir." The salesman understood the value of the *absence* of machine made perfection in a finely-crafted, one-of-a-kind object. His observation and comment assured the sale.

1

1 The most inane creative approach possible is to show a product simply as it is. There is no Christmas bonus waiting for the art director who says, "I've got a great idea: let's show a lawnmower in our lawnmower ad!" Add *something*: what if a lawnmower were a car? It would be adjustable to fit the "driver." A *feature* of this lawnmower is its adjustable handle. It is turned into a *benefit* by comparing it with a car's adjustable steering wheel.

What is the product?
Use the mind to:
Collect facts
Be methodical and comprehensive
Define how it feels, looks, and works
Determine target user
Identify what is good or bad about the product

What is the benefit?
Use the mind and emotions to:
Evaluate facts
Determine the position

How have similar products been positioned?
Can their positions be co-opted?
What position envelops theirs?
Can an opposite position work?

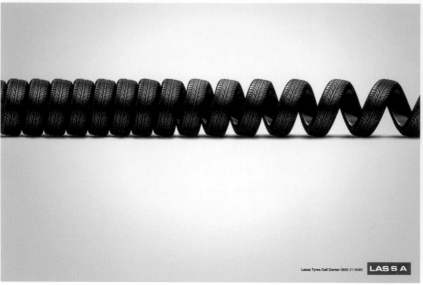

1

2

"Big ideas are so hard to recognize, so easy to kill. Don't forget that, all of you who don't have them," said John "Jock" Elliott, Jr., on his retirement as the chairman of Ogilvy &

Mather International in 1982. "I was a pretty good copywriter, but not good enough. I could execute campaigns, but never came up with the big ideas, so I went into a less demanding

kind of work. I became an account man."
1 A one-shot ad is an idea that can't be realised more than once. This combination of tires and telephone cord, promot-

ing the manufacturer's call center, is wonderful in its simplicity, but it can't be repeated.
2 The unique attributes of the product and humor are used to make this one-shot ad.

One-shot vs campaign advertising Coming up with a single ad that has a clear point made memorably is not an easy task. Creating a one-shot ad requires a compelling idea, fresh visualization, and clear, distinctive typography. Challenging as making a great one-shot ad is, clients almost always need an idea that is big enough to be freshly interpreted dozens or even hundreds of times over the course of a multi-year campaign. Such an idea, an idea that is campaignable, is called, naturally enough, a Big Idea. Creatives who can develop the Big Idea are in a minority of advertising professionals. Their skill is an extremely valuable commodity.

A campaign is an extended series of ads that are connected and unified by a common theme or idea. The theme can be expressed by maintaining a consistent attitude through the ad series ("Ugly is only skin deep and *we're proud of being ugly*"), or by repeating one headline (or by making

"Aeroxon Flycatcher" A startling demonstration of an insect control service is a one-shot ad. The billboard has stickiness in the shape of letters, which, over time, glue passing bugs and make the message visible. But can this be done in, say, a dozen permutations? Or is this installation about the end of the road for the idea – as well as for the bugs?

1

1 Though this is a great idea – that this toothpaste is natural and refreshing – and the ads are beautifully realized, this

campaign is really multiple iterations of the same ad. If you cannot easily imagine what the

tenth (or hundredth) version of the ad will be, you are not working with a Big Idea.

3

3 A campaign must have similarities, if not exact identicalities, in attitude, purpose, and design. Three ads from a 1959 Olivetti series show the product, a well-designed typewriter, as an evolutionary step forward in the history of writing. The layout changes, but the spaciousness, colors, and transparent overlapping treatment remain constant.

only slight alterations to a headline), or by using the same design throughout. A campaign must cross over media, as well. An idea might be wonderful for TV because it requires movement, but it must be translatable into print and be just as potent.

Ads in a campaign are never seen by the public in a cluster, the way they are presented on a critique wall. They are placed in publications or broadcast in intervals, so that repeated viewing makes an accumulated impression. Days or weeks may go by between viewings, so the ads must have a certain repetitiveness to them.

An advertising campaign can be made of scores of ads before it is retired and a new approach is developed in response to a changing business environment. Presenting a campaign usually consists of three print ads and two or three television commercials. These quantities suggest the campaignability of the Big Idea.

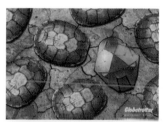

Camping equipment positioned as natural protection and expressed through simile: *a tent is like a turtle's shell*. Campaignable, Big Ideas are tough to develop. The creative process is best done as a two-person team, where ideas can be shot back and forth and improved upon and evolved from an unrealistic "what if?" to a polished idea. This campaign would be more fun to work on than the Aim campaign at left.

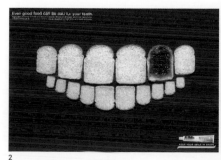

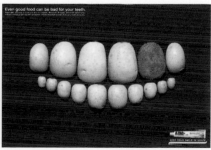

2

A campaign is a continuation of a defined attitude plus an idea big enough to be interpreted many times, each time as freshly as the first. Both the idea and the attitude must be flexible.
2 This campaign's strength is the idea that teeth can be represented by foods that teeth chew, like toast and potatoes. Can you imagine the twentieth ad in this campaign? It'll have to at least evolve into food that is not white if it is to be visible.

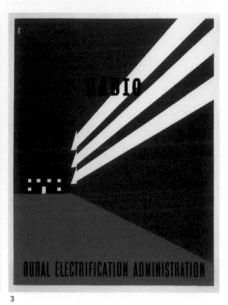

1

2

3

1 Lester Beall's poster series for the R.E.A. in 1937 promotes expansion of the U.S. electrical system.

2 Beall (1903-1969) saw no distinction between art and professional practice. These posters were silkscreened so their graphic simplicity was made necessary partly by technology and mostly by Beall's interpretation of Modernism.

3 Note Beall's thematic use of arrows and lines to indicate dynamic progress, and his use of colors, typefaces, and sizes.

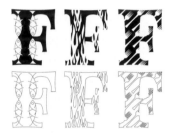

Developing a distinctive logo requires abstraction of both the type and imagery. This student's project develops three variations of a letter and object translation in assigned ways to help see similarities of shape.

An identifiable look for *every* client How can you make your advertising stand out from the ordinary, the work that we have all trained ourselves to ignore in all media? Understanding consumers and what they already see is part of the solution. Persuading clients to risk their advertising budget is another. But it starts with us, with our willingness to take risks and develop a look for each client for whom we work. It is a significant part of branding, or creating a consistent visual approach for all a company's materials that come before the public. A weak visual personality handicaps a branding effort: if a discernable character isn't recognized, your brand is seriously handicapped. A strong marketing character requires the risk of being different.

Get a message noticed by manipulating elements in an unexpected way. Abstraction of imagery and type produces new design solutions that a client can *own* without making the core idea unreadable.

Advertising
Design
and
Typography

1

2

3

1 Neville Brody for Nike, 1988: uses scale contrast of Franklin Gothic, print grows from tv commercial with moving type: young, hip audience.

2 Amtrak's campaign picks up the look of old railroad posters from the 1940s, which reinforces already existing ideas about scenic rail travel.

3 Torn paper and a loose painting style define this 1964 ad. **Opposite** Kurt Schwitters' 1924 ad for a writing ink manufacturer broke the design rules of the day. Schwitters was an artist associated with the Dadaists and helped found the *Circle of New Advertising Designers* in 1927.

PELIKAN TINTE

94

4001 Beste Buch- und Schreibtinte. Eisengallustinte, fließt bläulich, wird tiefschwarz. Liefert Schrift von unbegrenzter Dauer. Angenehm leichtflüssig.
5001 Buch- und Kopiertinte. Eisengallustinte, fließt bläulich, wird schwarz. Liefert auf der Kopierpresse 2 bis 3 Kopien. Kann auch in Büchern verwandt werden, ohne darin abzuklatschen.
3001 Starke Kopiertinte. Echte Blauholztinte, fließt violett-schwarz. Schrift und Kopien dunkeln schwarz nach. Gibt auf der Kopiermaschine 3 bis 6 Kopien. Auch nach längerer Zeit noch kopierfähig. Nicht für Bücher bestimmt.

3001   4001   5001

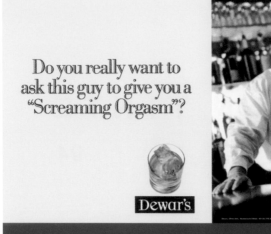

Drive it like you hate it.

1

2

Attitude, an essential consideration in advertising, should be consciously determined. Your campaign's attitude represents the product, so it has to be interpretable many times. If you can't have fun with attitude, pick another one.

1 Attitude is critical in liquor advertising: it alone differentiates products. For example, Chivas is *for those who have arrived*; Johnny Walker Red is for *those who aspire to and are almost there.*

2 Attitude characterizes mid-60s Volvo and VW ads. George Lois directly competed with VW by using similar design simplicity to emphasize toughness.

New York illustrator and typographer Daniel Pelavin has fun with the meaning of good design and expected conventions in his series of self-promotional materials.

Chapter 2 **The Four Levels of Advertising**

What makes an ad "good"? John Hunt, Worldwide Creative Director at TBWA\Worldwide, says, "Begin by admitting no one is fundamentally interested in what you've got to say. So *how* you say it had better be pretty startling… Lazy work is never good. Good doesn't even win awards. A good ad must earn the consumers' time. If an ad campaign is really good, consumers will seek it out…. You have to entertain to keep your audience interested, but when does that just make your ad a sponsored joke? On the other hand, take yourself too seriously and you kill the communication with self-righteous relevance. The geniuses of today seem to know how to navigate between the two… What defines a great campaign? (I used to say) 'an original thought enhanced by a brilliant execution.' Now I say 'an idea that comes from a different place.'"

Advertising
Design
and
Typography

1

2

3

1 Attitude grows from positioning. Campaigns grow from reinterpretations of positioning and attitude. Pepe's attitude is

of a *very* relaxed atmosphere.
2 A newspaper ad meant to attract magazine advertisers points out the natural needs of

young parents, the core group for the publication.
3 As the primary visual, the moon is provocatively used

to symbolize both night time and dusty dryness. The headline even implies sexiness. Excellent attitude.

"*The Running of the Bulls!*" (literally: "*Containment*")
1 This amusing consumer insert bound into a running magazine has fun with the 9-day festival in Pamplona, Spain in which people run in front of a herd of bulls.
2 "*Run, world, run.*" The first foldout reveals the subhead and shows bulls readying for the run by protecting sensitive parts and hydrating. The second foldout shows them stretching and applying Vaseline to reduce chafing. Finally, they are using the toilet, resting, and visualizing for the event. The back panel (not shown) lists retailers.

"Some people can only tell a good ad when it appears in an advertising award show," writes Mark Fenske. "Some people would say the only good ad is one that 'sells product...' How do you know – at the moment you've done it – that you've done a good ad... One word: art... When you've made art, stop. Until you have, don't. I believe it's that simple." Thomas Aquinas said, "Art is simply the right method of doing things."

Véronique Vienne writes in *Communication Arts*, "In our field, we seem to depend on competitions to define what's good and bad design... Other creative types have their competitions, but being 'good' is never the issue. Brilliance, originality, proficiency are what matter. Unlike us, they can be 'bad' and still get a standing ovation. Designers developed this strange do-good dependency in the early 1950s, when the modern design movement was still in its infancy. Between 1950 and 1955, designers were subjected to a grueling evaluation exercise sponsored by the

"It is our experience that if you rub minds with an artist you are pretty likely to strike sparks. Sparks are good things to put into every advertisement." Barton, Durstine & Osborn, Inc., 1925

"There's fun in this business when you get the right people together... then you get the right freedom of expression. An idea can come from copy or art. No difference. A really good ad comes along when the transition from picture to copy is so smooth you don't notice it. It's a unit: one image." Jim Hastings, AD, Campbell-Ewald Advertising, 1955

Four
Levels of
Advertising

4 What's the difference between this and comparable underwear? Fabric? Cut? Color? Detail? None of the above. It's attitude.
5 The attitude of a serious skier is revealed in the subhead: "And I didn't come here to sit around on the damn swings." The black area around the text is called a *mortise*. This one is not a random shape: it is an exaggerated parabolic ski form.
6 To those who don't pay attention, jeans are jeans. Make a brand stand out for a segment of the market with attitude. Know your audience and send signals they will receive. This ran in *Bikini* magazine in 1994.

1

2

1 A pun is a play on words. Puns are easy to make and hardly ever work as sales messages. The first job of an ad is to make itself seen: no design treatment will get a message across if an ad is invisible. The second job is to make a single striking point.

Puns may work for the first step, but they fail badly in the second, where the sales message is.
2 A pun on *pop art*: Campbell's

Soup deserves this foolishness. Andy Warhol used their label as a symbol of rampant consumerism in the early 1960s.

What makes an ad great?
1 Has an unexpected, fresh delivery
2 Uses simplicity so the message gets through
3 Image and primary type act as a unit for drama
4 Causes the viewer to become involved
5 Talks about the viewer, not the sponsor
6 Challenges curiosity
7 Causes an action or response
8 Causes thinking
9 Has well-designed, high-craft execution
10 Sells product (it may be good design, but not advertising)

highest authority in the field – the Museum of Modern Art… The design community was systematically and deliberately conditioned to equate Modernism with good design – and good design with good business… One of the originalities of the MoMA program was its taxonomy: instead of presenting gold, silver, and bronze medals, a practice popularized by international exhibitions in the late 19th century, the jurors only awarded an unassailable 'Good Design' stamp of approval. This democratic system of classification allowed them to dodge the difficult issue of defining by what standards they were assessing each entry… To this day, 'good design' is a lofty concept that evades definition."

What makes an ad successful? It depends whose doing the evaluating. A viewer considers an ad successful if it cracks through his defensive barriers and engages him by saying something valuable and actionable.

Advertising
Design
and
Typography

1   **2**   **3**   **4**   **5**

1 The urge to make puns can be powerful: resist it. What do baby chickens have to do with this Internet advertiser? Oh, they're *inexpensive*.

2 Can the pun be used for any other advertiser? *Thanksgiving* and *turkeys* certainly can. Bad cars, by the way, are called "lemons," not "turkeys."

3 "Dumbo" (the nickname for an area in Brooklyn) plus a new apartment building equals *a baby elephant*. How droll.
4 No, it's not.

5 A little less bad because boat nuts really may feel like they are wearing a vessel on their heads. *Spouses* of boat nuts would probably believe this ad.

Don't Let
Network Downtime
Wipe You Out.

InfoVista Lets You See
What's Happening Within Your
Network, Systems and Applications.

get the lead out of your ads   A prolific pencil is no substitute for a unique advertising idea. Creativity is an art not a technique at SH&L. Call PLaza 1-1250.

3   4

3 The primary visual of the surfer has everything to do with "Wipe You Out" and nothing whatsoever to do with the head-line's "Network Downtime," the subhead's "See What's Happening," nor the client's name or business. Perhaps the art direc-tor or marketing VP is a surfing fan?
4 The message in the text is valid – *pretty designs with no concept are anathema to this agency* – and the visual is a stopper, but the headline is a really bad pun.

A client considers an ad successful if it achieves the stated goals, increases revenue (directly or indirectly), and makes them look personally good to their colleagues, friends, and family. A creative director considers an ad successful if it achieves the stated goals (thereby covering her ass), makes the client happy (so it'll give more work to the agency), and makes the agency look good to colleagues, friends, and family. An art director con-siders an ad successful if it is creative (or at least new to himself) with the possibility of a submission to an awards competition, makes the boss happy (so *she'll* get a raise and/or promotion and year-end bonus from her boss), and makes the client happy.

What does not make an ad successful is mere "eyeballs," a term coined in the 1990s with respect to Internet viewers. This was prior to the Internet crash in which it was proved that eyeballs seeing something had little relationship to the eyeballs' owners actually buying what they saw

6   7   8   9

6 Unwind is like *untie*, we must suppose. Isn't there a more compelling way of saying "This vehicle is not for the office?"

7 Is this a pun or good sense? It is certainly manipulative: the reader has the rug pulled out from beneath his initial under-standing, so it risks alienation.

8 The charming play on words, i.e., puns, and a simple illustra-tive style make this Canadian poster series work.

9 A *good* pun is possible if it shows and says what the bene-fit is for the prospective buyer. This Bernbach/Krone classic gets the job done right.

1

2

A *cliché* is an overly-familiar visual or verbal idea. The best thing to do with a cliché is to not use it. By definition it is familiar and attention cannot be drawn with the familiar. The worst thing to do with a cliché is to use it without fresh interpretation.
1 *"What if the founding fathers on Mt. Rushmore are joined by a woman?"* Without that spin, this 1976 cigarette ad wouldn't get any attention at all. At the time, this was more provocative than it is now.

2 Use clichés in unexpected ways that serve the message: Santa is the husband; the smiley face has donated an eye and he's happy.

Point of view can make an ordinary scene, like people walking on a street (left) appear fascinating by looking straight down on them (right).

advertised. In fact, "eyeballs" is a modern version of CPM*, or "Cost Per Thousand," a determination of media costs that counted how many prospective consumers saw an ad or commercial. *M is *thousand* in Roman numerals.

Thinking verbally and visually Ask yourself, why would anyone read your ad? Why would *you* read your ad?

Who is the star of your ad? Is it the copywriter? Is it the photographer? Is it the typeface designer? Is it the art director, i.e., *you*? What have *you* done, what value have *you* added, to make the art director the star? Great art direction has to be more than picking the right image, photographer, and typeface. What intangibles make a good ad a great ad?

☛ **A great ad attracts the reader's attention** Use photography, illustration, type, space, color, and scale to get eyes to stop. No one is *look-*

1　**2**　**3**　**4**

1 An *analogy* is a comparison of similarity: "sunglasses are *like* glass panes on a beautifully-designed vintage automobile," or...

2 A Jaguar automobile is *like* a gorgeous woman.
3 *Borrowed interest* is a subset of analogies. Claiming a relationship where none actually exists plants an idea in the consumer's mind. This camera ad uses borrowed interest: it *says* but doesn't show the relationship to ultra fine wine.

4 *"It's like getting that little blue box."* This ad refers to the Tiffany blue box (see *Fig. 2 at top*), implying the product is equivalent to high-profile jewelry.

1

2

3

1 Hot dogs so long, they stretch your grill. You can laugh (or even be disgusted), but this ad increased sales 48%.

2 A burger so big, it'll tear your mouth.

3 A small car that is actually so big, it takes two and two quarter pages to show. This

ad recognizes the obvious fact that magazines have pages and *uses* that attribute.

ing for an interruption by an ad, so you have to actively attract attention. An ad strategy is a complete waste if you haven't first stopped readers.

☞ **A great ad holds the reader's attention** Having gotten a viewer, reader, or listener to stop, you have to hold his attention to get him through the message. This is done by providing a sequence of information, making the transitions from element to element effortless. Lastly, you have to get him to *do* something: sample, try, buy, call, or visit – or even think positively about the product. The perceived quantity of information is crucial to holding attention: it has to look like the ad won't take long to get through. Long copy is fine, but typographic principles (*see Chapter 8*) must be followed to ensure clarity.

☞ **A great ad breaks through people's ad-resistant shells** The world is resisting your efforts to communicate advertising messages. Don't you have a protective shell around yourself, avoiding sales pitches that at-

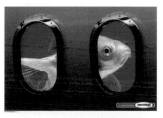

A toy vehicle so small, it makes a goldfish look enormous.

"Creativity is the power to connect the seemingly unconnected." William Plomer

1

2

3

4

1 Cans so small, you'll need a miniature straw. Scale is a powerful visual tool.

2 This newspaper is produced so fast and so timely, it can be used the same day as "proof of life" in a kidnapping scenario.

3 An unseen customized car so fast that it can only be caught by a jet aircraft.
4 Tires roll. This 1958 ad, made when four-color process print-

ing was still a novelty, shows motion by purposely offsetting the cyan, magenta, and yellow plates.

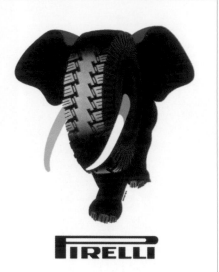

1

1 A car so tough – tougher than a police cruiser – that it is used as a shield in a shootout.

2

2 Tires so tough, they're like bull elephants. This Armando Testa classic from 1954 is every bit as great today as it was fifty years ago, demonstrating that simplicity always works.

One point per ad will smash through the reader's shell of inattention.

tack from everywhere, all the time? It is up to you to smash holes in those shells (*left*). The best tool for smashing through protective shells is a very pointy one, so be sure to have exactly one point per ad.

👈 **Creativity isn't useful unless it solves specific problems** Craziness for its own sake is amusing, but it isn't our job to merely amuse or entertain. If a problem hasn't been well defined, you'll know because it'll be hard to focus your creativity.

👈 **Put emotion into your work** Great actors don't *pretend* to be happy or sad; they will themselves to actually *be* happy or sad on demand in front of many people. That's what makes them valuable. Making your messages memorable comes, in part, through connecting emotionally with your audience. The more creative you are, the more sensitive you are to living and life. Use your innate sensitivity. Whatever you're feeling, find a way to apply it to your ads.

1

2

3

1 A marker so permanent that Jimi Hendrix's signature is still there decades later (he died in 1970).

2 *"155 miles of roaming and 70 restaurant refills,"* meaning a boot so comfortable, you will outlast it.

3 A car so powerful, it's like a passenger jet with two and a half times the normal thrust.

By not showing the car, this image implies extreme passenger spaciousness.

1

2

1 Use a medium fully: a rusty hinge is printed in the gutter of a magazine for this lubricant.

2 Lipstick transfers to the hood of a car on facing pages of a spread. This visual takes ad-

vantage of two obvious facts: lipstick is like ink because they both smear, and that a maga-

zine spread is more than two pages that just happen to be next to each other.

Paper is dimensional It has height and width, obviously. Not quite so obviously, it has depth (thickness) and opacity, both of which can be exploited. Paper bends, tears, and is bound into magazines. Pages are perceived in order, but that's only a convention to make reproduction easy. Isn't the *experience* of a magazine one long horizontal flow? Paper is covered in ink, which has properties of its own.

The surface of paper has texture. It wasn't until about 1750 that John Baskerville, a wealthy amateur printer in Britain, invented a way to make smoother paper, which lead to typefaces (including his own) with greater contrast. Some paper's texture is distinctive, but if you get close enough, every paper's surface is unique. The latest advance in anti-forgery technology is a microscopic scanner that can determine the precise kind of paper through its immutable surface characteristics. Paper, like any subject, is fascinating when you do some research.

How to be seen: "Where's the other half of this ad?" What if a spread ad is "interrupted" by other pages? Two facts being used: paper is opaque and pages are seen over time.

1

2

3

4

5

1 This 1957 ad for El Al airlines is perhaps the earliest example of paper's tearability in an ad. For its time, this was an ad that took risks.

2 The figure/ground relationship is ambiguous in this "torn paper" poster.

3 An ad for a magazine uses a torn envelope – the normal way

of mailing magazines in those times – to give a feeling of intrigue.

4 A product so loved, the ad has been torn out.

5 Paper has thickness, like a morgue's sheet. Turning the page reveals a second picture, as if the sheet has been pulled over the child's head in death.

1

2

3

Bad concept and bad design is the toughest pill to swallow.
1 Selling real estate is straightforward: just show the property

or a benefit of living in the property. An all-type ad like this is a total loss when it doesn't say anything.

2 Puns galore! Another Warhol ripoff via Photoshop filters. The copy begins, "Let's 'face' it… no real estate agency has more 'pop…'" Yikes.

3 This is probably a very good product, but the headline was written by the account VP and the presentation is so tacky, who would believe it?

"Is sloppiness in (design) caused by ignorance or apathy? I don't know and I don't care." William Safire

"Only the mediocre are always at their best." Jean Giraudoux (1882-1944)

"If you aren't fired with enthusiasm, you will be fired with enthusiasm." Vince Lombardi (1913-1970)

Poor idea, poor execution Quit. There is such thing as talent. It can't be learned, but it can be maximized. Read, absorb, experiment. Ask "What if…" Get out of the rut of the ordinary and the mediocre. Make every ad one that you'd be jealous of if you hadn't done it yourself.

Bad advertising may come from creatives thinking others will respond differently than they themselves do to their advertising. Reed Tucker writes, "Advertisers seem to be able to make themselves believe the consumer is going to react to their message in a different way than they would sitting at home… Think of how many ads a day you flip past in a magazine. How many you ignore on TV. (The client and the agency must) make it their goal to get noticed. To take chances. To buck expectations. After all, an ad can't be successful unless somebody sees it… (We must) create unique brand personalities with intelligent, entertaining ads instead of opting for sterile, fact-filled communication."

1

2

3

4

5

1 Straight out of the account department. They forgot to tell me why I should care.
2 Symmetry is a default design treatment just as facts are a

default concept.
3 Two noisy half-page ads competing for my lack of attention.
4 This is an example of defining design as *"filling in all the*

space." When selling maximum beauty, it simply *must* represent its own self.
5 Three type families and disjointed overlapping mortise

boxes make this a busy ad. Full-color printing was a new development in 1950, so perhaps this is a victim of technological exuberance.

4

5

4 Do investors actually *want* to feel manipulated into a relationship with their financial advisors in this 2005 half-page newspaper ad? On the plus side, Mac is an excellent mirror for those of a certain age who remember his entertaining tennis a couple of decades ago.
5 Though it looks organized, this ad has four typographic focal points, which is three too many. Space, which can be used to make an ad look easy to absorb, has been distributed evenly, weakening the ad's impact.

Sometimes bad advertising comes from dreadful clients. Clients choose an agency based on the agency's previous work and the quality of their pitch. In an ideal world, the client would then ask for – demand, really – the agency's best work. It is shameful for a marketing director and for the agency's own account executives to tamp down the agency's best work by asking for change after change, diluting the original ad and compromising its power to stop and inform readers.

But ideal clients are rare and the odds are that you don't work for them. Tempting as it is to blame poor work on the client, it remains the art director's primary responsibility to make great advertising. The ability to sell an ad to decision-makers is essential and comes with experience.

Meantime, don't make their roles as spoilers easy by making ads with more than one focal point, dull visuals, lame concepts, hard to read copy, and disorganized layouts.

Can this ad be any more visually noisy? Several type sizes and positions compete for attention and convey a sense of disorganization. If any old thing will do here, what will be the quality of the education they're selling?

Four
Levels of
Advertising

6

7

8

9

10

6 Design is a balance between contrast and similarity. Because they share the page with other ads, partial-page ads must err on the side of unity. These don't.
7 There are lots of typeface, position, and spacing contrasts in this magazine's ad, but not much similarity. It is a mess not worth pausing on.
8 Ditto.
9 Centrifugal type and no reason to care. Pretty picture, though.
10 Caution: this is a concept-free zone. This design has no personality and the text column is way too wide for effortless reading. Are they telling us they are the financial services company for dullards and masochists?

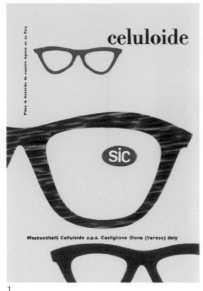

1   2   3

1 Eyeglasses are essentially a fashion product, so ad concept is generally less important than style. This 1958 ad could be a contemporary example.

2 The first words of text are *From $1 to $4 million*, so I expected a free car with the purchase of a home, or use of the car, or a session at a driving school, or

that the units come with garages, or even curvy streets in the development. But the BMW shown actually has *nothing* to do with the product.

3 This is probably the most blatantly manipulative headline ever written. Watch out for the bait and switch. Such ads just aggravate readers.

"This is not art for art's sake. This is art for advertising's sake." J.M. Mathes, Inc., Advertising, self promotion, 1955

"What a strange illusion it is to suppose that beauty is goodness." Leo Tolstoy (1828-1910)

Poor idea, great execution This is design, not advertising.

Stavros Cosmopulos, a founder of several agencies in Boston, wrote a series of amusing and truth-filled essays on advertising in the 1980s. One was called *Make the layouts rough and the ideas fancy*. An excerpt reads, "How many times have you seen advertising agencies present (work) where the beauty of the layouts and storyboards exceeds the beauty of the ideas being presented? They serenade you with crisp, comprehensive layouts, the typeface was selected after a lot of conferences about the style and its supposed subliminal communicative meaning... Elaborate storyboards are dazzling in their execution. Each panel is a work of art... Everything is there. Except for one thing. An idea... An obsequious account executive interjects that the client's name or product is seen and mentioned 14 times, twice in the first 5 seconds... All those hours and dollars spent is like putting makeup on a corpse. You can make it

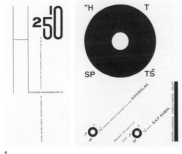

1   2   3

1 Three early ads by Piet Zwart for a Dutch cable manufacturer reveal his developing philosophy about design, c1926.

2 Is this velvet – at the time particularly extravagant and luxurious – in this poster for light bulbs, c1940? Is it brainmatter? If it's this pretty, does

it matter? The long diagonal bulb interacts with the two opposing headlines, mediating between brand and model.

3 Lovely image, but women fawning over human-size shampoo bottles maybe isn't an especially compelling reason to try the product.

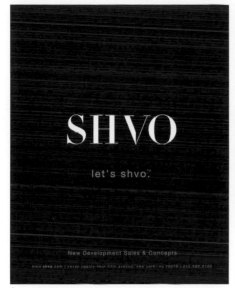

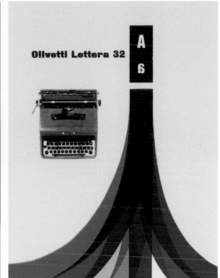

1

2

3

1 *SHVO*, which is distinctive with its customized *V*, aligns with the width of *New Development Sales & Concepts*. The mouse type at the bottom of

the page is sized to fill the live area of the page. But what does *let's shvo* mean?
2 ꟼORD risked illegibility, but only a little, to put the reader

inside a dealer's showroom. This is the first of a three-page sequence, hence no logo in the bottom right corner.
3 Italian typewriter maker

Olivetti's campaign is one of the most handsome in history. This ad shows the way keys swung into position to strike the ribbon.

look pretty, but the body is still dead… I'd rather spend most of my time working on the idea. Once you've done the research and gathered up as much marketing and demographic data as possible and established a direction, give it to the creative team so they can begin their distillation of information down, hopefully, to a single salient point. It is easier to penetrate your audience with one sharp, clean point than with a maze of half-baked, unremarkable, uninspiring ideas that will never motivate or be remembered… The poor production company is expected to transform some piece of crap into a thing of beauty through the magic of camera angles and computer graphics… The idea should be king. The words and pictures spring to life in your mind, stimulated by the strength and dynamism of the *idea*. Just imagine what a super presentation combined with all that technology could do for a good idea. Make the layouts rough and the ideas fancy."

"I don't know the key to success, but the key to failure is trying to please everybody." Bill Cosby

"Very few people do anything creative after the age of thirty-five. The reason is that very few people do anything creative before the age of thirty-five." Joel Hildebrand (1881–1983)

"Ninety percent of everything is crap." Theodore Sturgeon

Four
Levels of
Advertising

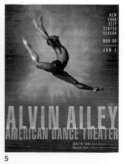

1

2

3

4

5

1 Karl Gerstner's 1964 poster for a Swiss printery uses shape, a simple grid, and bright colors.
2 Sometimes busy can be the perfect design solution. This

1967 ad for electric clocks is as active as the objects being sold.
3 An E is also an ampersand in this 2005 juxtaposition of typefaces, one stark and geometric,

the other organic and flowing.
4 Arresting visual: each finger ends in a hand. It says "five" loud and clear. It's a pity the ad isn't about "five" at all and

just a pun on "upper hand."
5 Beautiful photography is equalled by a distinctive type treatment, unifying the design of this brochure cover.

1

2

3

1 Excellent attitude and head-line. Interesting visual. So what happened? Someone won the argument for putting way too much information into this ad.

What if I had been *intrigued* in-to going to the Web site for all this detail? I'm not this commit-ted: make me fall in love with you before we get married.

2 Granted, there are many legal requirements in making pharma ads, but what if one paragraph of text was given priority – just to explain the headline a little?

3 Showing wait staff affected by their cities is a winning treat-ment, showing the serious steak-house has a sense of humor. But the space needs attention.

Two simple, clear ideas: water-proofness and big candy bar-ness. But in either case, what personality has the design added? How has the brand been promoted?

Great idea, poor execution This is a shame and must be redesigned. Poor execution can be at either end of the spectrum: *overdesigning* pro-duces a visually noisy ad; *underdesigning* produces a generic ad. Finding the perfect balance of imagery, type, and space is essential work of the art director. Overdesigning is any situation in which the design interferes with the message. Underdesigning is any ad in which the copywriter or account supervisor could have done the layout: it lacks artistry and craft. Would there be a difference in the copy if the account person had written it? There had better be, or the copywriter will soon be in a new business. Same for design. A great idea with poor execution is purely a failing of the art director.

Design is the way ideas are clothed. Overdesigning is like showing up to an office party in a combination of plaids, stripes, and polka dots. You will be noticed, but not for your good qualities and fine taste. Underdesign-

1

2

3

4

5

1 Oh! A picture of a backpack for a backpack ad. This is a waste of a terrific headline built on potent attitude. Quality photo-graphy, but poor art direction.

2 A letter to one's deserted couch: a great idea for an energy-boosting product. But elements are spread out: there's no grouping.

3 Great headline, but where's the design personality? Would you want to AD this account?
4 Youthful design relying on type is a good try, but it

doesn't show the idea well.
5 Great imagery and benefit of direct arrival at the destina-tion. But no design: this is just typesetting, not typography.

4 | **5**

4 Beautiful photograph: give the photographer a bonus. There's nothing *wrong* with the application of type, yet there's nothing *right* about it, either.

Design *rightness* is determined by *the clarity of purposeful relationships and contrasts*. There is no agreement between the type and image.

5 The contrast between the blinding optical art on the left and the exceptionally easy-to-read text on the right is key. Sadly, the text is set in bold (much harder to read than regular weight), has a tiny x-height, and has poor word spacing. Blame it on typesetting defaults and the AD's sense of contentment.

ing is like showing up in cutoffs and a t-shirt. Anyone who doesn't already know you will have to get beyond your presentation to see who you really are and be willing to hear what you have to say.

The middle road might seem to be khakis and an open neck buttondown with loafers. Classic, timeless, and universally accepted. But a person wearing it will not be particularly noticeable. You might say there's nothing *right* with that wardrobe: it's just generic invisibility.

Inappropriate "clothing" on great ideas detracts from the ad's ability to be noticed. Underdesigning either makes an ad less visible to begin with, or, if the visual is able to carry the load, the lame design doesn't contribute to the branding.

As Steve Cosmopulos says, "A good idea will shine through a poor layout, but a great layout will never help a poor idea. It will only make a bad idea more noticeable."

"Fashion is a form of ugliness so intolerable that we have to alter it every six months."
Oscar Wilde (1856-1900)

"The human mind treats a new idea the way the body treats a strange protein: it rejects it."
Biologist P.B. Medawar

Four
Levels of
Advertising

6 | **7** | | **9**

6 Get past the fine image and generic design is all that's left. Doesn't the client deserve a design personality they can reasonably call their own?

7 The disconnect between marriage and the cold, unemotional display type is purposeful. The text is unrelated.

8 A car so perfectly designed, it is like an egg, the epitome of functional design. The type, though, is set too wide for the page, and lacks a shape.

9 *"Thrills without spills. A tire that hugs the road and loves curves."* This Polish tire ad has a terrific visual, but the text type is absurdly small – especially so being reversed from black.

1

2

A great ad is elegant: it has all the parts necessary with nothing extra.

1 An imprint of a Levi's pant-seat as sound bars illustrates the clothing preference of a recording producer.
2 Opening the windows to the morning is the same position as holding an open newspaper. Full-page ad for Il Giorno ("The Day"), 1959.

An expressive billboard suited to its driving audience.

"Will it sizzle or fizzle? That depends. Depends on your insight into what makes people tick. On your courage to be different. On your skill to be graphically distinguished. When all three wind up in the creative solution – look out." Calkins & Holden, Inc., self promotion, 1955

Great idea, great execution Yes.

Great advertising ideas are so hard to develop. When they are presented with style and personality, they are in the highest level of advertising.

Testing ideas has become the preferred way of protecting the vast sums of money spent on advertising. Focus groups of laypersons chop away the best ideas because these ideas are – by definition – new, different, and unfamiliar. People don't like the unfamiliar. The same goes for design that dares to go beyond default sensibilities. An individual with a point of view is having an ever tougher time getting it heard.

Nevertheless, you have to dare to make mistakes to get your work noticed. I wonder if this partly explains why there are proportionally few creatives over the age of 45: do they get tired of being daring and pushing for their ideas to be accepted? Or is high-priced experience traded for low-priced youth? It is essential to make a creative splash early in

Advertising
Design
and
Typography

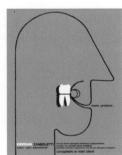

1

2

3

4

5

1 Weimer Purcell's 1950 modernist poster uses abstraction to express New York's energy.
2 Abram Games abstracts and combines a train and the map of England in this travel poster.
3 *"A newspaper that interests everybody."* Simplicity, elegance, and humanity in this 1959 ad for an Italian newspaper.

4 *"A strong simple selling idea... dramaticaly presented"* Benton & Bowles 1961 house ad must have produced a few inquiries, and several new clients.
5 *"Small problems... astringent, anesthetizes, antiseptic..."* J.P. Grivel's 1965 image-dominant ad mixes a dimensional tooth with a diagrammatic head.

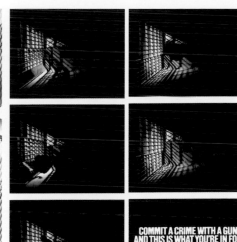

3

4

3 In order to say clearly that Swatch watches are from Switzerland, Paula Scher made an homage of a well-known 1934 travel poster by Swiss designer Herbert Matter (*right*), which happened to hang in the New York City Swatch offices. Though Scher credited Matter in the design of her 1985 piece, it did not deter critics from speaking out against her copying a design icon.

4 Demonstration on TV: half a minute of nothingness is the *feeling* of being in prison.

your career, or else you may not have an opportunity to get better.

Great advertising comes from pestilential attention to detail: copywriters getting every word just right, art directors getting every element just right, every type and spacing attribute perfect. As Steve Cosmopulos says, "Details make the big things possible. Without every grain of sand, there can be no beach."

Great advertising also comes from people who are a little unusual: they are easily bored, they love learning new things, and they are easily fascinated by the unexpected. If you ask the most creative people you know, they will probably reveal that they read at least a half-dozen magazines per week. They read autobiographies. They develop the ability to observe. They avoid unnecessary routine. They take different routes to work just to keep it fresh. If they work in advertising, they look at ads critically to see what's been done and buy annuals as a record of the best.

On creativity:
"I have never made the slightest effort to compose anything original... There is not a famous master whose music I have not studied through many times." Wolfgang Amadeus Mozart

"Originality is the most dangerous word in advertising. Preoccupied with originality, (practitioners) pursue something as illusory as swamp fire." Rosser Reeves

VINOPOLIS
CITY OF WINE

6

7

8

9

6 The senses of taste and sight are joyfully emphasized in this 1997 mark for a wine merchant.

7 Time Warner's eye/ear trademark was painted by hand when the computer-perfect version was deemed "too unemotional."

8 Can ugly *work*? An ordinary newspaper supermarket ad is undeniably ugly, but it has withstood the test of time *and it does work*. Like a hammer, this ad is a tool: it has a specific job and it does it well.

9 Skid control made visible, simply. The emptiness in the right column is clearly intentional.

Modern advertising timeline
adapted from Warren Berger's
Advertising Today

1959 Volkswagen "Think Small" ad and campaign develops at Doyle Dane Bernbach. Its roll-out the following year begins a revolution in advertising.

1961 Rosser Reeves presents the Unique Selling Proposition in his *Reality in Advertising*.

1963 Avis's "No. 2" campaign presents a perceived lack as a great strength.

Ronald McDonald is invented.

1965 The Pillsbury Doughboy is invented by the Leo Burnett Agency.

1966 Mary Wells becomes the first woman to head a major ad agency. She introduces a campaign the next year that emphasizes the disadvantages of Benson & Hedges long cigarettes.

1968 "Ring around the collar" coined and pushes Wisk detergent past its competitors.

1970 The "Spicy Meatball" commercial for Alka-Seltzer makes America laugh, but has questionable sales effect.

1971 Nike's "Swoosh" logo is designed at the last minute and accepted despite serious reservations which have since been overcome.

Frank Perdue, a third-generation Maryland chicken farmer, begins 150-commercial reign as a spokesman for his own product, saying "It takes a tough man to make a tender chicken."

Television is prohibited from airing cigarette commercials.

1974 Hebrew National hot dogs begins "We answer to a higher authority" campaign by Scali McCabe Sloves.

1979 Mean Joe Green softens for a moment when trading his game jersey for a Coke.

1980 15-year-old Brooke Shields sparks controversy by claiming, "Nothing comes between me and my Calvins."

Absolut begins its legendary campaign with "Halo" ad.

1982 Weiden + Kennedy opens in Portland with a single small client: Nike.

Federal Express uses the "world's fastest talking man" to present its fast delivery point.

1   2   3   4

1 *We try harder* is a convincing argument for using the not-as-good car rental company, 1963.
2 VW's big idea (c1965) is *ugly* *is only skin deep*, and their attitude is *we're proud of being ugly*.
3 Mary Wells turns a flaw (inconvenient extra cigarette length) into a benefit, 1966.
4 Frank Perdue, head of a family poultry business, is the spokesman as he brands chicken, 1971.

Advertising's greatest hits Advertising certainly existed before World War II, but it wasn't nearly the cultural engine it became in the 1950s and, especially, the 1960s. Advertising has been used as a way to explain and exploit: space-age references in product design and marketing in the late 1950s had everything to do with the threat of nuclear annihilation; post-War consumerism exploded as we were told to buy the newest, fastest, best products ever made – and keep the American manufacturing community busy.

Media evolved in response to the demand for more opportunity to promote mass-produced products. Television ownership grew from 3 million sets in 1950 to 32 million in 1955. Ad agencies developed from media agents to highly competitive think tanks for selling. The 1960s saw a creative revolution partly in reponse to the dreadful onslaught of advertising through the previous decade. Consumers were growing unrespon-

1   2   3

1 2006 becomes 1972 as the Alka-Seltzer classic "I Can't Believe I Ate The Whole Thing" is remade in celebration of the 75th anniversary of the brand.
2 Mean Joe Green shows his sensitive side when he trades his game shirt for a Coke, 1979.
3 "Fast delivery" described by the world's fastest talking human, 1982.

"SWOOSH" Design
1971

5   6   7   8

5 The Nike "Swoosh" logo is designed by Carolyn Davidson, a student at Portland State University for $35 in 1971. This is the current version:

6 Absolut is introduced with this ad in a still-going-strong campaign, 1980. Some of their best ads are limited edition magazine inserts (*see page 55*).

7 A very young Brooke Shields for Calvin Klein jeans, c1980.
8 Mahatma Gandhi for Apple Computers, a profoundly anti-consumerist spokesman, 1997.

sive to more of the same. So copy was shortened, visuals were emphasized (to better compete with television), and humor was added to the advertiser's inventory, though it didn't always affect sales as anticipated.

It's been said that advertising is "artificial truth." The best artificial truths are those that are accepted *eagerly*. Fashioning a message so it resonates with society at a particular moment is about as easy as setting out to write a hit song. Few can do it consistently and for those who can, gut instinct plays a significant role. Understanding people and their motivation is every bit as important as understanding the product.

Advertising's greatest hits really is a listing of campaigns that have resonated in our culture. These ads *contributed to* culture as much as they *reflected things already going on* in it. There were better ideas and there were samples that were visually significant, but these are the ones that lead the way in *cultural impact*.

4   5   6   7

4 Brains as a fried egg in a sizzling pan create discussion, 1987.
5 Energizer Bunny introduced as he barges into a campaign

of fake commercials, 1989.
6 ESPN's SportsCenter gets the mockumentary treatment in which athletes show up at the studio, 1996.

7 Budweiser amuses with its "Wassup?" campaign, popularizing an African-American term, 2000. It reaches its end when "Wasabi" replaces "Wassup."

1984 Apple's "1984" commercial tells Super Bowl watchers to think for themselves.

1985 Michael Jackson begins campaign for Pepsi, eventually setting his hair on fire.

1987 A fried egg illustrates a brain on drugs for the Partnership for a Drug-Free America.

1988 "Just do it" introduced by Nike and becomes one of the most famous slogans ever.

1989 The Energizer Bunny begins popping up in fake commercials.

1991 The Swedish Bikini Team debuts as a parody of sexist beer ads for Stroh's. Misunderstood, it is itself vilified as a sexist campaign.

Saatchi & Saatchi hires an actress to react to a British Airways commercial in London movie theaters.

1993 "Got Milk?" campaign is introduced.

1995 Calvin Klein jeans campaign features very young models in apparent porno film scenes.

1996 "Mockumentary" approach developed for ESPN's "This is SportsCenter."

1997 24 years after Washington Olivetto founds DPZ in São Paulo and begins a predominantly visual (non-verbal) approach, a Brazilian agency is named Agency of the Year at Cannes, the first time a non-U.S./England agency wins.

Apple uses Gandhi, the Dalai Lama, Alfred Hitchcock, and other worldwide luminaries to represent "Think different."

1998 Gaps "Khakis Swing" commercials air.

2000 Dot-com advertisers flood Super Bowl commercials.

"Wassup?" becomes catchphrase for Budweiser beer.

2002 The Mini is launched.

2003 Absolut Interactive site adds motion to print ads.

2004 Apple's iPod silhouette campaign.

2005 Target reinvents modernism and brands itself through design.

2006 Adidas makes the impossible in sports possible. The *futbol* match between two kids and their pro picks is a classic.

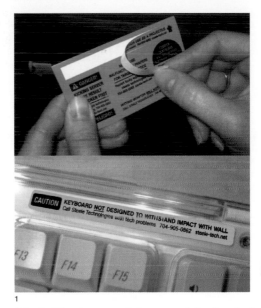

1   2   3

1 Peel-off business cards have witty phrases to be stuck on computer equipment as a reminder for future service calls.

2 Getting the logo into a prospect's wallet is easy: invent a prepaid "Burrito Bank" eating card which can be seen – and act as a reminder – every time a prospect pulls out her wallet.

3 Sitting and waiting for two seconds while the gate raises is an opportunity to remind. This is an unexpected installation – or is it a demonstration?

Chapter 3 **How to be Seen in Noisiness**

Advertising is everywhere It is inescapable: clothing is branded; ads are wrapped on the turnstiles at public transit stations; they are glued to the blacktop of parking spaces; they are pasted to the office water cooler; ads are digitally superimposed on baseball's backstop behind home plate; there are fake classified ads and ads on blogs; there is planned "word-of-mouth" and "guerrilla" marketing. Each of these are responses to the idea, "If I can't outspend my competitors, I can outsmart them."

The price advertising pays for this saturation (*opposite*) is an ever-thickening consumer skin. We – and they – are increasingly impervious to sales messages. It often feels like we *have* to be to retain our sanity.

There is only one way to successfully cut through the noise of

An ad on the top of a can of Coke is like watching commercials in a movie theater: you've paid for the opportunity of being sold to.

"You might as well fall flat on your face as lean over too far backward." James Thurber (1894-1961)

1   2   3

1 A program on the Oxygen channel is promoted on toilet paper rolls placed in bathrooms at bars near college campuses.

2 Temporary tattoos are handed out free, as this one for a type foundry.

3 Fans have been an advertising medium for generations. The message is in front of the consumer's face for hours at a time. The folding example is Italian from 1935. The contemporary example is from a Brazilian beer promotion that was distributed in New York City in 2005.

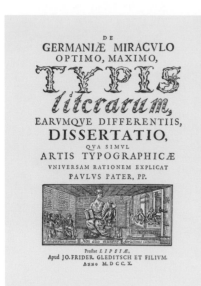

1

2

3

1 Clutter and noisiness is a relative condition; display types grew more elaborate as printed material became available, causing the necessity for differentiation. This is a 1710 title page printed in Leipzig.

2 Today, clutter and noisiness has increased so one extreme way to be seen is to make a *building-size* billboard.

3 Posters became the predominant advertising medium at the end of the 19th century. Posters had to stand out from the crowd of competitors on city streets. The most successful poster artists' styles were copied by less talented practitioners.

Like a moth on a tree trunk, advertising blends in with today's noisy media surroundings. The best way to be seen is to be simple and powerful. Visual busyness merely contributes to the noise.

advertising: keep your message crystalline clear and simple. Adding complication to a complicated world is not going to be seen: that kind of advertising blends in with its environment (*left*).

TV commercials can be skipped over with recorders, so marketers are placing their products directly into shows. "Virtual product placement" puts products into scenes after they've been shot. This allows advertisers to buy into specific regions and even to add products to reruns years after a show has stopped production. A leading provider of virtual product placement says, "We like to say it becomes part of the landscape of life." But placement saturation may cause viewers to rebel. Producers can sell placement in the release of the original movie, another in the DVD, and another in a portable video player release. In 2004, almost $4 billion dollars was spent on television, movie, and other media placements. That's a lot of advertising being sneaked into our "landscapes of life."

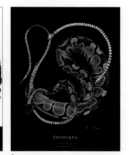

1

2

3

1 Poster made from actual newspaper pages.

2 Martin Casson's spread ad for Silk Cut cigarettes. One of the last in a 20-year campaign – forced to stop when cigarette advertising was banned – this campaign is among the most successful cigarette launches ever. Cultural differences may make you misperceive this as an anti-smoking statement. Note the lack of a sales pitch or even a logo: purple alone is needed to recognize the Silk Cut brand.

3 Similarity of form is used in this jewelry ad. A life-size snake is surely an audience repellant, but it is startling and memorable, a calculated risk.

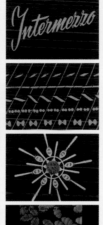

4

5

6

4 Artwork had to be simple, type large and easily read from a distance, and posters had to have a unique style, promoting many stylistic trends. The "Beg-garstaff Brothers," actually brothers-in-law James Pryde and William Nicholson, were artists who used poster design-ing to pay the bills so they could "afford the luxury of painting." They worked full size with a rough sketch, cut paper in basic shapes, then added type.
5 Making an ad look like a mini-poster is a cliché. Avoid it.
6 Before television, movies were *the* preferred entertainment. Theaters projected ads like these, often between films.

What about commercials on mobile phones? Phones are always on and they're carried everywhere. Because many mobile phones are GPS equip-ped, marketers send messages pitching nearby retailers. There are ads on every empty space imaginable. Now the "emptiness" of chatter, the time when your cell phone is not being used – what the phone companies, by the way, must think of as an added benefit to their customers – is being filled with pushed advertising messages. This is thought by many users and critics to be too intrusive.

Infomercials, like 30-minute programs on cooking devices and exercise equipment, are a $3–$4 billion dollar industry. Such programs have very high conversion rates, or percentage of people who watch and then buy. "Infotainment" is a category in which viewers can limit commercials to subjects they care about: the Food Network and the Travel Channel are two examples of branded entertainment.

1

2

3

4

5

1 Sufficient complexity to repel any but the most committed 1950s reader.
2 Simplicity and working with shape makes this poster visible.

3 White space in the form of newspaper (business section) columns are used to promote a women's magazine publish-ing a business issue.

4 An ad masquerading as a *comprehensive sketch* of an ad: the two areas of horizontal rules are the old way of indicating text type with pen and ink.

5 A fake ad for a hair care product is actually a vehicle for "taped on" messages from an investment company di-rected to women.

ABCDEF
AB
abc

Each era has its own noisiness
The 19th century saw an explosion of advertising as the Industrial Revolution spread mass production and mass consumption. In announcing products, advertisers began an escalation of visibility, and because printing was far better at reproducing type than imagery, the emphasis was on ever more elaborate letterforms. "Jobbing type" was type made for advertising use. The earliest, dated from about 1810 (though very bold decorative types were seen by 1790, they weren't legible at distance), were "Fat Faces," so called because they were the most extreme, heavy letterforms made. Fat Faces have exaggerated stroke contrast; each letter has both very wide and very narrow strokes. The usual Fat Face proportion of heavy stroke to height is 1 to 2½ (*above*). This is *Elephant*, a 60-point face shown actual size.

To make type *even bolder* and more visible than the competition's, serifs were thickened to the weight of the main strokes. Beginning in about 1817, these types became known as "Egyptians" (also called "slab serifs"), shown in BATTY (*right*).

By 1865, the use of Fat Face and Egyptian types was so popular and pervasive, the results defied legibility. This is the contents listing of a British news bill (*far right*). What a mess of expanded and condensed faces.

We have equivalent battles today to win eyeballs. The escalation of technology is our version of slab serif type.

3 **52**

Advertising
Design
and
Typography

WHITE CONDUIT

Licensed Pursuant to Act of Parliament, Of the Twenty-fifth of George the Second.

GARDENS,
OLYMPIC CIRCUS.

MR.
BATTY
SOLE PROPRIETOR OF
ASTLEY'S,

Most respectfully announces to his Friends and the Public in general, that he has made arrangements for the Gardens of this Fashionable and Popular Place of Resort, which, for the last Century, has been designated by all sects and classes as the
METROPOLITAN EDEN.
The Spacious Walks and Picturesque Beauties Create in the Minds of Lovers of the Romantic, a stirring interest, whilst the stilly Bowers court the Weary and Valetudinarian to the healthful enjoyment of Amusement without being compelled to inhale the baneful effects of Crowded Theatres. The

EQUESTRIAN ENTERTAINMENTS
Are arranged to take place in the
SPACIOUS & MAGNIFICENT PAVILION.
So recently erected by Messrs. CUBITT, which has been Re-decorated and Beautified, regardless of Expence, in order to vary so as to meet all tastes. The
ELEGANT THEATRE
Will still lend its charms to display an entirely new series of
CLASSICAL PORTRAITURES.
Arranged by the Original Inventor and Delineator of those admired Exhibitions, Mr. T. THOMPSON. In addition to these attractions, the lovers of TERPSICHORE will be gratified by a display of Talent seldom witnessed, even in a Continental Theatre; every arrangement being completed, THIS SPLENDID ESTABLISHMENT

WILL OPEN
MONDAY EVENING,
JULY 11th, 1842, with
THE LARGEST STUD AND COMPANY

ROYAL BIRTHS EXTRAORDINARY,

The Old Lioness whelped FOUR remarkably fine CUBS, three of which are in perfect health.

TO BE SEEN

WOMBWELL'S

Royal National Menagerie.

One of the most interesting Exhibitions which Europe affords, is a view of this Magnificent Collection of

FOREIGN ANIMALS AND BIRDS.

Mr. G. W. begs to announce to the Public, that the whole of his superb Menagerie will attend this place; it is indisputably he most rich, grand, and complete Collection of rare and beautiful Animals that was ever known to travel through any part of the orld; and is now offered for the Inspection of Amateurs, Connoisseurs, and the Public, by which an opportunity is afforded of iewing at one glance every kind of extraordinary, rare, and valuable Quadrupeds and Birds that ever crossed the Ocean, such as ways have been considered leading objects of Exhibition, exclusive of several Animals entirely new to this Country.—First,

That stupendous Animal, the Performing

ELEPHANT,

From the

TWO IM

LI

AN

THE

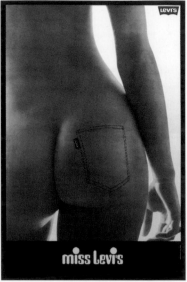

1 Benetton, the Italian clothing maker, has long embraced controversy in their advertising. Few ads actually promote the company or its products. Most are highly visible statements that "We exist!" Benetton's creative director, Oliviero Toscani, has an extraordinary sense of the outrageous and, often, the unjust. This ad – or statement – is from 1991.

2 Nudity always gets seen through visual noise. This 1971 Italian poster is simplicity itself. Updating the *miss levi's* is all that's needed to make this contemporary.

Utter simplicity allows a message to hit home, especially at 100kph, as in this Canadian billboard.

Getting attention in a crowded marketplace Simplicity and brevity are essential. There are three things an ad must do:

1 Get attention because an unseen ad is an unread ad. Art direction that produces an uncluttered initial message stops browsers. Image, type, and design must reinforce each other to make a single, unignorable impression.

2 Be read because that's where the sales message is. The headline and first few sentences are critical. Primary type cannot afford to be a mere label: it must promise valuable information. Make text large enough to be easily read.

3 Be acted on because advertising must ultimately produce sales, so some action like trying the product (just once – after that the product is on its own, regardless of advertising), visiting a store, checking a Web site, calling a phone number, or *any action moving toward a sale* is necessary.

3 **54**

Advertising
Design
and
Typography

1 Break through clutter by changing the point of view: what if the page is a sheet of glass?

2 Observe a person shopping for running shoes: they pick up everything. The most realistic representation of a product is the actual product itself. Shoes can't be bound into a magazine, of course, so a shoe, cut out on heavy-weight paper and sized to the width of the page, was printed separately and bound into a magazine on running. The back of the insert shows a tiny bit of copy and four locations where the shoe can be seen and tried.

Gimmicks get attention Three samples from the author's collection of dimensional Absolut inserts.

1 A real puzzle.

2 An actual-size knitted "sweater" to put over a chilled bottle.

3 A liquid- and snow-filled plastic packet bonded to the ad. There is simply no way to avoid noticing and being impressed by the effort made in these ads. Because of the high per-unit cost of these inserts, they are limited in their distribution by targeted zip codes.

"Nothing is so expensive as an unread ad." Anonymous

How to be Seen in Noisiness

1 No larger than a small poster, this installation and bumper sticker is surprising and memorable.

1

1 Advertising works best when readers recognize themselves in it. Here is a selection from a single issue of a magazine. What can be inferred from this description of the magazine's readers? If you were to develop advertising for this same audience, what should you know about your prospects? With regard to design, what techniques are used so this audience can identify itself? Or is the design of these ads suggestive of a generic audience, which is to say, without much audience distinction at all?

Editorial holds a magazine together by repeated patterning and texture. Ads stand out from that consistency and can be seen by riffling a magazine.

Magazine and newspaper noisiness A magazine is a three-dimensional object in which a sequence of repeated page patterns defines editorial matter from advertising. Good editorial practice adheres to house rules for departmental page consistency. These pages carry comparable content and appear in every issue and define the unique personality of the magazine. Editorial feature stories, by comparison, are designed to stand out in the editorial because their content is deemed to be truly special.

Advertising's function is twofold: to be seen and to be remembered. Advertising pages, being individual discrete bundles of energy, are engaged in trying to outshout each other and, much more easily, outshout editorial pages. The trouble is in making a given ad (yours) stand out among the other ads, each trying its hardest to outshout all the other ads. A magazine can be quite a noisy place. Because magazine makers understand they can't outshout ads, they rely on their continuity of pages to create a tone.

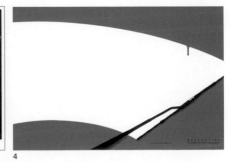

1   2   3   4

1 Go against the traffic: get attention by leaving most of the space empty.
2 Placing an ad sideways makes the message stand out. This interpretation is a bit different because of the blurry red car in the top left corner. Placed in the "normal" starting point for browsers, it indicates a legitimate beginning for a vertical ad. But the rest of the image obviously contradicts this verticality. The red car still reads correctly when the ad is turned sideways.
3 A new way to say "stiletto" with danger and sex.
4 A bloodied windshield describes "Quarantine: The delightfully violent driving game."

2   3   4   5

If you were to write a "recipe" for the design attributes of each of these eight ads, listing every treatment and characteristic so the ad could be replicated with- out visual prompts, how many ingredients would be shared?
2 Full-bleed; centered; head- line at top, small caps; serif type; diagram; bulleted list.
3 Head and margin bleed; head- line in image; subhead splits text; sans serif type.
4 No bleed; three-column struc- ture; secondary image; display reversed in mortised horizontal boxes; serif type; flush left text.
5 Logo and image merged into one; centered; lots of emptiness; full bleed; short sans serif text.

Forget color as a distinguishing characteristic. Many newspapers are printed in color and the rest soon will be. What differentiates the two media is size and space allocation. A newspaper sells advertising space by the column inch (one column wide, which varies from paper to paper) by one vertical inch deep. For example, a one-page ad is sold as 120 column inches (six columns, typically 2$\frac{1}{16}$" wide, plus column spaces, totalling 12$\frac{3}{4}$" x 20" deep, or 255 square inches) and a quarter-page ad is sold as 68 column inches (three columns wide by 10" deep). A newspaper page is typically peppered with ads, each competing for attention.

A magazine, on the other hand, has predetermined ad sizes. Magazines are trimmed in a variety of sizes, but their "live area," or the part of the page within the margins, tends to be shared by many magazines so that ad agencies don't have to make alterations to their ads to fit them. The page-size difference is visible in the margins surrounding ads.

One way to stand out in a noisy crowd is to whisper. More could have been done with this visual ("I know, we'll take a picture of the bottle with *two pills* in front!") to show the bone con- nection, but the type is orga- nized and purposeful, and the tone makes the ad visible in its printed context (*see noisy ads at top*).

"When ideas fail, words (or designs and executions) come in very handy." Johann Wolf- gang von Goethe (1749-1832)

1 A full spread ad (with mini- mal copy) uses a diecut fake subscription card insert that holds the sales message. This treatment takes intelligent advantage of subscription cards, a common attribute of magazines, while illustrating the single sales message: this vehicle is powerful.

SHORTS LOGO

HUNDREDS OF BORING LECTURES.
A SUMMER FRAMING HOUSES. A FIGHT
AT A REPLACEMENTS CONCERT. 5
FAKE ID'S. BACKPACKING IN THE
COHUTTAS. HELL WEEK. A STRING OF
DEADBEAT ROOMMATES. ONE DULL
POCKETKNIFE.

DUCK HEAD PANTS BORROWED FROM
WES McCLEARY, PURCHASED 1987.

YOU CAN'T GET THEM OLD UNTIL YOU
GET THEM NEW.

© 1993 DUCK HEAD APPAREL CO., INC.

CASTNER KNOTT, LAZARUS, ELY FEED
& TACK CO.

Section 2
Executions: Design

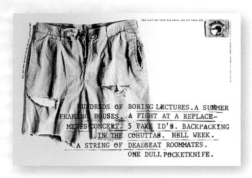

HUNDREDS OF BORING LECTURES. A SUMMER FRAMING HOUSES. A FIGHT AT A REPLACE-MENTS CONCERT. 5 FAKE ID'S. BACKPACKING IN THE COHUTTAS. HELL WEEK. A STRING OF DEADBEAT ROOMMATES. ONE DULL POCKETKNIFE.

"Dramatize the simple." John Hegarty

Over there's the manuscript. Here's the ad. Design makes the difference in this ad by Adam Levite, AD, with Andy Spade and Josh Miller, copywriters.

Why is design important? How a visual message is prepared, the quality of its design, can be compared to the way the lines of a play are delivered by the finest actors and by a high school troupe. Both may be performing Shakespeare, for example, but one show will be far more involving and believable. Design has precisely that impact on a *visual* message.

There are two primary kinds of design: one transmits information more or less for its own sake (editorial design) and the other promotes sales (advertising design). Though many believe they are quite different, they are in fact almost precisely the same activity. Why? Because readers are keen on being attracted by *any message* they sense will be useful or valuable to them. So poor editorial design will fail as badly as poor advertising design *from the user's point of view*, and theirs is the only one that matters.

Section 2 will look at the various aspects of making design decisions that will enhance, not hinder, the transmission of your messages.

What is "good" design?

Good design *comes out and grabs you. It says, "You want to read me. You'll miss something if you don't."*

Good design *invites a reader to stop a moment.*

Good design *gets the message across.*

Good design *is clean, clean, clean.*

Good design *is unobtrusive and unites a page.*

Good design *promotes the material in it.*

Good design *is something that coaxes the reader to want to read it – without reading a word.*

Good design *is functional by directing the reader through the parts.*

Good design *makes all the elements work in an understandable, easy-on-the-eye communication.*

Good design *is like perfume: it shouldn't overwhelm.*

Good design *gives personality.*

Good design *clearly and æsthetically communicates the intended message in an appropriate style.*

Good design *does not intimidate the reader.*

Good design *is uncluttered.*

Good design *"sells" the page to the reader.*

Good design *is art that facilitates reading.*

Good design *is radical enough to be visible and simple enough to be inviting.*

Good design *is like candy: the reader has to restrain himself not to gobble the whole thing up at once.*

Good design *is less.*

1

1 Designer attendees at a conference presentation I gave in Chicago were asked to write their definitions of "good" design. These definitions were forged in the heat of daily practice. Most are user-focused and address their needs.

Notice no one said, *"Good design is whatever I say it is."* Self expression comes with the design territory, but it should be in service to the message. With which of these definitions do you most agree? How can you make your work show it?

"To design is to have a plan, a concept in one's mind before it is carried out." F.H.K. Henrion

Chapter 4 **Design: Visual Presentation**

Why is design important? For information to be read, it must first be noticed. To be noticed, it must reflect back to the reader a preexisting sensitivity or need – for information, for a solution, for self-serving interest. In short, to be read, information must be useful. Information's usefulness must be immediately understood by the reader, so design is primarily about showing off the useful-ness of content.

John McWade, editor and publisher of *Before&After* magazine, writes, "Design has always been important, but ...it's no longer enough to have a good product; it must be a good-looking product. It's no longer enough to publish the news; it must be good-looking news. Good design sells products and gets noticed. To be noticed, information must also physically stand out from its surroundings." McWade continues, "Arriving

1 Design is not a random process. The futility of making arbitrary design "solutions" for real problems gets a send up from Stan Mack in his *Ad Age* strip. The fact is, account people do make design "recommendations," and the only known cure for this is for art directors to make account planning "recommendations" until it stops.
2 Herbert Matter's 1950 logo for Knoll International contrasts linearity with circularity.

Matter was a design consulant with Knoll for 20 years, producing hundreds of pieces including this 1957 poster. Another poster can be seen on page 45.

1

2

1 Good design reveals personality. These logos, designed and handlettered by Ed Benguiat, are examples of positive and negative spaces in perfect balance.
2 The same symphony represented four ways. Each expresses a different attitude and appeals to a different audience. Which is the most descriptive of the music, given that it was completed in 1888 in Leipzig? Which is the most random design? Which is the least interesting? Given this choice at a cd store, which would you be inclined to buy?

every day in our office mailbox is a thick stack of print advertising, which we sort over the wastebasket. Junk, junk, junk, maybe, junk, junk, and so on. How do we decide which to keep? Design."

Design is important because it helps reveal the content and makes it look valuable. Prospects will read your ads when they sense it is worth their time.

If a potential reader does not recognize the usefulness or value of the content, the ad will not be read. That is the definition of bad design.

If the design works, if useful information is presented as if it were valuable, it will be read. That is good design.

Good and bad design ought not be defined by likes and dislikes, unless they are the likes and dislikes of readers. Ego and art are unavoidable in any creative activity, but the prospect's needs must take precedence. Prettiness has nothing to do with this.

"Design is so simple, that's why it's so complicated."
Paul Rand, 1996

"Basic design is the advanced study of fundamentals. It is a... process (that) involves the reduction of visual ideas to universals (that) transcend pure aesthetics... Basic design isolates factors of visual perception so that they can be easily observed, analyzed, played with, controlled, learned, transposed, and applied." Daniel Friedman, c1979

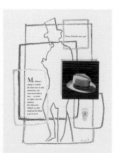

1

1 Selections from a campaign by Paul Rand for a hatmaker, circa 1949. The differences between ads are self-evident. What makes them interesting as an example of compaignability is their unity, provided by tan, brown, and black; variations of the top-hatted mascot; the squares; setting text in unusual shapes; initial caps; pictures of hats; and the company crest. It is evident that a limited palette allows creative freedom. Rand became one of the most influential identity designers as the post-war economy grew. His IBM logo and applications helped define modernism in 1956.

Principle 2 *Gestalt*

Principle 3 *Space*

Principle 1 *Unity* is a condition in which all elements are in agreement. It makes a design look *purposeful*. This example's unity comes from the models and the three containers having similar variety of shape.

Principle 2 *Gestalt* A design makes an overall impression, which is its *gestalt*, a German word. Another way to say this is a design is more than the sum of its parts.

Principle 3 *Space* can be either positive (a *figure*) or negative (*ground*). Good design addresses negative space as a shape. Space is used well in this partial-page ad.

> "*Every generation laughs at the old fashions but religiously follows the new.*"
> Henry David Thoreau (1817-1862)

> "*It is easier to be a genius when you don't have to pay the rent. We live in a world that values dependability over brilliance. The time to explore and take bold risks is a luxury few of us can afford once we leave school.*" Kate Wing

Layout vs design Lay out, a verb, is the process of organizing elements into an attractive composition, close to "order" and "deploy" and with more thoughtfulness than "arrange" or "unsnarl," as in: "I want you to lay out these pictures, captions, headline, and text to fit a spread ad." Layout, a noun, is the presentation of pieces in a composition: "This layout is a miracle of ingenuity that makes nineteen pieces look like a single statement."

Design is a more complex term. As a verb, design means *to plan*, to simplify a message to its essence, to cut away the extraneous so that

Advertising
Design
and
Typography

Principle 7 *Balance*

Principle 8 *Color*

Principle 9 *Emotion*

Principle 7 *Balance* Symmetry is formal and makes space invisible. Symmetry is a default layout style because it is easier to ignore the use of space. Asymmetrical design is dynamic because it requires the manipulation of space. This example balances the narrow deodorizer with the wide room.

Principle 8 *Color* is used strategically to organize, unify, emphasize, and direct. Color should not to be applied randomly as decoration.

Principle 9 *Emotion* A communication is a *connection* between sender and reader, and emotion is integral to connecting between people.

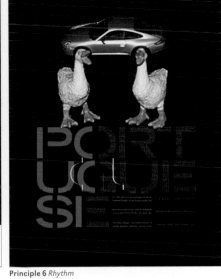

Principle 4 *Dominance*

Principle 5 *Hierarchy*

Principle 6 *Rhythm*

Principle 4 *Dominance* The result of contrast between elements in which one dominates the other by size, position, style, color, or shape. This example is image dominant.
Principle 5 *Hierarchy* Managing dominance to reveal elements' inherent order of importances. Readers generally do not perceive more than three levels of importance: most, least, and all the rest as a single middle level.
Principle 6 *Rhythm* The way time is revealed in design by repetition of elements or space. Rhythm is shown here in the spacing of letterparts and groups of text lines.

which matters most is revealed. As a noun, design encompasses layout, or composition, but also connotes content and communication. Design is a more specialized, thoughtful process than layout. But design cannot succeed without great sensitivity to layout.

Layout and bad design decisions overlap. Using a red liquid-looking background is an *elective* treatment for, say, a lightbulb ad, but it is an *idea* when used in an ad for a blood bank collection drive. Random designing is really glorified layout when the motivation is only to prettify.

"The designer is an interface. He's an explainer. He is the link between the thing and the user, between the company and the customer."
David Bernstein

Principle 10 *Memorability*

Principle 11 *Genius*

Principle 10 *Memorability* Ads must be remembered if they are to be acted on. Messages that rely on visual information are better remembered than verbal (typographic) designs. Two contrasting visual ideas are the best remembered of all. This example combines images of Richard Wagner, a German composer, with a reference to the interpretation of Japanese conductor Kent Nagano.
Principle 11 *Genius* *"Green Price Labels. Live like the rich!"* Genius is the slight but significant difference between competence and authority, as in this artfully-crafted poster for a large French department store.

1   2

Editorial design typically tells stories over sequential pages, whether paper or Web (*see below*). The pages are unified by shared design characteristics.

1 This magazine story's design "recipe" includes black and white bleed images, narrow columns of type, and a distinctive display treatment defined by variations of red, four lines of depth, and overlapping ascenders and descenders. Note how this display type treatment is carefully reinterpreted on each spread.
2 Advertising also uses repetition, but this must work over time, as ads are not ordinarily run on sequential pages.

"Advertising is an area where design has to be so good that it disappears." Brian Miller

"If you manage to do something following your instincts as closely as possible, then you have succeeded, but that is truly exceptional. It very rarely happens." Francis Bacon (1561-1626)

Kinds of design: editorial and advertising Many university design programs separate course content into advertising and editorial design. Why? From the *reader's* point of view, all visual messages are equivalent because they are looking for interesting content or entertainment. Visual cues come to them from both sides: editorial to convey content, advertising to convey sales messages.

Both editorial and advertising are in the story-telling business. Editorial stories tend to be longer, while advertising stories have to make their points very quickly. Editorial design decisions are made in the service of the story. Advertising design decisions are made, oh… also in the service of the story. So they are in many ways the same. Visual thinking is visual thinking and design principles are applicable to everything, regardless of the design's purpose. This is how readers see things, and their viewpoint is what matters.

Advertising
Design
and
Typography

1   2   3

Web page design is more like editorial than advertising design: it is a compilation of many pages, all sharing shared attributes. Design consistency is achieved by creating grids and typographic styles, both of which shape *space between elements* as much as they shape the elements on the page.

1 Information design for MoMA and the Whitney Museum. Simplicity on the home page… **2** leads to a richer selection on subsequent pages. Characteristics include a structured presentation, open linespacing, allcaps light type, and a bright red. **3** Pop-ups appear to reveal a third layer of information.

Glow global
Intense colors and natural textures
that easily translate into
your own personal style.

1

2

What all design has in common Design is a process of simplification, of finding and revealing meaningful differences and balancing them with an overall impression of similarity, or *design unity*. Design should reveal a plan, bringing a sense of order and predigestion to the information. The samples on this page have been chosen for their ambiguous design: are they examples of advertising or editorial design? As a reader, don't they all compete for your attention equally? Isn't each simply a superior example of *no-qualifier-needed design*?

1 Catalog spread (sales)
2 Advertising

1

2

3

There is order in good design. Readers have become accustomed to a host of design principles. We are comfortable with them. Designers may flex these principles, they may experiment with them, they may break them, but if they go too far they risk losing their audience. Interpreting the principles of design unavoidably becomes *style*. Style and fashion are similar and they change purely on the need for "new" and for many designers to follow others' lead. The easiest way to avoid current design fashion is to look to any area of the arts *other than advertising and editorial design* for inspiration.

1 Editorial cover
2 Advertising
3 Editorial spread

Design:
Visual
Presentation

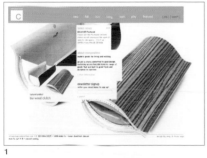

1

2

3

4

Design principles are perceived subconsciously by readers, because principles are the things that make reading – and looking – *familiar*. An informed designer knows the principles, has mastered them, and bends them as the content asks for fresh, attention-getting visuals. This tension between the familiar and the fresh is one of the primary attractions of being a designer, and should be embraced and exercised.

1 Web (sales)
2 Editorial cover
3 Editorial spread
4 Advertising

1

2

1 Inherently interesting content Interesting is in the eye of the beholder, and the beholder is always the reader, not the advertiser or creative team.

"What would our targets find interesting?" The human body in a new way is, and the aerial photo of London is likely quite fascinating to Londoners.

2 Arresting pictures A beauty shot is not as interesting, for example, as an information- or attitude-filled photo. Crop and size to reveal importance. Type

size naturally shows importance. Why not handle images the same way? This is animal fur shaped like a hurricane for New Orleans pet recovery.

"Communication that doesn't take a chance doesn't stand a chance." Carlos Segura

"A life spent making mistakes is not only more honorable but more useful than a life spent doing nothing." George Bernard Shaw (1856-1950)

What makes readers respond It is a fact that hummingbirds are attracted to red. If you want to lure hummingbirds to your window, you have to put out a red feeder, regardless of how pretty or novel some other model might be.

The same goes for readers. Readers – and readers are much more alike than they are different, though some have special requirements, like larger type for older people – are accustomed to certain design at-

5

6

5 Headlines that make readers want to know more The job of primary type is to get the browser to the secondary type: be provocative or compelling.

Questions rarely work: readers don't care *yet*. This headline is a non sequitur that causes the reader to check at least the first two words of the text, if

only to resolve the peculiarity.
6 Subheads that illuminate the headline The job of secondary type is to expand on the headline and give enough

information so the browser can decide whether to commit to the text. In this case, hand lettering and color contrast add visibility.

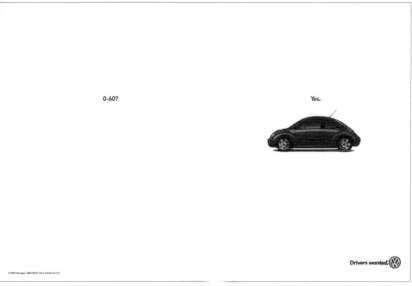

3 **Multilevel readership** Three levels of importance – primary, secondary, and text – makes a message progressively interesting. Primary type catches readers and should make them want more; text contains the sales message.
4 **Space** makes the page look accessible and inviting. Browsers, by definition, have no commitment to your message, so it has to look immediately effortless. This is an extreme example of empty space, but *everyone* who sees this ad reads it. So is getting everyone to read a short message better than getting only a few to read a longer message? You decide.

tributes and gravitate to them subconsciously. Knowing these attributes is essential so that when you diverge from them, you do it on purpose as specific situations require – or maybe just as they request. Listening for solutions from a problem is invaluable.

There are eight ways to get readers to pay attention. They are nearly impossible to use one at a time: consciously combining design characteristics is one of the best ways to develop unique design solutions.

"Never mistake motion for action." Ernest Hemingway (1889-1961)

"Less heat, more light." Anonymous

7 **Intriguing captions** Captions are display type: they are read before the text and should describe the importance of the image. This caption is the display *and* text for a provocative ad for the Scratch-Win Brazilian lottery.
8 **Well-built text** Text is literally built one attribute at a time. Typeface, size and column width, weight, linespacing, letter spacing, word spacing, and paragraphing all contribute to making text reveal ultimate craftsmanship. The highest quality text settings also need finessing by the copywriter to avoid bad word breaks and inconvenient spacing patterns.

1

2

Over- and underdesigning is a question of degree:
1 *Overdesign* is a condition in which too many design relationships have been made.

The result is that none of the relationships is dominant. An overdesigned ad looks noisy and repellant. This has too many type sizes, caps/lower-

case, and alignment issues.
2 *Underdesign* is a condition in which too few design relationships have been made. Elements are each "one of a kind"

and don't agree with the others. The result is a somewhat random assemblage of pieces. These have too many contrasts and not enough similarities.

"Overdesigning and under-designing are equivalent expressions of a lack of design relationships. *Over-designing has too many re-lationships which is seen as busyness. Underdesigning has too few relationships which is seen as randomness. Perfection is, as usual, found in balance."* Saša Bílý

Overdesign and underdesign An overdesigned ad is one in which the reader becomes distracted by the flashiness of the graphics and whose purpose is primarily decorative rather than communicative. Is being overdesigned only a subjective determination? Or is it possible to take the measure of flashiness? It is certainly possible that "overdesigned" is a euphemism for "unfamiliar." In many cases, "overdesigned" is another word for "ugly." Overdesigned documents have lots of personality, but the flashiness is misplaced and doesn't reveal meaning.

Underdesigned documents have little personality. They are to design as vanilla is to ice cream flavors: suitable, if bland.

A balance between personality and clarity is what's needed. Design that works makes people see the content. If a design decision fails to add to the ad's clarity and communicativeness, it should be rejected. Make design decisions in favor of the content and the reader.

Advertising
Design
and
Typography

1

2

All the ads for Broadway shows on this page appeared in an is-sue of *Where*, a New York City arts magazine, so they are di-rectly comparable. The designs

must compete head to head for attention and persuasion. These four designs have been arranged from less designed (more random relationships, **1**)

to more designed (less random relationships, **2**). There is a link between the precision and pur-posefulness of design relation-ships and the level of sophisti-

cation of the content and the intended audience. How would the message change by pour-ing *Faith Healer* content into the *Hairspray* design?

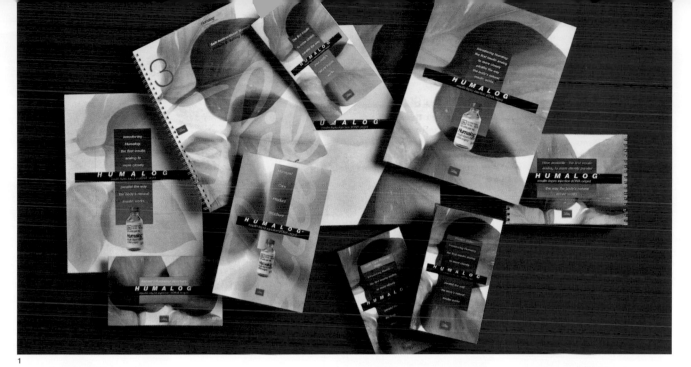

1

1 Humalog, an insulin medication, gets a full breadth of printed materials at its launch. Note that each piece is different to accommodate its specific needs, but that each undeniably fits into a common design treatment. This is a good balance between design contrast and design similarity. If one must make a mistake in this regard, it is far better to err on the side of similarity and consistency than contrast and variety. Repetition helps build brand awareness.

Primary and supportive materials Every communication from a client, whether a TV commercial, spread ad in a newsstand magazine, or point of purchase display or brochure, should reinforce a core message and be designed as part of an ongoing conversation. This is a definition of *branding*. Art directors get bored with a brand long before the public does and should be very careful when making changes to it.

Brochures can be as simple as a folded piece of paper, or as complex as a bound booklet. They are often thought to be inferior aspects of advertising, which is a pity since they usually cement the sale. A friend of mine works for a pharmaceutical advertising agency in New York City. One of her clients is a drug company that makes anti-rejection medication for organ transplant patients. This manufacturer's advertising campaign focuses on brochures and items given directly to prospective transplant patients. That isn't lesser advertising.

Catalog as enormous poster: Diesel's seasonal collection shown in a single image (*top*), with details extracted below.

1   2   3

1 The Vitra USA showroom in Chicago, designed by the Boym Studio, is as identifiable as a logo could ever be. Done in part to meet economic necessity, the resulting illustrated walls imply the details of a room and set off the dimensionality of the company's furniture. This spatial design was inspired by the children's book, *Harold and the Purple Crayon*, and has won numerous prizes for its simplicity and artfulness.

2 Bob Gill's 1965 POP displays for slippers still look fresh and charming.
3 Gert Dumbar's 1993 Dutch police branding system.

1

1 "A strong logo creates the power for an effective brand image. Can you identify these renowned corporations (by their abstracted blots)? Could

someone do the same with your company's logo blot?" – Jonathan Gauthier, an identity expert in Ft Lauderdale.

2 Bruno Munari's faces show a variety of distortions and abstractions made possible by the existence of Pablo Picasso's work some few years

earlier. This variety of interpretations from a single person shows us the infinite ways that exist to present any object or idea.

◆ **Previous spread** Walk into a supermarket and you will find examples of brands that have thrived for generations, becoming icons of American consumerism. Each has been carefully nurtured and protected from marketing ploys that would injure the product and its image. It is an interesting exercise to deconstruct these design personalities and see what makes them successful. Often, *familiarity* is the key, and that can't be duplicated by newer competitors. Maintaining the brand is a tedious job for these products' art directors because novelty and invention isn't generally useful or wanted.

Branding and identity A brand began as a permanent sign of ownership of an animal made with a hot poker. It was subsequently used to burn a mark on casks of wine. A "brand-mark" came to mean a "trademark" or "brand." *Brand* was formally adopted as a term in 1929 when Standard Brands (now Kraft) resulted from the merger of several food manufacturers.

The American Institute of Graphic Arts defines a brand as a person's perception of a product, service, experience, or organization. David Ogilvy, founder of Ogilvy & Mather in New York in 1949, is credited with developing "brand image," the idea that of two identical products, people can be persuaded that one is in some way better. Ogilvy says in his 1983 book, *Ogilvy on Advertising*, "Image means *personality*... The personality is an amalgam of many things – its name, its packaging, its price, the style of its advertising, and, above all, the nature of the product itself."

Perceptions are developed in *touchpoints*, instances where people come

Advertising
Design
and
Typography

1

1 The maple leaf is Canada's national symbol. It was adopted in 1834 to represent French Canadian nationalism. By 1860, it was accepted by all Canadi-

ans and is considered symbolic of self-reliance. Shown here are 18 interpretations, a mere skin-deep sampling, representing only a few companies that

use the device. To design a new version of a maple leaf symbol is challenging. What new, memorable trick can be used to create distinctiveness?

2 Coca-Cola considered redesigning its aluminum cans to look more like their iconic glass bottles, thereby reinforcing their brand.

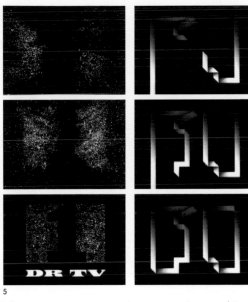

3

4

5

3 Four outstanding marks designed by Herb Lubalin. Each is a unique interpretation of the name. The top example started as the "flag" for a magazine and later was expanded into a popular typeface.

4 Hugh Dubberly's diagram of branding activity is shown here far too small to read, but

sufficiently large to suggest how complex branding can be. The chart can be downloaded at dubberly.com/brand

5 The Danish National TV identity uses motion graphics and the logo's shape, which can be infinitely interpreted. This makes the station a dynamic entity in viewers' lives.

in contact with a brand, which include advertising, editorial, packaging, store displays, and product use. Art directors and designers are responsible for a brand's expression, or visual identity as it appears throughout a campaign (including its name, trademark, communications, and visual appearance).

Brands are developed by *branding agencies*, firms that develop and manage *brand-building* across media. They define *brand attributes* or distinctive features that are considered *benefits*, or perceived advantages. In addition to art directors and designers, others who work on branding include strategists, marketing directors, advertising planners, Web developers, public relations specialists, and copywriters.

The point of creating and maintaining a brand is to encourage *brand loyalty*, which is the preference for one brand over its competitors, usually measured by repeat purchases.

"In the new impersonal mass selling era, the burden to manufacture customers will not be limited to strong pre-selling done by advertising. It will also necessitate, more than ever before, planned tie-ins of a product's promotion in mass selling media outside of the point of purchase." Ladislav Sutnar, designer, 1955

Design:
Visual
Presentation

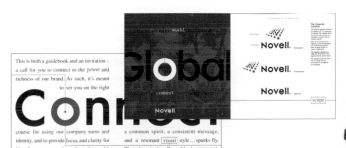

1901

1930s

1946

1970

3

4

3 A corporate identity is more than just a logo. It includes rules for the logo's use and complete development of its application in every foreseeable

need. These are two spreads from Novell's Corporate Guidelines brochure for their own employees.

4 Oats were a commodity until, in 1882, the owner of the first automatic oatmeal factory invented rolled oats as a breakfast cereal and branded them.

He merged his company with several others and, in 1901, the company took the name of one of its subsidiaries. The Quaker Oats Company was born.

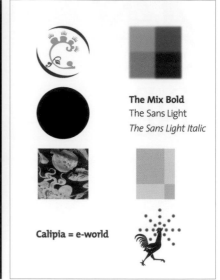

1

2

3

1 Among the earliest branding systems were 13th century European merchant's marks (*top*). Before the age of printing, they were applied by hand to identify the owner, the maker, the quality, or the provenance of an object. That a symbol had to be repeatedly drawn or painted by hand kept symbols relatively simple. In the mid-1400s papermakers began marking their product through use of a *watermark* (*above, middle*), a design impressed into the paper while it is being formed. A still later trademark development was the tissue paper that wraps fruit (*above*). Growers in Italy and Spain used the woodblock-printed tissue paper to both protect their produce and identify their brand.

2 Using the border design treatment of the American Express card, this campaign reminds us that charged items are automatically insured

against, in this case, breakage. **3** The *trade dress* are the marks, color and shape palettes, typefaces, image and

page treatments, taglines, and sounds that are used consistently in a branding effort to make it recognizeable.

Because consistent presentation is essential to a branding effort, there have to be rules for the application of design treatments and all other aspects of the brand. The branding rules are kept in a *branding manual* that is supervised by, and I kid you not, the *brand police*.

One global company begins its branding manual: *"No one ever got in trouble for following a company's branding rules. Why is that? A brand is, in part, a consistent impression that a company projects. A consistent impression gives a company the appearance of vision, organization, and intellectual authority. That is no small thing. (This company) believes its reputation for excellence and innovation is well served by the clean, distinctive visual branding described in these pages. It is essential that (this company's) offerings and communication maintain a consistent visual brand identity with integrity and consistency across all media. Our identity will help current and potential customers recognize our many prod-*

Advertising
Design
and
Typography

1

2

1 The CBS eye was designed by William Golden in 1951 in the early days of television's growth. Shown also is the very first instance and a contemporary use

of the logo. Golden ran CBS's marketing as if a sovereign: when changes were suggested, he would hand over a pencil

and ask that the faultfinder design an improvement. **2** Occasionally, a trademark can become a symbol for an entire industry. One such mark is the

Woolmark, which represents "Pure New Wool" as designated by the International Wool Secretariat.

Bob, I've got emphysema.

1

2

1 This 1976 Marlboro ad is iconographic in its simplicity. Full-bleed images of western life with the "Marlboro Country" headline reinforced the brand over decades. Cigarette advertising was subsequently banned in the U.S.
2 California sponsored a 1997 anti-smoking campaign that imitated the Marlboro campaign. This is known as *culture jamming* or *subvertising*, the act of modifying ads to subvert their original intent.

ucts, services and events and it will present a clearly focused imprimatur *that will become synonymous with our reputation for excellence and innovation. This graphic system provides the flexibility needed to accommodate the various forms and formats of our printed and electronically delivered materials. It will enable our many communications professionals around the world to produce visually compelling materials that are graphically compatible with those of their colleagues and worthy of (our) brand. As a representative of the company, it is up to you to be sure these guidelines are properly and thoughtfully applied."*

Branding differentiates a product from its competitors. Enhancing perceived differences – not actual differences – between products along with defining the personality of your product is often the purpose of a campaign. Liquor, being as much a parity product as any, is one example of the value of creating a branded personality.

"What is the difference between unethical and ethical advertising? Unethical advertising uses falsehoods to deceive the public; ethical advertising uses truth to deceive the public." Vilhjalmur Stefansson, Explorer & ethnologist (1879 - 1962)

"Mediocrity knows nothing higher than itself, but talent instantly recognizes genius." Arthur Conan Doyle

4 75

Design: Visual Presentation

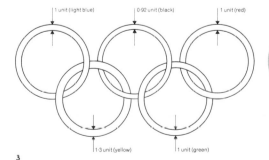

3

4

3 This rendering of the International Olympic Committee symbol is by Otl Aicher, who made adjustments for equivalent optical weight of each colored ring. Being lightest, yellow requires the widest ring. Black, being darkest, requires the narrowest ring.
4 The five candidate city's marks for the 2012 Summer Games show the application of Aicher's Olympic rings in five variations. The winning city uses the winding shape of the River Thames – which runs through London – as a model for the multicolored ribbon. This gives their mark a strong sense of place.

TRINIDAD, KINGDOM OF RUM

10CANE RUM

SACCHARUM OFFICINARUM

40%
LC/VOL

750ml

DISTILLING PERFECTION
FROM FIRST PRESS
CANE

IMPORTED

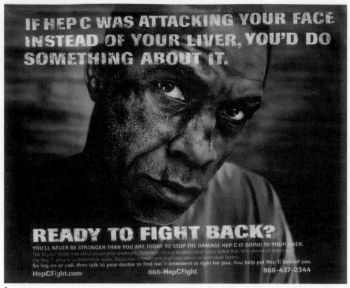

IF HEP C WAS ATTACKING YOUR FACE INSTEAD OF YOUR LIVER, YOU'D DO SOMETHING ABOUT IT.

READY TO FIGHT BACK?

HepCFight.com   866-HepCFight   866-437-2344

1

1 Ads that have no shown sponsor are often pharmaceutical, as in this half-page newspaper ad. The subject is Hepatitis C, and there are two actions suggested: visit the Web site or call the toll-free number. But the sponsor could be The Hep C Foundation of America, Concerned Physicians Against Hep C, Hep C Survivors, or, as is the truth, Roche Laboratories, which is introducing a new drug.

A recently introduced rum was developed first as a brand, then it became an actual beverage. The advertising team was given a bottle shape and crest. They developed these two elements into a brand roll-out that included print ads, films, an interactive Web site, parties for bartenders to discover the product, and a magazine showing the product's evolution at its Caribbean distillery. The brand came about as a consequence of research done on the island, in informal chats and formal meetings with various people directly and only peripherally related to the product. The resulting tone is goofy, amusing, a little old-fashioned, and different. That last is essential and not easily achieved.

If you can make a brand a friend, a real mirror of the consumer's aspirations, you will make a conversion into at least a trier. After having tried your product, a trier may become a buyer, but that will be based mostly on the experience of the goods themselves, not on your advertising.

Advertising
Design
and
Typography

Ad with logo   Same ad without logo

1

GRAFFITIEX
SZYMANSKI-CLEAN-MANAGEMENT
it's easy to clean.

1 If you cover the logo on an ad, does it still communicate the sender's identity? It should, because advertisers deserve an overall visual identity.

2 An all-image ad in which the repeated logo alone does the talking.
3 The type for this plant care firm is neutral and handsome, but not noteworthy. The thumb prints around the door handle, though, are unusual, descriptive, and humorous.
4 This business card for a German graffiti removal service is printed with scratch-off silver ink. When removed by the recipient, the message is fully and memorably revealed.

1

2

Guerilla marketing is defined as marketing that is seen in unexpected places or in subverted presentations.

1 This ad, part of 2005 campaign to introduce a new telephone service, is printed on vinyl and glued to the floor. "Try not to die" is a sarcastic comment to the older, more stuck-in-their-ways customers who feel threatened by technology.
2 An actual-size model of the end of a subway car and real paving stones and emergency cones are used to draw attention to the topic of "unexpected guests" on behalf of a coffee company.

Guerilla marketing doesn't look like advertising. It is born of an environment in which consumers shut out advertising pitches almost without regard to their merits or personal interest. As soon as a message is recognized as being advertising, it is closed out. Guerilla marketing cuts through that defense by making its pitches with great stealth, using non traditional channels to advertise, so the recipient doesn't recognize he's being sold to. For example, a person, seemingly normal and perhaps a bit passionate about her beverage, might begin chatting up a few people in a particular bar. Turns out she's being paid to get a little chatter going for a brewery or a distillery, one influential customer at a time. It's called "influencer marketing."

Or "rip-away" wild postings in which the posters are meant to be taken, or car wraps, or wraps of the entire interior of a subway car, or live billboards, or legal graffiti, or viral and blog marketing, or projections, or...

"The word 'quality' is one of the worst in the language. It means so much that it means nothing. It is so often used wrongly that it cannot be used rightly. The only way to convey the idea of quality in an advertisement is to leave the word out... The word 'advertisement' must be stretched to cover every single piece of (information) that reaches the eye of the public. Each must possess and show the good taste, the quality that is in the goods."
Calkins & Holden, Inc., self promotion, 1925

Design:
Visual
Presentation

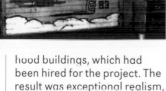

1

2

3

1 Nike installed fake street signs, premarked with graffiti, at various sites in Amsterdam.

2 Fourteen inches of snow crust is not remarkable – unless it's on a car's roof two weeks before any other Swiss resort opens. This is a plastic mold glued to a car for early season visibility.
3 A beer's ad agency hired local graffiti artists to paint one-of-a-kind statements on neighborhood buildings, which had been hired for the project. The result was exceptional realism, authenticity, and credibility.

1 | 2 | 3

1 Type and image similarity: both are wrinkled, torn, and bent on this 1966 poster. This is the result of a design *pro-* / *cess* and was achieved before the advent of easy Photoshop effects.
2 Design unity is where all the / parts work as one: 1 (image) + 1 (type) +1 (space) = 1 (unified design). The *S*-shape at the bottom of the photo, a carved / turn in skiing, is the element that joins the parts.
3 Simple form and flat color make a simple message clear.

Chapter 5 **Design: Unity and Clarity**

Stock illustration has replaced illustrators. Stock photography has replaced photographers. Stock ad design templates are replacing designers. If a Web site displays a design template for an ad that can be downloaded and costs, say, fifty dollars, what on earth would compel a client to pay thousands for your time? Remember, clients are business people: they buy low and sell high, so saving on labor costs is very attractive. Indeed, it is almost a mission for many of them.

I have two words for you: *value added*. Designers have to add value to a message by transcending the competency of stock design and offering customized, distinctive design that is better than stock. That doesn't sound very hard, until you come face to face with the next design problem. It is a fair question to ask, "What exactly makes your design better

Advertising
Design
and
Typography

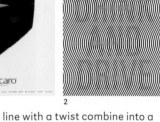

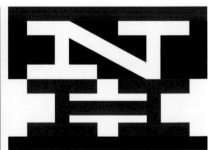

1 | 2 | 3 | 4

1 "It is easy to make an astonishing piece of furniture: all one has to do is extract from the wood all the Saccaro it contains." Elegant photography and a head- / line with a twist combine into a deceptively simple message.
2 "Don't Drink and Drive." The act of reading causes mild nausea in this modern op art poster.
3 Typeface choice matched to the style of the illustration creates unity.
4 Letter shape unity, the similarity of form between the *N* and / *H* and their extremely large serifs, defines this classic 1954 mark for the New Haven Railroad. Note the precise management of negative space.

1

2

3

1 Total integration of type and image were largely invented by the Stenberg brothers in the period between the World Wars. As a consequence of so-

cial change, the cultural status quo was questioned, leading to remarkable changes in art and design between 1915 and 1940.

2 Design equilibrium is realized in Land Rover's 50%-50% page division between packing list and car ad. The risk they took is in purposefully

making the two page halves look completely unrelated.
3 Paul Renner's early sketches for Futura reveal his search for unity among letterforms.

than decent stock, which costs hundreds of times less?" This book is filled with outstanding advertising design. But don't be lulled into thinking the ad world is chockablock with such quality. The huge majority of ad work is invisible – and worse. Many of these ads would probably be better had they used a template. At least they'd be clearly organized.

As an art director, the greatest value you can add is a killer idea, brilliantly realized. As a designer, the greatest value you can add is to bestow *unity* on the elements in your work. Rather than having, say, six elements all doing independent duty on one page, get them working together to make a single impact. Do this by making them agree with one another: by form, color, position, or style.

Design is a *process*, not a *result*. Choose the right process and the result will follow. The artistry of design and art direction comes with the understanding that unity is the most valuable commodity designers offer.

Though a subtle feature, the extension of the diagonal line through the *S* of *SCOTSMAN* gives both image and type a shared attribute, unifying them. It is exactly such details that separate the extraordinary from the plain.

Design:
Unity and
Clarity

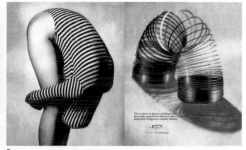

1

2

3

1 Cubist illustration of a dancing figure with modernist lettering of similar form unifies this c1930 poster by Marc F. Severin, a Belgian ad designer.

2 A combination of rough lettering and image plus limited color palette unifies Anton Clave's 1953 French poster.

3 *Form* – or shape – is repeated to convey the point in this 1992 spread ad for a fashion company. While the images

are unified, the type in this example is not as successfully handled as in the other two examples to the left.

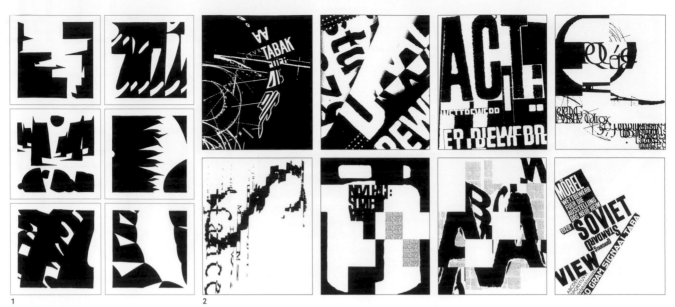

1

2

The figure/ground relationship is fundamental to design. To master it, you must see the empty space as easily as you see the figures within it.

1 These are hand drawn figure/ground studies from my first-year students. They abstract parts of a single letterform and use the parts in expressions of

direction, organic/geometric contrast, rhythm, texture/mass contrast, and balanced asymmetry.

2 The second exercise is to abstract *word groups* using provided materials. These studies also require abstraction (legibility is specifically prohibited) ⤳

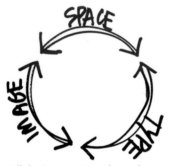

All design uses just three elements: space, imagery, and type. Visual drama happens where these elements meet and a form that is one element can be mistaken for another element.

The three design elements: space, image, and type All of design uses exactly three ingredients: space, image, and type. The difference between mediocre, average, ordinary design and superior, eyecatching, career-making design is your use of space. It is the forgotten sibling of the three. Why is this when space (or time in a TV commercial) is the very first thing we start with in a design? My theory is that we are more interested in *what is* than in *what isn't*. And space and time are simply background absences. We misperceive our jobs as visual communicators when we think we are supposed to *fill in the space*; we aren't: we are supposed to *utilize the space* for a message.

Space is the unavoidable opposite of fullness, of busyness. It is the background of everything we see. It is ignored by all but a few who understand its power and usefulness to create contrast, drama, or rest. In order

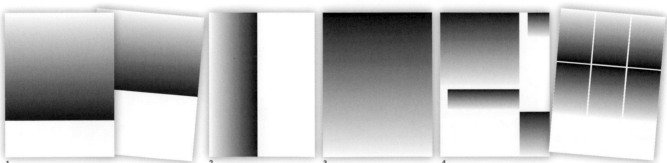

1

2

3

4

1 A single dominant image at the top half (or two thirds) of a page is the most viewed arrangement. The headline beneath the picture in this layout is

like a caption: it has a natural secondary role. This layout is known as the "Ayers #1," after the N.W. Ayers agency that made it popular.

2 A page split vertically is not as easy to arrange intuitively.
3 Full bleed can be arresting, though type placement becomes more difficult when it is

dictated by the image.
4 Random arrangement of images is confusing. It is better to arrange them to be perceived as a single visual element.

3

and illustrate design ideas like internal (organic) and external (grid) design relationships, hierarchy, order, and spacing attributes.

3 The third exercise expresses a real message in set type. In this project, legibility is required, along with the expression of unification vs isolation, direc-

tion, rhythm, texture and value, and spatial depth.
4 The fourth exercise is adapted to ads, translating relationships in the second exercise to

the new copy. Students must use their own photographs and be prepared to defend each decision they made in the translation.

4

to *use* space, you first have to be able to *see* space. It is a learned ability that takes time and practice.

Emptiness in two-dimensional design is called white space and lies behind the type and imagery. Other names for white space are "negative space," "trapped space," "counterform," and "leftover space." More than mere background, white space works for – or against – clarity and usefulness, depending on the expertise of its manipulation. When used to its fullest, white space becomes foreground: background becomes a positive shape and both positive and negative become intricately linked.

One of the earliest and best lessons I learned about design was the aphorism, "If the white space is well designed, the occupied space will be well designed." It does not follow, though, that well-designed figure leads to well-designed ground. This may seem odd, but it is true.

The lack of managed white space results in a noisy, busy design. Pur-

"Teen sports have just gained more space in São Paulo." Magazines sell space to advertisers. This diagram announces FT magazine's larger format and bigger space.

Design:
Unity and
Clarity

1 A close up of a human face has natural power to stop because we *like* looking at each other. And we are hardwired in our DNA to look at each other.

2 Background and foreground are one in this 1958 ad for an Italian sewing machine. It is such visual trickery that causes the human eye to linger a little

longer. The grays have been removed on the right to make the continuous color evident.
3 Emptiness and fullness are contrasted on purpose in a

three-page newspaper ad from 1986, the early days of the Macintosh. This ad introduced the first desktop network, which required lengthy explanation.

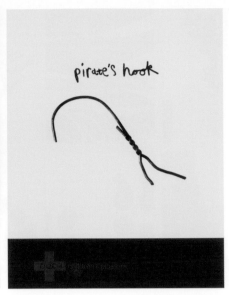

1 2 3

1 Typical pre-Bauhaus design, c. early 1900s, in which space exists only in the background. Its shape is completely determined by the type and illustra-

tions in front of it. This poster is by an unknown Russian artist.
2 Space became a plastic entity with the Bauhaus' efforts to revisualize it. Herbert Bayer's

magazine cover, with its precise type alignments, may look tame by today's standards, but it and other work similar to it were revolutionary in their time.

3 A life-size piece of a shirt hanger and child's writing in an empty gray field removes distractions from the statement that *kids need bandages*.

Tight headline and small images interplay to *show* "filled up-ness."

poseful noisiness is a good treatment for ads about, for example, anxiety, video interference, or the extraordinary muchness of a flea market. For most other messages, a degree of dynamic clarity serves both the reader and the message.

Space is defined by its perimeter. This may be the physical edge of a poster or magazine page or the shape of a TV screen, or it may be a drawn box, what is called a *framal reference*.

But it takes on size and meaning only when an element is placed in it. Suddenly, the space becomes large or small, high or low, tall or narrow. This primary relationship is called the *figure/ground relationship*, of which there are three kinds:

☛ **Stable figure/ground** The figure is definitely in front of the ground and dominates it. Symmetrical design is stable: white space is behind and around the figures. Stable figure/ground is the easiest to design.

Advertising
Design
and
Typography

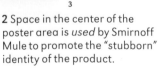

1 2 3 4

1 Negative space used in the title. The use of old-fashioned wood types is consistent throughout the client's materials for branding.

2 Space in the center of the poster area is *used* by Smirnoff Mule to promote the "stubborn" identity of the product.

3 *"Keep chopping."* White space signifies *absence*, as in the lumber necessary to mill the ax handles ironically used for tree felling.

4 *"Don't wait too long to get rich."* Space is divided horizontally, giving the text a broad area in which to agree with the angle of the magazine's spine.

1 *"The bonus plan of fidelity."* Negative space, in this case the white of the paper, is well used in this black and white campaign for a Swiss bank's credit card awards program. The ambiguous use of space makes these two ads sophisticated versions of the studies shown at the top of page 80.

2 How do you show that these beef boullion cubes are "packed with flavor"? Exaggerate the scale of cow in space.

➡ **Reversible figure/ground** The figure and ground are seen equally and interpenetrate. There is a tension between the balanced foreground and background. Reversible figure/ground produces a dynamic design and is much harder to develop.

➡ **Ambiguous figure/ground** Similar to reversible figure/ground, but elements may be in the foreground and background simultaneously. A designer must be able to see shapes abstractly for this.

Stores that sell expensive goods are almost invariably spacious. They understand that a bazaar-like atmosphere is good for bargain hunters, but not for luxury goods. Similarly, white space communicates quality and class, so long as it isn't wasteful.

Managing space is the greatest single benefit to readers and to your advertising and design samples. Most art directors don't understand it and avoid it. If you doubt that, just look at most advertising.

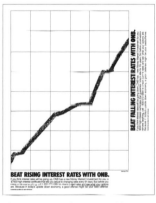

The page can be turned for a second, entirely different point of view, as in this ad for Old National Bank.

1 Nearly life-size product shot with fish hook but without distractions in the background simply alludes to an alternative meaning to the sport of fishing.

2 White space dominates in this unusual spread ad in a Japanese fashion magazine. The result looks almost like editorial columns with empty areas where ads were *supposed* to run but didn't. But it makes you look, and catching eyes is Step 1 in advertising.

3 White space denotes status, quality, prestige, and, above all, luxury. Porsche has had many years to perfect its "shiny mirror" in which its audience can see themselves.

1 Images may be color, gray-scale, or bitmapped. Each mode evokes a different feeling, ready for an art director's intentional exploitation.

2 Photos, ordinarily used for accuracy, can be abstracted and be both startling and communicative, as in the high-tech look of this hotel ad.

3 The illustrated poster by Abram Games, a British designer active in the mid-1900s, promotes the use of the subway to the London Zoo. Note his use

of *ZOO* as the train and the London Underground symbol (⊖) in the tiger's body, a clever way of creating design unity.

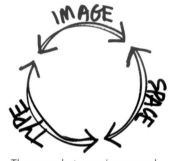

The areas between image and type and image and space provide rich opportunities to develop design unity.

Image Advertising is often created as one visual with an explanatory headline. The visual is the primary element overall and the headline is the primary *typographic* element – but it is meant to be seen after the visual. An image will look quite different in full color, grayscale, and bitmap (*above, far left*), especially when each version has been carefully adjusted with brightness and contrast sliders to optimize detail.

Image is defined as any visual, whether photographed, drawn, or – let's not overlook this one – set in type. Ads typically have one image to ensure that only one point is being made. But more than one image may be used, just as more than one size of type may be used, to create *hierarchy*, or order of importance.

Imagery has characteristics other than the content, of course, that can be used in specific circumstances to help craft a message. The unity of an image with type is enormously important. Their characteristics should be

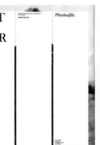

1 *"Our virtual support makes the difference."* Manipulation of part of an image creates contrast and emphasis.
2 Illustration styled to make a

bank *look* friendly, not just say it in the headline, supported by space and very short copy.
3 L.L. Bean is selling a state of mind, not just clothing.

4 The image is purposefully obscured by columns normally reserved for text. It is no coincidence that about a thousand words would fit on the page.

5 A close-up photo of the texture of a paper towel adds to this advertiser's meaning. Texture is an overlooked resource that carries near-subliminal value.

1

1 Bleeding an image makes it look as large as it possibly can. It also makes the image the ground, that is, on the plane behind every other element. It takes careful planning with the photographer to get sufficient empty space, or at least relatively "quiet" areas, so that type can be overlayed and still be legible. Keep in mind that text on any background is considerably more difficult to read, so the reason for its overlapping had better be worth the reader's effort.

made to agree in some way. For example, a predominant color or texture in an area of an image may be applied to the headline. Or part of the image may be made to interact with the headline, though with great care so the type remains legible.

Image and space have a relationship that stands ready to be exploited, too. Other than a rectangular picture placed in front of space, how can space appear to be in front of the picture?

Obliterating the image/space relationship requires the removal of space altogether. Extending imagery to trim is called *bleeding*. An image that extends to trim on all four sides is said to be "full bleed." This is an image that can't be made bigger. It presents the image as if it were a little closer to reality, not a cropped photo of reality. If you think of a spread as a window, a full bleed photo seems to look right through the reality of the page surface.

> *"Content is the most important part of an ad, with execution a close second. The layout is the third most important aspect of a message that will stop readers."*
> Stephen Baker

Design:
Unity and
Clarity

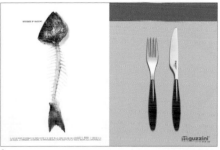

1   2   3

1 *"Schubert Evening."* Contrast between image and type completely fills the space in a 1965 poster for an evening of chamber music.

2 An image looks larger next to a smaller one. This creates hierarchy similar to a headline with text: one takes precedence, one creates the contrast. Notice that the logo is made visible by having been placed in a quieted, monochromatic corner.
3 Simplicity and elegance make this filleted fish and product shot stand out. Space, as blank paper (or a placemat?), are consciously shaped. Type is simple and acts as the supporting player.

1 Display type can be manipulated to resemble either space or image to attract readers with abstraction and well-crafted design.

2 *"Learning Greek (and Arabic and Japanese) the easy way."* Letterforms that evoke their country of origin, but spelled in German, for a language school in Germany.

3 Dull, bad design gets a send-up in this ad for an insurance company that means to make investments clear to its clients.

Type is more than choosing a typeface and it is much more than typesetting. "Typography" means "drawing with type." That is the activity of using type differences and similarities to show off meaning and to create the impression of "frozen sound."

We are most familiar with reading left to right, top to bottom. Such an obvious point is one of many type conventions that we generally don't think about. Yet art directors are paid in large measure to think about precisely these conventions so fresh interpretations can attract attention to their clients' messages. For example, can you imagine that there are circumstances in which organizing type backwards or right to left makes perfect sense? Learning typographic conventions is necessary so they can be broken at will to bring life to and solve a specific problem. The discipline is simple: just keep an open mind (*above*).

1 A single letterform can be interpreted an infinite number of ways. These are illustrations representing the majors at a professional art school.

2 Part of a broad identity program, this stock image agency wanted to be perceived as being less conservative. Similar to a watermark or a branding,

their new logo is run over the top of images.

3 Contrast of short and simple versus long and complete: this is a model of display and text.

First get the reader involved, then deliver the goodies.

4 Type can be an illustrative element, as is this ribbon in a precommunist Cuban poster.

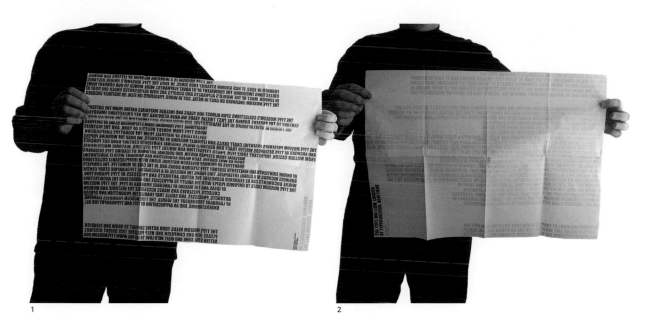

1 The message on this poster for a type museum has been printed in reverse on the back of translucent paper. The fact that there are far too many characters per line and that the text is set in all capitals is a conscious decision, given the intended audience of typog- raphers and designers. There is simply no way to read this poster without becoming aware of the act of reading. Under any other circumstances, this would be an example of pretty much everything not to do to readers. Breaking the rules, though, works here.

Type can be separated into two groups: display and text. Display type is *any type* meant to be read before the text. Text is the (usually) small type where the persuasive message is. The purpose of display type is to entice and cause the reader to move progressively toward the text. Any- thing that interferes with that goal – getting the reader into the text – is very bad typography. Text is less pliable: having won readers with display type and imagery, it is unwise to make reading difficult at the granular level (where the message is).

Type's default position is *in front of* image and space. Integrate type with image and space by putting it behind one or both of these other ele- ments. Make type visible by making it subordinate to them.

When type's width is equal to the height or width of an image, they are unified. A treatment, for example a texture or a shape, given to both im- age and type will unify them.

1 Letterforms are shapes that can be merged into an image as well as characters that can be merged into words. Put im- agery into the letterforms (as in this c1962 Fiat ad) or...
2 Put letterforms into imagery, making the meaning of the word inseparable from its ex- pression.
3 Type and space can be joined by letting space dominate type forms. Notice the similarity of this ad with the type and space samples at the top of pages 80 and 81.

1

1 Hierarchy in image and type is well used in this campaign. There is a *primary visual* whose attributes are photography, full color, full bleed, and the cars are about the same size (this is not a coincidence). There is a *secondary visual*: a diagrammatic drawing explaining the claim, sized smaller than the text column width. There is *primary type*: serif, all caps, letterspaced, one word larger for emphasis, reversed out, centered, near top of page, with its own label above. There is *secondary type*: the centered caption placed above the art. And there is *tertiary type*: centered text, black, open line spacing.

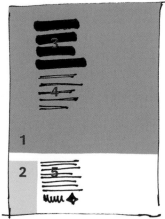

Hierarchy is ordering *kinds* of information. 1 Primary image; 2 secondary image; 3 primary type; 4 secondary type; 5 tertiary type.

Other design components The three design elements are space, image, and type (which is discussed at length in Section 3). These are ingredients. Then there are ways of cooking the ingredients: hierarchy, contrast and similarity, dominance and equilibrium, balance, alignment, repetition, scale, depth, juxtaposition, and color. This is a finite group of ideas to master, but remember as you go through them that design is a tool for expression, not a surface decoration.

Hierarchy Really good design moves the reader effortlessly around the page, whether paper or electronic, in order of the type and images' significance. Thought of from the readers' point of view, exectly three levels of importance is ideal: most important (to catch attention), least important (to ignore if the reader doesn't want to commit), and everything else made similar as middle importance (to explain the primary material and

1   2

1 There are two images in this spread ad: the road sign and the vehicle. Of the two image elements, the more important is the speed limit sign because it explains the headline: that this car gets *55 MPG*.
2 Space is divided into two strongly horizontal areas. The reward is above and a nearly lifesize guitar is below in these magazine spreads. There is something about these ads that presents the product as an object more than a utilitar- ian music-making instrument. Is it the glossy surface? Is it the extreme close up only a lover could have? If you play, you will lust after one of these toys.

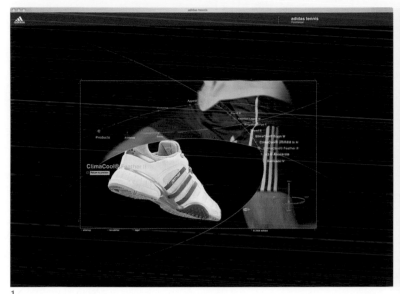

1 When motion is added to a design, as on a Web page, be careful that the message does not get lost amidst the visual excitement. The Adidas site has as much excitement as anyone's, but they have muted the basic type contrasts to color, size, and position. Even the backgrounds have been made as invisible as possible (black and dark gray) so all attention is on the products being shown.
2 Image-dominance and a visible grid structure make subtle type contrasts sufficient to show hierarchy. A "snowman" is an 8 stroke hole, and readers of the golf magazine that this ad appeared in would know it.

peak interest in the third-level material). There is no reason to divide this middle category into subgroups. It only confuses the reader with complication. Is it better for them to understand this thing is *slightly* more important than that thing, or is it better to make the ad's overall impact a thing of effortlessness, clarity, and ease?

Three-level hierarchy is applicable to imagery and type and can be expressed through any contrast: size, weight, color or value, style, or position. Size is the contrast most frequently used. A big picture is more important than a small photo. A piece of big type is supposed to be read before smaller type. To be creative and fresh, turn that normal approach on its head: make the smller picture or the smaller type the focal point.

But don't challenge your audience to read or decipher your message, because they won't. Would you? If design gets in the way of the idea, you aren't doing your job as art director.

"Designers, it appears, cower behind a camouflage of complexity, taking refuge in confounding rather than clarification." Stephen Doyle

"It is what we think we know already that prevents us from learning." Claude Bernard (1813-1878)

Design:
Unity and
Clarity

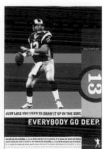

1 Three-level hierarchy seen in a 1768 announcement in a New York City newspaper.
2 A small part of a large photo is the focal point of this spread ad. The primary type at top left (the natural starting point for readers) forces the reader diagonally down to the brief sales pitch and logo in lower right, ensuring every square pica of remoteness is seen.
3 Hierarchy can be revealed by even one lone contrast, in this case type weight. Using fewer contrasts produces more sophisticated design.
4 Hierarchy is clear when differences are distinct, yet similarities still retain design unity.

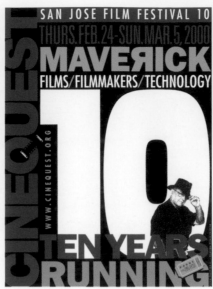

1

2

3

1 Image dominance tells the story in this 2005 Jeep ad – by hanging the vehicle upside down from the garage rafters, the advertiser implies its vehicle is just another outdoor toy.
2 Type dominance in a series of posters. The images are the only elements that change, but their sizing and definition of neg- ative space within the numeral *10* make each poster different.
3 The Fat Chance Bird Food mark uses black and white lines that aren't – *but look like* *they are* – equally thick. Even the eyes differ. These slight ad- justments give the symbol de- sign unity, a sense of whimsy, and quality and craft.

Kinds of contrasts
large/small
heavy/thin
simple/complex
refined/crude
comforting/unsettling
formal/informal
stable/unstable
man-made/natural
new/old
light/dark
shiny/dull
sharp/soft
straight/curved
smooth/rough
geometric/freeform
horizontal/vertical
high/low

Contrast and similarity are flip sides of the same coin. They cannot be separated. Design is the act of equalizing these two attributes so a message is at once eye catching *and* unified. Too much contrast and you have a mess. Too much similarity and you have gray oatmeal.

Similarity is not the same thing as unity. Similarity is simply the condi- tion of having shared characteristics. Unity is the condition of elements relating to one another for artistic or editorial purposes.

Maintain unity by keeping the design simple; having an internal grid for alignments, creating a group of type styles and sticking to them, and working on ways to make type and image agree.

Dominance and equilibrium *Dominance* is making one element more important than another. It is related to *contrast* since there must be con- trast for one element to dominate another. Dominance is created by al-

1

2

3

4

5

1 Image dominance while using type and space intelligently.
2 Image dominance is clear by the nearly complete lack of type in this 2005 Polaroid ad that suggests the effect of shutter release overuse.
3 The headline is integrated as an LP label with the primary image in this c1959 beer ad.
4 This is more than image dominant: it is *imagecentric*. The display type labels parts of the image and the box rule highlights a part of the image.
5 Overlapping geometric circles provide stark contrast of form with lines of type placed in a horizontal rectilin- ear shape.

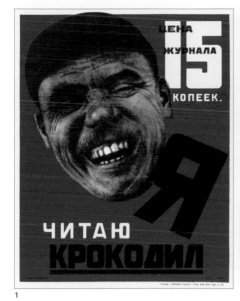

1

2

1 *"I read 'The Crocodile' magazine."* Equilibrium is a balance between image and type and between figure and ground.

This 1930 poster by an unknown Russian artist achieves the former because type impacts on art and vice versa.

2 Type and image are in equilibrium in this series of ads for a nightclub. Each is drawn and lettered by a different illustra-

tor, making this campaign identifiable for its *consistent inconsistency*. This is a very creative approach.

tering size (also called *scale* when comparing two elements), positioning, color, style, or shape. If insufficient contrast exists, the design will fail because the elements compete with each other for attention. Readers are challenged to find their own entry point, which most will subconsciously decline to do.

Creating a focal point is an act of determining dominance through contrast. Designs are most effective when there is a single focal point because readers have an obvious starting point from which they can be guided to adjacent levels of information.

Equilibrium is a state of balance, stability, tranquility and calmness. These attributes can sometimes be useful in advertising, but because advertising has to be in some measure intrusive and attention-getting, equilibrium often works better in editorial design. Equilibrium is, however, a valid tool for careful use.

Equilibrium can also be a default result of *lack* of contrast or hierarchy. This ad suffers from having had the type spread out equally over the page in bits and pieces.

Design:
Unity and
Clarity

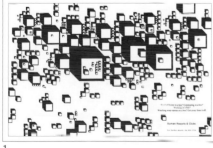

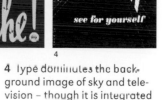

1

2

3

4

1 The cubes symbolize compartmentalized urban living in this ad that promotes vacations.
2 The type takes up only a little more space than the image,

but it is far more intricate than the image, the indication that we are supposed to linger there.
3 *"Alas for the Neocid! Alas for the bugs!"* (A reference to

Cicero's (106BC-43BC) "Alas for the times! Alas for the manners!") Type dominance is used with life-size flies appearing to crawl on the type.

4 Type dominates the background image of sky and television – though it is integrated into a single element – in F.H.K. Henrion's dramatic design.

1 *"No better nipples in the world. I want to suck them 'til I'm old. Rubbery."* Symmetry is ordinarily not dynamic, but it can be when, for example, complementary colors are used abundantly.
2 Symmetrical design doesn't have to be a perfect left-to-right mirror image: the off-center turtle does not make this an asymmetrical ad. The centered *get it* and secondary type with logo are stronger elements.
3 The minor "infractions" don't invalidate the symmetry of this ad, either.

Balance is the state of equalized tension. It is necessary to creating design unity. If a design is balanced, the overall impression is one of organization and clarity. If a design lacks balance, the individual parts become more visible than the whole. There are three kinds of balance.

☛ **Symmetrical balance** is centered on a vertical axis, like a mirror image. It is balance through similarity. Symmetry is a static arrangement based on form that confers stability, formality, and classicism. White space is forced to the perimeter and appears in the background. Background is *passive space*. Symmetrical design is all about the figure and barely at all about the space. Symmetrical balance does not require a precise mirror image: any close similarity of left and right sides will produce the appearance of symmetry. In other words, if it *looks* symmetrical, it is.

☛ **Asymmetrical balance** doesn't look the same on both sides, but when done properly, the two halves are in a state of equilibrium and are said to

Advertising
Design
and
Typography

The benefit of a symmetrical design is that design doesn't interfere with the message.
1 Typical advertising design, c1900.
2 An ad for the brand new city of Las Vegas, featuring a nuclear explosion, which had been tested within viewing distance in the surrounding desert, 1952.
3 An original Slinky ad with the added Christmas gift message.
4 I swear... If only this elegant 1960 ad had a visual reference to "natural dark ranch" mink.
5 An aluminum car park seen from above matches the width of the headline.
6 Display and text switch expected sides for a change.

1

2

1 Asymmetry is the condition in which the left and right sides are definitely not mirror images of each other. This spread is divided into wide primary photo and narrow product shot, with the difference in size denoting relative importance. The separation of logo and small headline forces the reader to tra-verse the entire visual story.
2 All information is made to fit into a column – except the headline, which bumps out to the left. The roundness of the pro-duct is shown to great effect by contrasting it with the rectangularity of the type and secondary images in this premium-brand speaker ad.

be in a condition of "balanced asymmetry." It is balance through contrast. *Asymmetry* is informal balance with dissimilar sides, which helps create a more active, dynamic design. Asymmetry uses white space and, be-cause there is more than a simple vertical alignment of elements as in symmetry, requires sensitivity to each relationship and element on the page. Asymmetrical design confers modernism, forcefulness, and vitality. Asymmetrical design developed in the 1920s, and Jan Tschichold codified the principles in his 1928 book, *Die neue Typographie: Ein handbuch für Zeitgemäss Schaffende ("The New Typography: A Handbook for Modern Designers")*.

☛ **Overall, or mosaic, balance** looks like wallpaper: everything is more or less equally distributed, without much regard for hierarchy or con-trast. Overall balance results in noisy design that disguises rather than clarifies design relationships for the reader.

Tschichold designed this poster for a lecture on *die neue typographie* in 1927. The asymmetrical empty shapes and careful alignments were revolution-ary, as was the all lowercase setting.

1

2

3

4

The benefit of an asymmetrical design is that space becomes active and enlivens the message.
1 The lettering quality and pre-cise alignments in this 1913 auto ad distinguishes it. Oswald Cooper, its art director, was acclaimed for combating ugli-ness in American advertising.
2 Piet Zwart's ad leaves most of the space empty and relies on exacting alignments for a new formal organization, c1927.
3 Empty black space and extra tight cropping dominate this ad.
4 The image of a smoking brain is far more interesting than the off-center type treatment in this ad for an online business de-veloper.

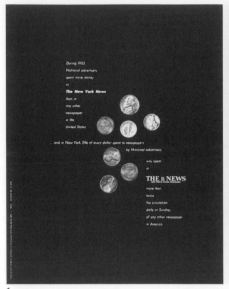

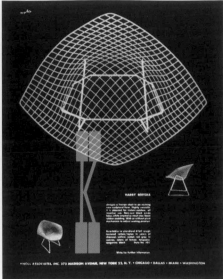

1   2   3

Alignment is the simplest physical relationship: elements look like they belong together because they are in spatial agreement.

1 The flush left alignment of the two areas of text makes the placement of the 29¢ in coins and the central part of the text (doing duty as a very subtle headline) look random.
2 There are *no* accidental alignments here. Herbert Matter and Florence Knoll collaborated on this ad for Knoll's *Bertoia* chair.

3 These baselines agree: they are both horizontal, but they put half the headline upside down – on purpose. Rotate the ad to see the second message.

Snap-to-guides alignment can look like misalignment because shapes vary along the aligned edge. Triangular and circular shapes are especially noticeable. Typeforms need the same attention, particularly at display sizes. Some programs have an Optical Margin Alignment feature that can do this automatically when it is selected.

Alignment organizes elements and makes a layout look clean, neat, and simple to read. The surest way to have proper alignment is to consider whether the space is aligned, not just the figures being placed into the space.

There are two kinds of alignment: *measurable* alignment and *optical* alignment. Because shapes vary, compensation is necessary to make things *look* aligned rather than merely *be* aligned. Of the two, optical alignment is of a far higher quality because it is apparent alignment. Measurable alignment is also called *digital* or *snap-to* alignment and is easier but produces poor results with anything besides rectangular shapes. This is because it organizes elements by their perimeter box. If an element isn't rectangular, it gets treated as if it were, which presumes space is inconsequential. By now, it should be clear that the handling of space is one of the vital characteristics of outstanding design and art direction.

5 **94**

Advertising
Design
and
Typography

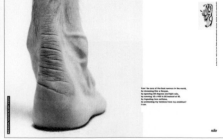

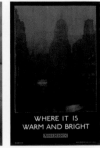

1   2   3   4

1 The type is aligned flush left, so the clean edge relates the type to the bicycle spoke.
2 There are two kinds of information here: that which aligned horizontally (the sales pitch, which is big and bold, and the logo), and that which is aligned vertically (the identity of the heel's owner – who is also the writer of the text, and the shoe image and information).
3 The ball aligns with the logo to triangulate with the player.
4 Centered alignment is a system that can be broken for the focal point, as in this softsell poster that makes the Underground more than transportation in rainy, chilly London.

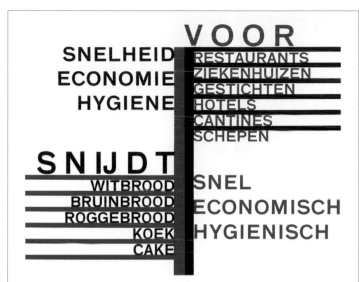

1

2

3

1 Alignment along a vertical center axis, three sizes of type, and strict color use unify this 1927 Dutch poster by Paul Schuitema.

Repetition builds cohesion because it cannot be done accidentally.

2 Repetition is used humorously to illustrate a software offer for teachers in this 1985 Canadian newspaper ad.

3 There are many ways to show five men holding drinks, even in a vertical partial-page ad. This one uses repetition in position, clothing, and hand placement. This is purposeful design decision-making that bestows order and simplicity.

Repetition Any idea that is repeated – position, size, color, shape, type, or use of graphic elements like rules, background tints, and boxes – provides unity. Repetition, which is related to *similarity*, produces *rhythm*, a time-based design attribute.

Design is the process of stripping away unnecessary complexity to achieve design unity. Repeating similar elements, or making diverse elements appear to be similar by repeating them, is an effective way of removing distracting differences.

Advertising uses design repetition in the series of ads that make up a campaign. The ads share multiple attributes that, with repeated viewings, reinforces the core message. When developing campaign repetition, balance must be achieved between sameness (so every ad looks almost the same as the others) and too much difference (so that every ad looks like a one-shot rather than part of a campaign).

Repetition of shape will unify disparate objects. This principle can also be applied through similarity of position, size, color, type, and other attributes.

1

2

1 Repetition of the mouth in motion is used as a central element in a collage of images. It contrasts with the simplicity of a pair of fine shoes.

2 *"Not all homemade things taste as good as Pfanni. Love you can taste."* This campaign uses repetition of artistic medium, scale, lack of background detail, logo and tagline position, and headline treatment. This last is interesting: the words, typeface, type size, and type's color remain constant. The shape and position change, but the four similarities are far greater than the two differences, so the treatment is campaignable.

1

2

3

Scale plays with our expectations of size relationships.
1 Scale is used to excellent
effect in this 1936 poster for
a Prague shoe store by Emil

Weiss. Asymmetry and unusual hand lettering with extreme
weight contrast contribute sub-
stantially to its impact.
2 Scale shows exaggerated

happiness in this business-to-
business ad promoting a color
copier, whose output can be
significantly marked up.
3 Extreme scale change will

abstract a visual element. A
closeup of a three-part layered
cocktail is so large that it becomes a colorful eye-catcher
as it dwarfs the product shot.

Image-to-image scale: Toy
cars held in realistic position
shows incongruous scale.

Scale A perceived relationship between two or more elements: comparison against known size. "Small" and "big" are relative terms in comparison to nearby elements. A startling change in scale makes people stop
because of our natural affinity for abstraction and because scale shows
something familiar in a new way. Scale can be used to make an element
come forward: make the foreground large and cover parts of elements
meant to look "behind." Scale is closely related to hierarchy, because a
change in scale means a change in the order of seeing.

Depth is space. We live in a three-dimensional world that has width,

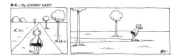

height, and depth. Because of reproduction limitations of print and television, most
advertising takes place in two dimensions:
width and height. Adding the third dimension, depth – whether implied

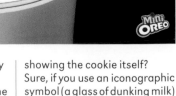

1

2

3

1 A stylized abstraction of a bee
is scaled to make the headline
and product appear very small.
2 This head is about life-size,
but it looks huge because of the

scale of the product shot and
the type. Note the management
of white space, making the
copy and product a single element in this 1967 magazine ad.

3 How do you say really, really
tiny? Adjust the scale of the
glass of milk with the size of the
splash. And is there a way to
have a cookie ad work without

showing the cookie itself?
Sure, if you use an iconographic
symbol (a glass of dunking milk)
for that *particular brand* of
cookie.

1

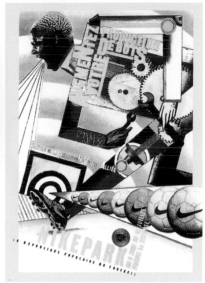

2

a

Depth is implied on a flat plane by overlapping elements. **1** Printing type on a wrinkled label, photographing it, and placing that photo partially over another image creates the illusion of its being in front of the bottle. Here is a version with the overlap reversed. **Juxtaposition** places objects in unanticipated situations.

2 Nike's series of posters for a month-long soccer event in Paris quite consciously recall the mid-1920s Russian Constructivist style.

or actual – gets much closer to reality. Implied depth is a visual trick (see cartoon strip). Layering, drop shadows, transparency, and other digital manipulations are illusions that suggest depth. Transparency will cause ambiguity: what is in front and what is in back? Die cuts, bas relief (embossing), folding, and multiple pages are ways of using actual depth. Adding the fourth dimension, time, is a necessity in TVCs, but it is an overlooked possibility in print. Multi-page ads on a sequence of right hand pages, for example, are seen over time. The illusion of depth is heightened by blurring an element, since only a "real" thing can be in motion.

Juxtaposition is the result of placing an element in an unexpected environment. This presents a puzzle to the reader, and makes him look. Care must be taken not to abuse this power: the juxtaposed element cannot be a random act of creativity. It has to make a reasonably obvious point.

"In an ideal world, humanity will no longer exist." Replacing a rifle with a trombone makes this a startling juxtaposed image for a French magazine. The type's flush left arrangement relates it to the vertical post on which the victim has been tied.

1

2

3

1 Contrast of size between the wing in the foreground and the planes apparently below creates the *illusion of depth* in this 1941 poster by Joseph Binder.

Compare it to the same view with no planes and one in which the planes are considerably larger and look "closer."
2 Replacing one element with another, in this case hundreds of ants in the shape of a slice of cake, encourages a double take in a Brazilian ad for sugar.
3 *"It was born in American football. It lives today in our futbol."* What appears to be a football goalpost becomes a futbol 18-yard box when rotated.

1

2

3

Color creates personality.
1 Color used sparingly and in flat shapes in this 1960 ad for a sofa which is still being made and is a modernist icon.

2 A large grayscale image contrasts with "the excitement of color" in this 1965 RCA television ad. Shows broadcast in color were a novelty, so the

copy includes a promise, "Crisp, clear black and white pictures, too." Note the pairing of the rustic cabinet with the subject: the cast of "Bonanza."

3 *"Friendship is something you enjoy more in life."* Color used to bring foreground in with warm color and push background away with cool color.

Color used to highlight a portion of a grayscale image for emphasis.

"Color is a creative element, not a trimming." Piet Zwart

Color Like good writing and good design, color is a raw material to be used strategically for a clear purpose. Color contrast has the same potential for communicating hierarchy as typeface, type weight and size, or placement contrasts, and its random application works against clarity and understanding just as do any other random changes in design. Define what's useful and indicate its potential value with color.

🔊 **Color aids organization** Develop a color strategy. Limit color use as you limit font use to communicate real differences. Plan color use from the start: if it is added on at the end, its use is likely to be only cosmetic. Use color consistently. Along with typography and spacing attributes, a unique color scheme can be an identifying characteristic.

🔊 **Color gives emphasis** and ranks elements in order of importance. Regardless of ink color used, every element has a color – or perceptual emphasis – that must be considered. Type itself is said to have "color," or

Advertising
Design
and
Typography

1

2

3

4

1 Long black text is used to interrupt a short red headline in this type-dominant ad.
2 Red advances and cool green recedes. The juxtaposition of

the magazine's cover in the background makes a statement (perhaps) about living vicariously through the pages of this publication.

3 Black is a color and has its own connotative meaning, too, as this sexy 2005 spread for a Mideast skyscraper forces the viewer to notice.

4 Bright red and green on a background of neutral tan makes this early-1900s poster for Singer Sewing Machines visible.

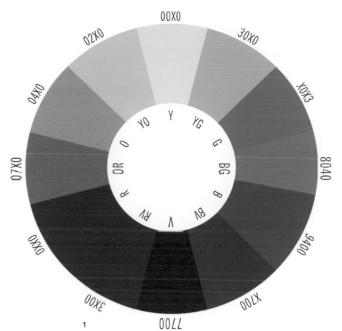

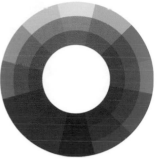

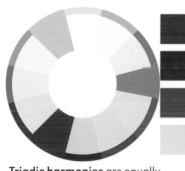

Tints are colors with white added. This reduces *saturation,* shown on the outermost ring.

Shades are colors with black added. This reduces *saturation.*

Complementary colors are opposite each other on the color wheel.

Analogous colors are next to each other on the color wheel and always look good together.

Triadic harmonies are equally spaced on the color wheel.

Monochromatic color is a single hue with its tints and shades.

Achromatic colors are shades of black, or they can be made by mixing complementary colors, which neutralize each other when mixed or overlapped.

1 The color wheel describes the interrelationship of colors, which are properly called *hues.* *Value* is the lightness or darkness of a hue. Saturation (or *chroma* or *intensity*) is the brightness or dullness of a hue. *Primary colors* are red, yellow, and blue. *Secondary colors* are orange, violet, and green. *Tertiary colors* are yellow-orange, yellow-green, etc.

gray value, that can be used to create hierarchy. Darker type is seen first, so display type is usually bolder and bigger. Color codes information, simplifying complex data, but color's highlighting benefit is quickly exhausted and devolves into a colorful mess. Color highlights elements of importance if it is used sparingly; **you read this first, didn't you?**

🔖 **Color provides direction,** relating parts to each other. Warm colors make things appear closer while cool colors move elements back, so a warm tone should be applied, for example, to display type that is in front of an image to further the illusion of depth. Experiment with graduated tints; it is said there are no flat colors in nature.

Black type on white paper has the most contrast possible. Color applied to type will make the type look weaker. Counteract this effect by increasing type weight from, for example, book to regular or bold to black, and increase the type's size a little for optical equivalency.

1 Yellow is a basic building block of this corporation's campaign. It is used as consistently as typeface choice, subhead and text sizes, column structure, and the text's wraparound of the primary visual.
2 *"For colors that stay."* Strategic color is a significant element in this campaign for a laundry detergent. "Longlastingness" is illustrated by the use of recognizable few-hundred-year-old master paintings.

1

1 Space is the fundamental raw ingredient. It has height and width. It can be organized symmetrically or asymmetrically. **Image** uses scale, color, and, when there is more than one image, hierarchy.
Type includes headline, subhead, caption, text, and tagline. It is organized hierarchically and relates to image by size, alignment, or style. Display type gets the reader into the text, but text makes the pitch.
Logo Normally put in the lower right corner or centered at the bottom. It can be a product shot with a label or other interpretation.
Time to read, or to turn the page, or to be captured and wowed by a TVC.

"Tell me sweet, tell me true, or else my dear, to hell with you." Anonymous, on advertising's brevity

"The big change in the last twenty-five years is the transition from word thinking to visual thinking. There has been a definite change in the relationship between illustration and text. The trend today is to illustrate the message visually where possible and to use supplementary text to expand the message for those who want more details." Wallace F. Hainline, AD, 1955

Putting it all together There are five parts of an ad: space, image, type, logo, and time. Each has a specific role to play and has conventions for its use. These conventions are waiting to be bent by conscious design decisions, but always in service to the message.

It is easy to simply *have* elements in a design. Copywriters can do that. It is considerably harder to *use* every element toward a singular purpose. That takes an art director's sensitivity and understanding. It is artistic added value. Without it, art directors are considered mere overhead by the bean counters. Be sure you are adding value to the ads you make. Study design and typographic history: it's all been done before. Study art and design and people and how they communicate. If design doesn't get you excited – if the concept is the only thing that fascinates you – quit this design thing and be a copywriter. You will thank the art director who is passionate about visual presentation as well as the concept.

5 **100**

"I chose these corporate colors because they say 'responsive yet reserved.'" Adjectives are applied to colors that make art directors' decisions appear less subjective. Is it real or is it wishful thinking? Which of the four combinations below best applies to each of these terms?

Stable	**Unstable**	**Extroverted**	**Introverted**	**Other**
Calm	Touchy	Sociable	Quiet	Prosperous
Even-tempered	Restless	Outgoing	Unsociable	Supernatural
Reliable	Aggressive	Talkative	Reserved	Permissive
Controlled	Excitable	Responsive	Pessimistic	Free
Peaceful	Changeable	Easygoing	Sober	Valorous
Thoughtful	Impulsive	Lively	Rigid	Graceful
Careful	Optimistic	Carefree	Anxious	Innocent
Passive	Active	Leadership	Moody	Presumptuous

C	M	Y	K	R	G	B
40	50	40	20	140	112	112

C	M	Y	K	R	G	B
20	50	60	10	189	134	96

C	M	Y	K	R	G	B
90	60	0	10	0	63	122

C	M	Y	K	R	G	B
50	10	10	20	52	123	146

C	M	Y	K	R	G	B
100	60	30	40	0	44	67

C	M	Y	K	R	G	B
30	100	100	30	131	16	29

C	M	Y	K	R	G	B
20	70	100	0	197	107	35

C	M	Y	K	R	G	B
100	40	80	20	0	96	75

C	M	Y	K	R	G	B
10	5	30	10	216	215	178

C	M	Y	K	R	G	B
30	20	40	30	144	144	121

C	M	Y	K	R	G	B
10	60	60	0	176	192	172

C	M	Y	K	R	G	B
30	10	30	10	221	131	97

ADVERTISING DESIGN
Campaign with type and space

Malcolm Mansfield 1962

Bradbury Thompson 1959

Bob Gill 1956

John Massey 1978

Dietmar Winkler 1969

PURPOSE

To develop a three-ad campaign and one :10 TV spot that uses type and space (no images) to make its point.

PROCESS, PART 1

Shown at right are five examples of type's malleability. The first two use imagery, which for this exercise is off limits. Find three typographic executions, one each from a decade since the 1950s, in which type is used to illustrate its own point. The samples may be either advertising or graphic design. Scan and print scaled to maximum size on separate 8½"x11" sheets of paper. Write a description of what makes the design's type work, year of publication, and your name on the back.

PROCESS, PART 2

Choose one product:

1 Airline route between Burlington VT and Westchester NY Airports;
2 Anti-static Wipes;
3 Solar backpack; or
4 the local Literacy Volunteers.

Research your product and document your findings, then develop responses to each of these topics on a single sheet:

Client Airline; Anti-static; Backpack; or Literacy.

Job description Develop a campaign to run in (define) media.

Marketing objective What your client wants to achieve with your ads.

Target audience Be very specific.

Problem How does this product solve a buyer's problem?

Unique Selling Proposition What does your product have that no one else has (or is talking about)?

Copy points What additional information will be included in the text?

Action to be taken Stop by; call; visit Web site; other (that you specify).

PROCESS, PART 3

Type has inherent plasticity. Use it in an ad campaign of three 8¼"x10¾" vertical pages or three 11"x16¾" horizontal spreads, plus one :10 TV spot. | There are four ways to make type a focal point: Position it to stand out, using space prominently; contrast its color; contrast its size; or bend, chop, distort, tear, or otherwise "damage" it to become the focal point.

Other things to think about as you develop your designs: Use one of the following design principles, which, *when expressed in the extreme*, will cause a dynamic design: contrast of direction, break in rhythm, texture/mass contrast; organic/geometric contrast; balanced asymmetry; the relationship of elements to the framal reference; abstraction of elements to make them at once readable and noticeable; and positive/negative space interaction. | Experiment with

form, but information must be legible. | You may use any typefaces you like, but your campaign must be a coherent set. Simpler letterforms work better than complex ones when abstracting them. | You may use non-representational elements, but they may not compete with type and space for attention. | Execute all preliminary layouts full size. | Explore radical spacing ideas and use of the page's trim size. | Flirt with illegibility, particularly in the primary typographic element. | Display type must be created in Illustrator or Photoshop so you think of and treat type as shape. | Compose finished ads in Illustrator and convert all type to outlines. | Print final compositions on bright white paper. No tiling. Flush mount on ledger and letter your name lightly in pencil in the back, bottom right corner.

PROCESS, PART 4

Develop a ten-second TV spot that uses only letterforms and space. Choose one of your print ads and animate it. Be sure your TVC has exactly ten seconds duration. | Make the spot in a motion graphics program of your choosing. Add sound and voiceover. Export or convert as a QuickTime file. | Burn the file on a descriptively-labelled CD.

:10 seconds

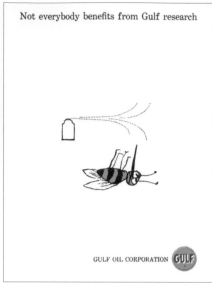

1 A tree rendered in tooth-paste – joining "nature" with dental care – is an abstraction of image.

2 *Simplicity of form* is another way of thinking of abstraction: removing every extraneous detail from the core idea.

3 Type can also be abstracted by removing all but the essential parts of the forms. This implies depth and adds mean-ing to the headline. In this instance, it is not a gratuitous treatment, given the product and message.

Design is interesting when it is developed in the areas *between* the three elements designers use: type, image, and space. This chapter explores the area between type and image.

Chapter 6 **Design: Words and Pictures**

Words and pictures are the ingredients we think about most. Space is not widely understood and so it gets sniffs of suspicion and raised eyebrows. But look at any of the examples on these pages and deny that space exists in these ads. If it exists, is has to be planned.

But words and pictures get the super-ginormous share of attention. And it has been ever thus: the Egyptians almost always placed their hiero-glyphics ("sacred writing") near images, like lengthy captions, so the words and pictures would work together for clearest communication. It makes as much sense today as it did forty-five hundred years ago.

There are three fundamental rules to know about words and pictures:

☛ **Words and pictures are teammates** If words and pictures are in the same ad, they should be working toward a single purpose, to make a

1 Egyptian papy-rus showing words alongside images for maximum com-prehension.

2 Images and letters carved into a single piece of wood was a technological improvement over slow manuscript writing, but it lasted only a few decades

before the invention of movable type in 1450. Hasty hand tint-ing, as in this 1420 example from Prague, indicates its pur-pose for the ordinary citizen.

1

2

1 Display type can be subordinate to the image by serving as a caption to the most telling part of the overall image.
2 Text appeals to rational thought, pictures appeal to emotions. Brain hemispheres specialize in one or the other, and this car is positioned to appeal to both. This is a variation on "a picture equaling a thousand words."

single point. They shouldn't duplicate each other, and if one does all the work, the other should be given permission to either get useful or sit this ad out.

☛ **Words and pictures have a flexible relationship** It is *expected* that words and pictures together convey advertising messages. What is not expected is to have them in an unusual relationship together. Shake it up a little: can a picture replace words? Or can words replace the picture? One must dominate the other. Try reversing their importances. Try telling the story without one of them.

☛ **Words and pictures can be abstracted to maximize their attention-getting capacities** The first job an ad has is to stop the browser. Display material (and space) are the tools to do it. How much of a word or a picture of an object must be there for it to be understandable? Legibility is not important in *getting attention*. It is essential in text.

Being literal is dull and uncreative. How much abstraction in pictures and words can you get away with to bring life to your message?

3

4

3 This three-page ad starts with words and turns into (almost) all pictures. With so much contrast, typeface and margins become very important unifiers. Note the "leaders" at the bottom of the first page, which are perhaps the biggest clue that these pages do, in fact, belong together.
4 Non-stop flights from New York to Tahiti are illustrated with a single, non-stop line that shows the Empire State Building and a Tahitian thatch-roofed house. The Web address is the only lettering in this ad and it, too, is part of the continuous line (*shown in the detail*).

1

2

1 A focal point is a single element that the viewer is supposed to see first. It may be either a visual element, usually a photograph, or a typographic element, usually a headline made large to communicate importance. Here the focal point is made visible through contrast of color.

2 The focal point in this ad is the metal serving lid because it is the lone illustrative element.

Focal point Having a single focal point is essential to breaking through readers' barriers. The focal point in advertising is most frequently an image with the headline in a secondary role. Being aware of this typical approach provides the opportunity to work against it creatively.

Though inherently different, pictures and words are almost always seen together. They come with plenty of contrast. The designer's challenge is to make them harmonize by crafting shared attributes. For example, pictures and images can be the same width, the same size, the same color, or the same texture. Such harmony leads to design unity, which in turn is what makes messages break through the surrounding visual noise. Simplification of any three elements into two, or, better still, three elements into *one*, makes a message considerably more unified and much more appealing. This is design at its best, adding to clarity and understanding.

1

2

3

4

5

1 The focal point is immediately visible in the center of a design. This is enhanced by the use of spiral facial features.
2 This centered design, a 1956 classic movie poster (and titles sequence) from Saul Bass, uses cut paper and rich colors.
3 Generous white space surrounds the brief foreign language accolades of the car, which are translated in the footnote salespitch.
4 Type and image have been joined into a single element in this early-50s TV promotion.
5 The best focal point is the reader herself. This mirrored sidewalk installation was mounted on a construction-site wall.

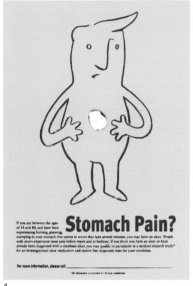

3

4

5

3 The focal point is the element that contrasts the most with its surroundings. To make a focal point, get everything *except one element* in agreement.

The angled, color image of the open datebook is the most dissimilar element in this financial ad, so it is the focal point.

4 A focal point can be something that *isn't there*: the hole in this poster for a medical study was actually burned away with a blow torch.

5 An ordinary picture of a vehicle becomes a focal point by making it the largest element and abstracting it and tipping it sideways.

A focal point is at once the element that is made to look different from the other elements on a page, and the result of everything else being made to look similar. There are five ways to develop design similarity:

🖐 **Eliminate clutter** Make things agree. Scrub away any arbitrary differences; they are too insignificant to mean anything to the reader.

🖐 **Use a grid** A grid limits dimensions and positions. If you can't do just *anything*, what you do will be more considered and consistent.

🖐 **Unify image and type** Manipulate their shapes, color, texture, and direction so they appear as a single element.

🖐 **Adjust spaces** Two distances are needed: a wide one that separates and a narrow one that joins. A 2-to-1 ratio makes these distances distinct.

🖐 **Develop a style manual** This may be as simple as type and spacing specifications. Or it may include more comprehensive data like image treatment and use of color and other non-representational elements.

(continued)
Structure
Organized–Chaotic
Serif–Sans serif

Size
Large–Small
Long–Short
Wide–Narrow

Color
Light–Dark
Warm–Cool
Bright–Muted

Texture
Fine–Coarse
Reflective–Matte

Density/Gravity
Transparent–Opaque
Light–Heavy

Design:
Words and
Pictures

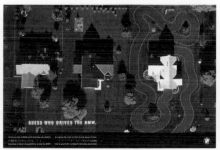

1

2

3

1 *Series* or *sequence* is shown in this half-page vertical Honda ad. Though it lacks a focal point, the rhythm of the four nearly identical frames

commands attention.
2 Image dominates in this spread ad by sheer overwhelming size. But there is real craft in the type: the headline and

text align on the right column edge, and the type and logo align at the bottom, indicating a grid's use.
3 Internal structure – the rela-

tionship of vertical edges of fabric "skyscrapers" to column edges of type – dictates the design of this spread ad by Herbert Matter, 1965.

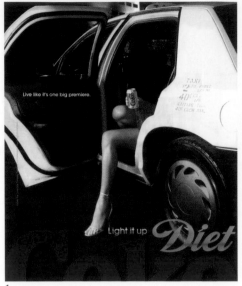

1

2

3

Internal structure reveals relationships between the particular elements in a design.
1 The headline is positioned horizontally near the can. The

logo is abstracted as it bleeds off the bottom of the page. *Diet* is scaled to fit in the hole to the right of the *k*'s ascender. The tagline tucks in next to the

stiletto heel and aligns with the median of *Diet* and the right vertical of the *k*.
2 The product name agrees with the vertical edge of the

curtain. It also aligns with the right edge of the text block.
3 The perimeter of the text area aligns with the edges of the briefcase.

"All languages are methods of communication. Advertising makes use of pictorial language. Communicated to the public through creative design, the advertiser's ideas are translated into sales." Westvaco Inspiration for Printers, Number 203, 1956

Internal and external structure Elements can either be related to each other or fit into divided space, which is better known as a grid.

Unlimited choice is both a blessing and a curse. Having four brands, three flavors, and six sizes of ketchup makes shopping for *sauce tomat* as much a problem to be solved as a tasty condiment to be enjoyed. Having 2,000 fonts makes choosing *one* a more complicated process than having 200 – and it makes *deciding* more important than *using* type. When faced with a blank screen, time is wasted investigating dead ends and aimlessly playing with design elements. After all, when *anything is possible*, there is no starting point and no obvious end, other than the project deadline. Can't design be more objective than this? Designers should take a clue from physicians, who don't aimlessly do things to their patients. Doctors diagnose the problem and solve it. Designers should spend more time diagnosing the problem (identifying similarities and

1

2

3

1 A print campaign for a German machinist uses a grid system that ensures consistency. Headlines, which may be broken in one, two, or three lines,

are positioned flush left with either text column, which are always eight lines deep. The logo is base-aligned with the bottoms of the text columns.

The image treatment gets the utmost from a single ink color.
2 *"Our advertising is door-to-door."* Use of a grid organizes seventeen elements into a unit.

3 There is a grid here, but the type refuses to play: the grid is not producing unity. This proves *having* and *using* are not the same thing.

1

2

The grid organizes space and is usually visible only by the alignments of the design elements.
1 Spaces between type and trim are equalized around the perimeter of this spread. The two images begin and end along the same lines. Nothing breaks the unifying effect of conscientious alignment.

2 The type in this dramatic sample adheres to a grid while the image contrasts in almost every way. Space is particularly active, being sliced into vertical and horizontal strips, and left in a great chunk on the right half of the poster.

contrasts and distilling the message to its abstract essence) than in designing the message. Until a problem is completely absorbed, its design treatment is likely to be arbitrary.

👉 **Internal structure** Materials have their own inherent structure. A serif type is fundamentally different than a sans serif face. A picture of a product from the front, say, is exploitable in a wholly different way than a picture of it from above. These differences come built in, but it takes sensitivity to recognize the interconnectedness between slightly differing parts. This is "organic design."

👉 **External structure** A grid is a division of space onto which the parts of a design are fit. The essence of using a grid is abiding by its dimensions. Elements can start and stop only on grid lines. There is no sense in having a grid and then breaking it more than once: for the focal point only, to make it stand out from its surroundings.

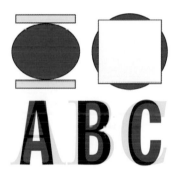

A tomato sandwich looks quite different from the side than from above (*top*). Similarly, serif and sans serif versions of types give essentially different form to the same core letters. Such differences can be exploited in organic design.

Design:
Words and
Pictures

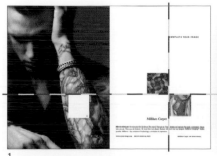

1   2   3

1 Extracting a piece of a tattoo and comparing it to carpet design is certainly a value-added approach. The grid has only two axes. The other elements are less precisely positioned. **2** A revised design increases the headline to match the width of the text block; enlarges the name to match the width of the carpet sample; pulls the phones into the text block; and positions the tagline under the tattoo extract. **3** VW uses a grid of 1½" squares to force unity on the multitude of different shapes. Note the focal point is the lone break with the grid. The *contrast* makes it visible.

1 *Image dominance* is determined by more than just the acreage that is covers. This full-bleed ad is, in fact, image dominant, but not because it has a large picture. What's impressive about this ad is the image's manipulation of perspective: the headline misrepresents a horizontal photo of a stone wall (*inset*) as a road surface.

2 *"Lengiz Publisher: Books on All Sorts of Knowledge."* Though there is more type than image on this classic 1925 Constructivist poster by Alexander Rodchenko, the image is dictating what the type must do. It is therefore *image dominant*.

Type and image in equilibrium look pretty missable. This is not design for communication, it is arrangement for fit. If advertising were fashion, this sort of design is a housedress.

Relating type to image The first step in developing a type and image relationship is recognizing that type and image are fundamentally different languages. The challenge is to develop similarities so that two different things look like one single thing. Anyone can design a *thing*, but to design a *good thing* takes the ability to find and exploit relationships.

The second step is deciding whether the type or the image will be dominant. The image, as a default "non-decision," is usually dominant. Dominance ordinarily refers to quantity: one element dominates when it is the largest thing in a design. But dominance can also occur when one element imposes itself on another element. A subordinate element is one that is imposed on by another.

The third step is to create the relationship, to design the parts so they look like they belong together. There are three basic relationships, with an infinite number of ways to execute them:

1 Type dominates this ad for acceptance and, nominally, music lessons by mail.
2 There is a great swath of beautiful image here, but the type has all the fun.
3 Image determines where the headline goes, but it's the type that makes us look at this ad from precommunist Cuba, 1950.

4 A backward-reading headline, letterpressed into textured paper then photographed – with instructions to look in a mirror – make this an unexpected typographic illustration.
5 Image dominates as shoes tumble counter-clockwise out of the scene. The fifth style is for the dog?

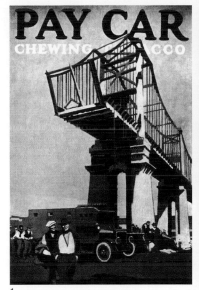

1

2

1 Proximity Elements that overlap have the closest relationship of proximity, as seen in the product's name and bridge.

2 Size Headline and text sized to fit the width of the largest photo. The headline is a caption: it presents a contradictory idea that focuses the reader's understanding of the image. Without it, we might think the boots are suitable only for airplane mechanics. Note how the photo panes are "stitched" into place, using the boot's rugged threading as a visual device.

☛ **Relate by position or *proximity*** Things that are closer look more related than things that are further apart. The ultimate nearness is on top of, so *layering* is an ultimate expression of proximity. Image on top of type makes the image look more real by adding implied depth (but if too much type is covered, it makes the type hard to read). Type on top of image is much less persuasive (and it negates the reality of the image and makes small type hard or impossible to read).

☛ **Relate by size or alignment** When the height, width, or starting and ending positions of the image is equal to the type, they are unified. Coincidental agreement is not as persuasive as cutting off part of the type to make it match the size of an image.

☛ **Relate by shared form** or characteristic treatment, direction, color, texture, or idea. This is a huge category. One example may suffice: If the headline and visual are centered, red, and sideways, they are unified.

"THE MOST," "PLA(ZA)," "EXTRA." Type in the style of the Batman television series explodes in front of images in this TV spot. The idea grew from the comparative sizes of their packs: cigarettes as Batman and Robin.

Design: Words and Pictures

1

2

3

4

1 Proximity Christ: *"Como my chosen one."* Mary: *"My beloved calls me."* Type as speech in a detail from The Coronation of the Virgin, c1355, Sebald Woinschröter, Nuremberg.

2 Alignment The all-caps headline is centered at top; the all-caps logo is centered beneath the right column.

3 Size Primary, secondary, and tertiary images each have paired levels of typography, giving a clear sense of organization.

4 Shared form *"Work with no fear, your rifle is near."* Type and image are inseparably intertwined in a poster made in 1920 during the Russian Revolution.

FUTEBOL-ARTE, SÓ COM CERVEJA-ARTE.

BRAHMA

BRAHMA

BRAHMA

"Joga Bola" by m3h

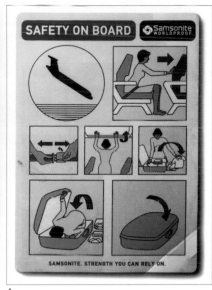

1 2   3   4

1 (*opposite*) *"Artistic football can only be compared with artistic beer. Play ball."* The shape of the headline is a consequence of the shape of the player's legs.
2 The image takes the shape of the letters, making them a single element.
3 *"Bobby Fisher lives in Pasa-dena."* The type can be inserted directly into the illustration, as in this sign hung on a mesh fence for a German theater poster by Gunter Rambow.
4 Type is put in place and in the style of a source document. This replica of an in-flight safety card makes the case for the strength of the luggage brand.

Shared form Form is another word for anatomy, appearance, arrangement, configuration, fashion, guise, manifestation, shape, species, style, or structure. From these myriad (from the Greek for *ten thousand*) choices, when we talk about type and image sharing *form*, we're talking about getting them to have the same *shape*.

Shape can be defined as bringing design treatment, direction, color, texture, idea, or one of dozens of additional attributes into agreement. This is an important aspect of advertising design, so let's look at them individually.

As you look through the next few pages, it may occur to you that there is an overlap where you think an example could be in another category. You may well be right. That you are considering precisely what kind of type and image relationship is shown – whether it is rightly or wrongly categorized – is the important thing.

"Like the egg, so mysteriously pregnant with promise, so wonderfully simple in form, an idea cannot be handled too carefully! For there is nothing so exquisitely painful as the hollow anguish that is left when an idea, from its fragile perfection, is suddenly a mess." Jack Tinker, President, McCann-Erickson, Inc., 1955

Design: Words and Pictures

1   2   3   4   5

1 A Nike Web page looks like an "undesigned" scrap book to appeal to its target audience: young, street- and Internet-savvy hoopsters.
2 *"White."* An ad for an Italian department store, c1935, integrates type and image into a single element.
3 Alexey Brodovitch uses hand-drawn letterforms in positive and negative versions of the same 1924 poster.
4 Images, sized to fill holes in the headline, are at the mercy of the type.
5 *"Formidable advertising support for your sales"* Similar to Fig.4, the images fill in gaps in the type in this B-to-B ad.

Treatment 1 Mismatched wood and metal type and stock "line cuts" in the printer's library are used to random excess in a 1923 Dadaist poster.

The purpose is to create shock through apparently haphazard confusion.
2 Image and type cascade together in a movie-like se-

quence. The *dénouement* is the panel with Rock! and Doris! and the movie's title! on red: irresistible and inexorable!
3 Paula Scher's celebration of

dance unites the image with type that emits the *emotion* of the show. This is a spectacular solution that breaks type rules for the whole design.

1 This type treatment, which clearly connects the type to the image, can be slapped on any image, for any product, at any time. That's not neces-

sarily a good thing. Here it is in 1955.
2 And here it is in 2006. Sure, its festive and spirited. Even youthful and irresponsible.

3 Handwritten copy added to a photo of an open travel diary conveys a feeling of immediacy. Who doesn't like peeking at some else's diary?

4 The smoking dummy is *in* the window and the type is distorted as if *on* the window. This would have been stronger as a single "unretouched" shot.

Advertising
Design
and
Typography

1 Type shares the angle of a leaning bicycle in A.M. Cassandre's 1925 poster.
2 The illustration affects the type, showing how everyone

should work together, in this World War II–era poster by Jean Carlu, 1942.
3 Type explodes from the drums in Max Huber's 1946 poster.

4 The two lines of type are aligned with the upper left edge and the lower right of the dual image. This is a simple, elegant layout that lets the con-

tent speak for itself – and gets out of the way of the technical-looking chart. This isn't selling a car so much as an idea and an emotional connection.

1

2

3

Direction 1 Type on an angle, normally a tricky move, succeeds here because of the definite relationship of the figures with the lettering. The relationship is furthered by the shared weight of the lines in the grid around the letters and within the drawing.

2 A diagonal line connects the primary figure with his family, about whom he is preoccupied.

3 A vertical line is implied between the plate and the headline. This is called "completion," or "closure."

👉 **Treatment** Whatever you do to the headline you do to the image. Bend both. Put one into the other. Rather than letting them look like they just happen to be on the same page – with maybe a nice alignment to make them look designed – type and image should be caused to relate.

Type may be placed on a surface in the image, they may share a shape, or the image may be altering the type.

👉 **Direction** Direction is inherently dynamic. Emphasizing one direction over any others avoids static balance.

Our natural tendency is to look from top to bottom, and from left to right. Working with direction in any other way is perfectly fine, so long as you anticipate a subconscious barrier from your readers. Make your atypical directions apparent and worthwhile.

Direction may be vertical (*above right*) or horizontal (*below left*), or diagonal in two (*above left*) or three dimensions (*above center*).

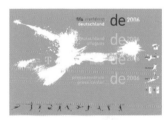

This horizontal figure is extremely dynamic and expressive. These two qualities are revealed by contrasting it with the structure of precise vertical type alignments.

1

2

3

1 The radio station call letters are embedded in the headline of this 1955 trade ad. The condensed vertical letterforms contrast with the long horizontal strips of white space, the headline itself, and the lines of text. There is nothing one could add or subtract from this design.

2 The headline curves because of the orange in this vertical magazine ad. The straw opening is at the top left corner, where browsers look first.

3 Intimate interaction of type and imagery are shown in a balance between horizontal headline and art with vertical columns of text.

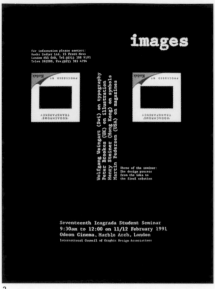

MITTEILUNGEN D. BUNDES DEUTSCHER GEBRAUCHSGRAPHIKER E.V.

BDG BLÄTTER 1927

DRITTER JAHRGANG

NEUNTES HEFT · ALS MANUSKRIPT GEDRUCKT

images

1

2

3

1 Color Inspired by expressionists and cubists, color use was reinterpreted at the Bauhaus. Under the direction of Walter Gropius in 1919, the applied arts were reinvented, expanding the use of color along with codifying and using asymmetry and emptiness.
2 Color is inverted for type's legibility and white so the yellow "eyebrows" become most visible. Had the type been made yellow, the "eye sockets" would have been given prominence.
3 Partly through color (the teeth have to be white) and partly because of the idea, this late Art Deco Italian toothpaste poster emphasizes the type.

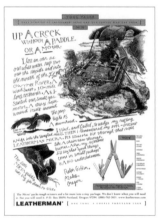

Scratchy and idiosyncratic lettering (including peculiar color changes) is matched to a scratchy illustration style for design unity.

☛ **Color** can be extracted from the image and applied to the primary type, making them unified. Or color can be contrasted to create relationship. The most natural color contrasts are complementary colors (see pages 98-99), colors that are opposite each other on the color wheel.

☛ **Texture** is a surface that is best described by the sense of touch. In two dimensional design, a feelable surface must be translated into a visual description. Such a translation of texture is often mistaken for *pattern*, which is a repeated decorative design. A pattern is a textural translation when it describes a surface. Actual texture is so uncommon in advertising that it alone, as on an insert or package, can demand attention.

☛ **Idea** By far the most interesting way to create design unity is through concept. The opportunities for making the message its most potent are the greatest in this category. However, the results are dependent on the thorough blending of visual materials.

Advertising
Design
and
Typography

1

2

3

4

5

Texture 1 Rough images share rough-hewn lettering in these 1997 posters by James Victore.
2 Type and image are chopped into descriptive, dimensional texture in an ad for a Broadway show.
3 The headline reads *Snow Removal*, but the ad is for television repair. The "snow" is visual broadcast interference.
4 Consistent type color and tight linespacing allow empty space to describe the subject of this poster.
5 Lettering applies the texture of facial hair to the book title in this c1975 design by Alan Peckolick.

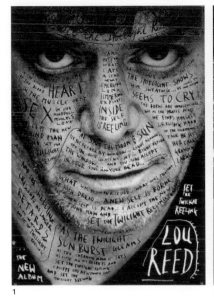

Idea 1 What is the best way to show the notably personal nature of song lyrics on a poster of the musician? Stefan Sagmeister, who has

scratched lettering into his own skin for self-promotion pieces, merely handwrote the lyrics on a photo of Lou Reed's face.

2 This is a campaign an art director could love. The images show predictions visibly, yet naturally, in everyday situations. Note that the text is very

hard to read. Knocking type out of process colors is asking for trouble. Using a bold weight of a serif type also increases readers' difficulties.

1 An ad to increase magazine subscription rates makes use of a false front cover and matching fake address label, where the message is.

2 The type is backwards in this detail of a Sharp Electronics ad shows a droll scene from an exceptional point of view: from inside the television screen

looking out at the viewer.
3 The structure of the outer columns (and careful text wraps) contrast with the looseness of numerous comments,

set in red for ignorability, about the spaciousness of the vehicle. It is remarkable that so many copy points are included in what is mostly empty space.

1 A 1958 retail fashion ad shapes text into image, making it a lot more visible but a little harder to read.

2 Headline as imagery: the quotes of praise are literally raining down on the car featured in this ad.

3 The headline snakes in and out of the building, showing the trail of the people in the picture.

4 A full bleed conflagration on the left is balanced with a nearly life-size toasted marshmallow on the right. The humor puts the horror in perspective.

1

2

3

1 A contemporary Nike ad is a pure Ayers No.1: a page in which about two-thirds of the page is image; the primary type is placed beneath the image as a large caption; and the text and logo are at the bottom. The headline could be cleaner by deleting both periods and letting the line break separate the phrases.

2 A business-to-business ad from 1956 layers transparent type and image. Flush right/ ragged left text is hard to read.

3 It's still an Ayers No.1 if the image doesn't bleed, as in this 1959 Corvette ad. By today's standards, this is fairly long copy for a car ad.

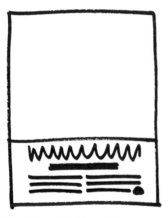

The Ayers No.1 layout presents information in the most logical order: image, headline, sub-head, text, sponsor's logo.

Design transparency: the Ayers No.1 is the simplest, most transparent form to give an advertising message. It shows a picture, a headline, and the lesser elements in their naturally descending order (*left*). The Ayers No.1 is as *invisible* a presentation as possible.

Another benefit of the Ayers No.1 is that readers are used to it, so they *look through it* to the content.

The weakness of this format is, of course, that it makes your ad look very much like everybody else's Ayers No.1 ads.

The remedy is to give your ad a twist:

☛ Run the headline into the image so it acts as a bridge between the picture and type areas.

☛ Make the type asymmetrical or leave most of the bottom area empty.

☛ Put a secondary image in the type area.

☛ Relate the image to the headline by shared treatment.

Advertising
Design
and
Typography

1

2

3

4

5

1 Ayers No.1 with no text and asymmetrical "logo" in an almost three-to-one ratio.

2 Scale and proportion are explored with a text area that is only about an eighth of the overall height.

3 Elegant column structure, typeface contrast, and empty space in a two-to-one ratio.

4 White type on black background is harder to read, but three lines is perceived as "few," so readers will not be put off by this treatment.

5 The expanse of empty tan makes this image dominant, but all that emptiness makes the product look like a sad, lonely, friendless celebrant.

4

5

4 Though there is no division between image and text area (the white of the page bleeds up into the image), this Japanese ad for French water is an

Ayers No.1. The shared form of bubbles, the tops of the round glasses, the bottle cap, and round cutouts on the gloves is excellent art direction.

5 An Ayers No.1 as a spread. Beyond the charm of the way in which "six generations" are shown and the quality of the photography, this wouldn't win

any *design* awards. Its simplicity could be mistaken for being underdesigned, but its simplicity is a win for the client and the consumer.

● Cut the image off in a shape rather than a horizontal line.

● Put a texture from the image into the type area or ghost the primary picture and put it behind the type area.

● Put the headline and text sideways in the type area.

● Make an upside down Ayers No.1 with the headline and text at the top and the image at the bottom. It works nearly as well as right side up.

Just about anything can be done without harming the Ayers No.1 format. The most defendable decision you can make is, naturally, the design treatment that furthers the existing branding style. The Ayers No.1 is so versatile, it's like vanilla ice cream: you can add *anything* to it and it'll taste great.

Other formats draw attention in their own idiosyncratic ways, but the Ayers No.1 will be here forever, transparently letting the idea come through – and winning awards for copywriters and photographers.

An inverted Ayers No.1 puts space at the bottom two thirds of this ad, which is used well to indicate room for fainting.

Design:
Words and
Pictures

1

2

3

4

1 David Ogilvy's wordy 1950s Rolls Royce ad gave prospects plenty to consider when learning about a $14,000 purchase. Thirteen numbered points break

the text into moderate pieces.
2 An inverted Ayers No.1 with headline and text at the top. It is amusing that this layout variation features a rock climber who

is dangling downwards.
3 A pair of inverted Ayers No.1s. The scratchy treatment behind the type extends the demolition idea perfectly.

4 It's still an Ayers No.1 If It doesn't have a headline. An owl is hidden among a forest of charmingly hand-rendered trees.

A B C D E F

G H I J K L

M N O P Q R

S T U V W

henry wolf

X Y Z

which leaves H, A, B, E, R; which is <u>more</u> than enough!

HABER TYPOGRAPHERS 115 WEST 29 STREET NEW YORK LO 5-1080

1 2   3   4

1 (*opposite*) Henry Wolf was a master at using type alone with only minimal trickery, 1961.
2 An all-type newspaper ad has very long text to explain its apparently peculiar logic.

Illness can be emotional, but this approach is intellectual.
3 *"They mix alcohol with gasoline. (Sound of a blender as type gets mixed.) We use Bardahl Top Oil."* This Brazilian

commercial uses animated lettering, a perpetually undervalued technique.
4 Jan Tschichold designed this poster (*top*) in 1930, as expressive asymmetrical typography

was being invented. That type has shape (*middle*) was a radical departure from the traditional centered arrangement (*above*).

All-type ads Sometimes the best way to tell a story is with type alone. These are the instances when the meaning and power of language is at its most persuasive and it takes an alert ear to notice this. In these circumstances, simple letters simply arranged are enough (*above left*). It takes design discipline to be willing to get out of the way of the message and simply set two or three sizes of type. It is the most benign advertising design possible (*below*).

After typeset ads, there are four methods to create all-type ads, each increasing the level of abstraction and exacting a greater toll on legibility. Consequently, execute these ideas on display type only. Text is too fine, and readers too harried, to tolerate much fooling around with legibility at small type sizes.

1 Type arranged to illustrate its meaning Keen observation, free imagination, plus strong intention can make words *show* what they mean. This is

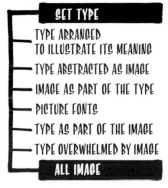

This chart shows the organization of type's *interaction of form* with imagery. This is distinct from their arrangement on the page.

Design:
Words and
Pictures

1   2   3   4   5

1 Oswald Cooper's hand lettered all caps, all centered ad, Chicago, 1927.
2 Flush left type contrasts with centered in this 1955 trade ad.

This is not a font that looks like typewriter type: it is immensely-enlarged typewriter type.
3 All type and lots of attitude make this poster effective. With

copywriting this striking, adding a visual would probably be counterproductive.
4 Though this is "just typesetting," color is essential to this

poster's meaning.
5 Solid black space represents earth in this simple all-typeset depiction of burial. Breaking for sense helps a lot, too.

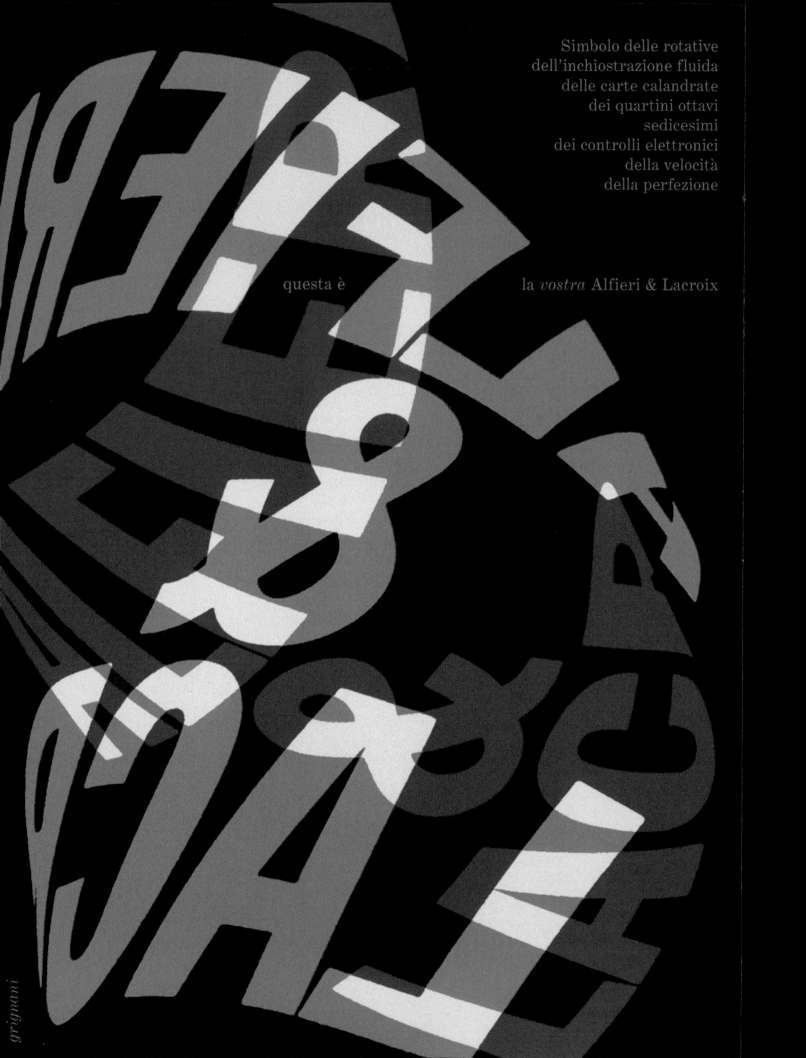

Simbolo delle rotative
dell'inchiostrazione fluida
delle carte calandrate
dei quartini ottavi
sedicesimi
dei controlli elettronici
della velocità
della perfezione

questa è

la *vostra* Alfieri & Lacroix

grignani

1 2   3

1 (*opposite*) *"Symbol of the ro-tating press and fluid ink and of smoothed paper..."* A poetic statement about printing quality is interpreted with type

made flexible and transparent for an Italian ad agency.
2 An exception to the rule that diagonal type is ugly because

it so rarely relates to the content. This 1961 poster by Pierre Monnerat *uses the angle* by playing with the *Z–N* similarity.

3 Type weight used to illustrate its own meaning. No type family has this many weight members, so this is a custom lettering job.

more than typesetting, in which breaking for sense is about the maximum intervention, and an all-type ad taken to its extreme interpretation, which becomes *type as image*.

2 Type abstracted as image Letterforms are segmented or separated or letterforms have been heavily processed so the first impression they make is not necessarily one of pure legibility. Working with type as image requires developing figure and ground shapes and is well beyond typesetting, which may be all that's needed in a conventional all-type ad.

What makes a type as image ad potent is that it distills an idea to its essence. It is so pure, there isn't even a need for an image to go with the headline. It is usually startling in its directness, too. It is almost oxymoronic to have a homely type as image ad. That may be true in part because designers who excel at this approach have a more sensitive feel for typeforms and space in general. It is great discipline to get in the habit

Simple typesetting on a small billboard attached to a bench apparently misnames the object in a visual juxtaposition.

Design:
Words and
Pictures

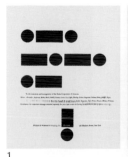

1   2   3   4   5

1 Paul Rand used Morse Code, a passion of a potential client's, in trying to win an account.
2 The wonderful orange shapes happen to reveal a quote mark

in their negative space. A character made large enough will become its surrounding shapes.
3 Simple typesetting with some characters rotated 180°.

4 An all-type identity makes faces for a Spanish candy manufacturer.
5 Hand printed wood type of the contestants in an international

rugby match is carefully crafted to fit together. Its even spacing and dark color become an illustration of a pint of ale with *England* as the foamy head.

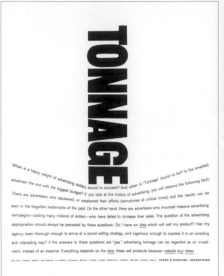

1 Don Eggensteiner's house ad for Young & Rubicam warns against spending sheer volume of advertising dollars. "Every-thing depends on the *idea*. Ideas sell products because *people buy ideas*."

2 Type shaped into a renowned façade for a 1977 poster by Ivan Chermayeff.
3 An anti-establishment mes-sage is expressed by moving the type on a scanner as it passes, producing a new take on the UPC barcode.

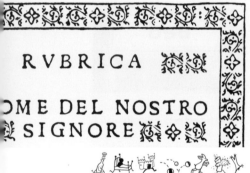

of trying to come up with an advertising idea using type alone. It doesn't always produce persuasive results, but the exercise forces a different perspective on a problem and often leads down unexpected paths.

3 Image as part of the type This is type dominant design in which letter-forms that have been merged with image (*opposite, top*). Image may be in the shape of type, or image may be arranged into readable letters and words. Letterforms are not subordinate, and legibility is willingly sacrificed. The illustrative subject should be appropriate to your message, either in agreement or in sharp contradiction.

4 Picture fonts (including *dingbats*, *symbols*, and *ornaments*) are col-lections of keystroke-accessible images and illustrative characters (*left*). They are ordinarily used as bullets for emphasis, as in the arrow at the beginning of this paragraph, or, when repeated into lines, as borders and separators. Some picture fonts are fanciful letterforms and others,

Advertising
Design
and
Typography

1 An exaggerated reply form has plenty of sarcasm so readers might recognize themselves as potential subscribers.
2 *"Applications"* Futura type-face was introduced 30 years before this promotional book-let cover was designed in 1960.
3 The CBS logo replaces 'I' in the headline of this 1955 self promotion during the eye's intro-duction, when pictures were toppling words as the primary language.
4 Herb Lubalin's 1971 animated type promotion for public TV.
5 Most text-as-skyscrapers isn't legible, but one "building" is.
6 Geometry reigns in a 1930 Dutch ad for Cirkel coffee.

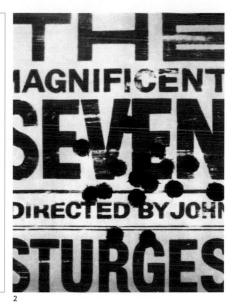

1 This is a photo of type on a roadside trailer sign seen in rural areas where fishing is popular. This is a full-spread business-to-business ad for tackle shop owners.

2 Saul Bass scores another movie poster success in 1961. The bullet holes are representational, but it's the type's cropping that gets our attention.

not quite as legible, may be used in semi-coded messages. The first picture font was a set of type fleurons (*"flowers"*), made by Giovanni and Alberto Alvise in 1478.

In addition to these four all type – and mostly type – methods, type can be subordinate to image in two ways:

☛ **Type as part of the image** Image dominates as type is inserted into or substituted for a part of an image. Similar to the third category (*opposite, "Image as part of the type"*), but with emphasis on image. This method is especially effective when a message's meaning and execution are unified.

☛ **Type overwhelmed by image so it nearly disappears** Extreme image dominance. By definition, type plays a very subordinate role in this category, though it is part of the design. The next and last category beyond this is all-image design with no type at all.

Max Huber's poster for the Italian Grand Prix mixes perspective and transparency to represent motion and speed.

Design: Words and Pictures

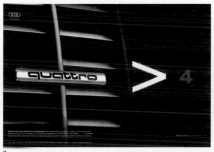

1 The letter *K* structurally diagrammed – stroke ends and meeting points – and drawn dimensionally, 1952.

2 A three-dimensional letterform construction (with perfect craftsmanship) represents a large Italian department store.

3 The imagery of an auto's front grille is incidental to this all-type ad alluding to more features than all wheel drive.

4 *"Life is perfect!"* Type is image in this poster using red and black caviar, which lets the art material be the type.

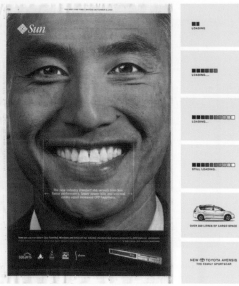

1

2

3

Charts 1 The Angolan flag is more than a backdrop: its three colored areas are used as proportional indicators of illnesses and medical care in the southwest African country. **2** The width of a CFO's smile is measured in Sun Microsystems' newspaper ad, giving measurable proof of their product's performance. **3** An internet banner ad makes use of a visual pun of the familiar "loading" chart to illustrate the car's substantial cargo space.

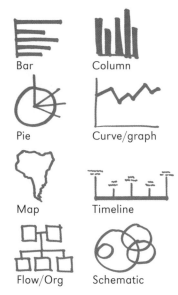

Bar   Column

Pie   Curve/graph

Map   Timeline

Flow/Org   Schematic

Charts and diagrams A chart is a pictorial composition that represents numerical or quantifiable relationships. A diagram is a simplified drawing showing the appearance or structure of a thing. Both are useful in advertising as opportunities to display data and promote the client's design personality and brand.

There are fifteen categories of charts and diagrams. The most familiar are bar and column charts, pie charts, curve charts (or graphs) with *X* and *Y* axes, maps, timelines, flow charts and organization charts, and schematics. Charts and diagrams are useful in speeding information along when words would only slow things down.

The characteristics of a good chart or diagram are *elegance*, the simplest solution for the problem; *clarity*, making the conclusion obvious; *ease*, putting labels near parts; *pattern*, using similar treatments for similar charts; and *simplicity*, removing unnecessary details.

Advertising
Design
and
Typography

1

2

3

1 In a three-page ad, Nike trail shoes are followed by a trail made to look civilized, as if it were a track.
2 Piet Zwart's 1926 ad for Nederlandsche Kabelfabriek (Dutch Cable Manufacturers) at Delft, a major client for whom he designed hundreds of ads, brochures, posters, and catalogues. The very tall, very condensed zeros are made from existing curves and straights of geometric rules, normally used by printers for borders. **3** Molecules meet halftone dots in a chart exploring Einstein's brain. No explanation is given for the scientific-looking treatment above his head.

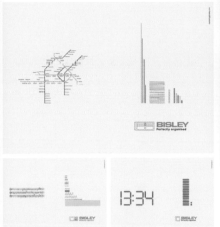

1

2

3

1 An audio equipment knob set to eleven is an unambiguous reference to *This is Spinal Tap*, the 1984 mockumentary on *really loud* rock music.
2 A company that makes office storage furniture uses *disorganization* and *decomposition* in chart form.

3 Quantities are shown in color then captioned in an explanatory key.

1

2

3

4

1 Telephones could be any color in 1962 – as long as they were black, when colored phones were introduced by Western Electric. This chart promotes the relative popularity of each color through scale.
2 Different kinds of files take up different amounts of space, so a lifesize thumb drive is seg-mented to show capacity.
3 *"Your contribution plus our contribution equals..."* shown graphically in a house ad for Red Cross contributions, 1955.

4 An ad for paper shows rolls of paper and trimmed sheets with tabs placed between sections of a job, labelled as a calendar.

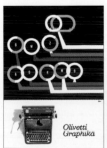

1

2

3

4

5

Diagrams 1 Olivetti presents their 1958 manual typewriter as a high technology machine. Cover the graphics and see how much a diagram can add.
2 Two arrows indicate rotation (red) and extraction (blue) in this 1965 diagrammatic ad.
3 The familiar boot shape of Italy is detached as an illustra-tion of the damage land mines do to human limbs.
4 A map highlighted by hand with life-size Post-It® notes per-sonalizes this ad for neighbor-ing real estate developments.
5 A typographic flow chart showing the proliferation of dogs when they aren't neu-tured avoids showing breeds.

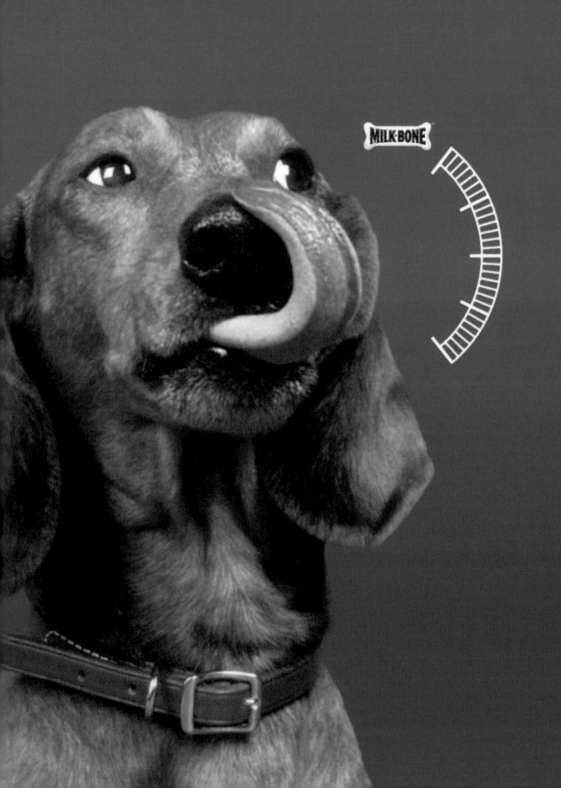

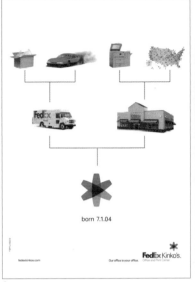

born 7.1.04

FedEx Kinko's.

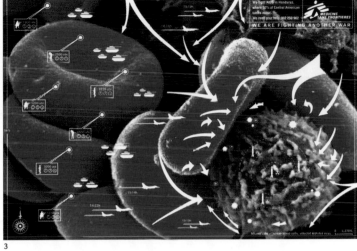

1 (*opposite and above*) Let a chart and great stock images of dogs do the work. According to the creative team, "99.9% of dogs don't read, so we opted for a simple visual solution…that Milk Bone creates dog excitement. The other .1% of dogs received a 230-page report…"

2 A flow chart showing the heritage of a new business entity.
3 Doctors Without Borders often works in war zones. Their efforts to fight AIDS are abstractly represented at the cellular level as if on a battle invasion diagram of the HIV virus.

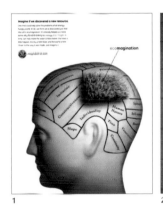

1 A diagram of the human mind reveals a new and fertile area.

2 A bank of light switches shows which bodily functions and nervous connections are working in this ad for Multiple Sclerosis.

3 A stadium seating chart superimposed on a photo of a car implies either being the center of attention or having perfect concert seats in a car with a great sound system. Either way, those are positive messages (unless you are a hapless bystander forced to endure the passing racket).

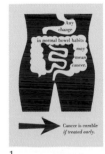

1 Leo Lionni's 1950 poster for the American Cancer Society diagrams the human gut.
2 Type indicates nearby landmarks of a new residential building in New York City. The scaled titles show their proximity while emphasizing the city's verticality: height has great value in New York.

3 "Opposite ends of the scale" is used to show selection.
4 A map of a runner's route with his stream-of-consciousness thinking as its headline.

5 A drawing of sports clothing with numbered callouts gives this ad the feel of scientific authenticity, a goal of the branding for this company.

Art
is knowing what to
LEAVE OUT.
– Anonymous

FURNITURE MANUFACTURER

SPORTING GOODS

FASHION

AUTOMOBILE

FOOD

PHARMACEUTICAL/MEDICAL

ADVERTISING DESIGN
Redesigning an already good ad

PURPOSE
To explore visualizing selling ideas in familiar ways for unfamiliar results.

BACKGROUND
There are four levels of advertising:
1) POOR CONCEPT/POOR EXECUTION
2) POOR CONCEPT/GREAT EXECUTION
3) GREAT CONCEPT/POOR EXECUTION
4) GREAT CONCEPT/GREAT EXECUTION
Shown at left is a headline that can be interpreted many ways. Beneath it are six product categories. Apply the headline to three one-shot ads for a product from any three categories. | You will have to do some research in advertising and design annuals (or other sources of juried design excellence) for additional source material.

PROCESS, PART 1
Select an all-type ad and list its design attributes. Make two versions of this ad: an exact duplicate substituting its words with your new copy, and an interpretation of the design attributes you wrote down.

PROCESS, PART 2
Select a type-dominant ad and list its design attributes. The proportion of type to imagery must be 75% type to 25% image. Make two versions of this ad: an exact duplicate substituting its words with your new copy, and an interpretation of the design attributes you wrote down. Create an image from scratch for these two ads.

PROCESS, PART 3
Select an image-dominant ad and list its design attributes. The proportion of imagery to type must be 75% image to 25% type. Make two versions of this ad: an exact duplicate substituting its words with your new copy, and an interpretation of the design attributes you wrote down. Create an image from scratch for these two ads.

ADDITIONAL INFORMATION
On the first version of each of these Parts, make as few changes as possible as you reinterpret the original design.

The design decisions you will need to make (for example typeface, imagery, and spatial organization) in the conversion process of Parts 1, 2, and 3 will be the grist for discussion. *Your decisions in the process of adapting new content on existing design are what will reveal the rightness of your design thinking.* Always provide the source design with your studies so the fidelity of your interpretations can be evaluated.

All preliminary studies and final ads are to be 49p0 x 63p6. *No other sizes will be evaluated..*

One Part must be bitmapped, one Part must be grayscale, and one Part must be RGB, and each must be *used*, not merely *had*.

If you aren't sure about a particular decision, *do it two or three ways.* True to advertising conditions, time doesn't allow any delays in this process. Explore, abstract, and interpret.

Six final cropped high-resolution prints on bright white heavyweight paper. Lightly pencil your name and a full accounting of the study's attributes on the back bottom right corner of each study. *Identifying the attributes thoroughly is essential.*

All preliminary and final work (with additional full-size 300dpi tiffs in bitmap/grays/ RGB formats) must be grouped and burned on a labelled cd.

As an art director, everything you touch should look — at the very least — loved. Promote yourself as being one of the best young advertising minds around. Your immediate competition are your classmates. Outdo them because they will be trying to outdo you.

These are examples from a similar exercise. Note the variety of solutions that this process generates.

1 Celebrating the 10th anniversary of Italian television, this 1964 billboard installation captures the feeling of the young image-dominant medium.

2 This bus stop billboard is a product demonstration. Stacks of fake money (with fourteen real bills on top) are sandwiched between sheets of shatter-resistant security glass.

3 *"Isn't that the Japanese flag hanging there."* A billboard campaign can be site specific. To promote the idea that they cover local events fully, a Swedish newspaper had one-of-a-kind signs made, each referring to a nearby object or landmark.

All imagery, all type, and type as imagery (using details of inventions and constructions of the modern world).

Chapter 7 **Design: Print Design vs Billboards, TV, Web and Interactive, and Radio**

Readers' preferences in print have had centuries to develop: bigger means more important; bigger is easier to read than smaller; there must be a balance between contrast (which makes things stand out) and similarity (which gives a design singular impact); hierarchy guides the viewer through the parts of a message; and consistency unifies a multi-page document. Because of their familiarity and their inherent rightness, each of these design principles can and should be applied to other forms of advertising media.

Print vs billboard design Billboards are defined as "outdoor media," so giant size and roadside location are not the only criteria. Billboards

1 "Damaged" billboards is a startling way of getting attention. Billboards can be site-specific, as is this one at the entrance to a Canadian theme park. The body is a realistic dummy, not just a printed silhouette cut out.

2 A billboard and its surroundings can interact, as in the sheets of rubber "bubblegum" covering trees.

3 Real objects (like a car) attached to billboards are spectacular.

4 So are self-referential cracked and peeling panels.

5 Motion can be added to billboards, as in the pendulum swings between candidates.

1 A billboard can cover an entire wall, as in this trompe l'œil (French for "*fool the eye*") example pasted on a blank brick wall in Santiago, Chile.

2 Posters with die cut head shapes pasted over existing cracks and damaged surfaces use the walls' properties in- geniously for a Chinese head- ache medication. This is such a natural solution; it seems obvious and it makes you imagine, "I wish I'd thought of it." Notice the very small, non- competing ad message in the lower right corner.

do tend to be really big posters, but they also include bus and train cards, and installations. Though the number of billboards has remained relatively constant for the past few years, billboards are a growth in- dustry with sales increasing by more than 5% per year. Their sales have increased because, in an age of audience specificity, they are a sure way to reach a breadth of viewers whose only common denominator is their precise location on the planet. That breadth leads to shared experience and, it is hoped, discussion and action.

The best billboards have visual messages that are self-explanatory and very easy to understand. Many big billboards are located near highways. Drivers can't devote more than a moment to a billboard: seeing partly with their peripheral vision, copy of any length is a waste of space. So keep it visual and keep the headline short. More creative opportunity exists in smaller billboards that can be read with a few seconds more leisure.

Use the surrounding space: the sky and the pole.

Design: Print vs Billboards, TV, Web, Interactive, and Radio

1 "*We wish you a peaceful Sun- day.*" A billboard for a German magazine shows a contrast of images to promote their news and sports coverage. Direction and scale are consistent, but an unexpected and jarring break in synchronicity (helped by contrast of black and white vs color) demands our attention.

2 Printed in water-soluble ink, this poster drips away in Singapore until the message is barely legible.

3 Printed backwards so it will be right-reading when seen in the the mirror in women's rest- rooms at bars and restaurants.

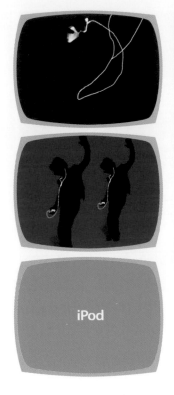

1

This is admittedly one of the simplest campaigns to come along in a while, but it is fantastically successful, too.
1 TVCs, billboards, and magazine ads are treated identically as...
2 Posters, which are shown in a TVC dancing to the sound of a passing person's iPod music.

2

"Over the years I've had a foot in each of two worlds. I worked first as a graphic designer, then as a filmmaker, then as a graphic designer, then as a filmmaker. And it seems to me that each has informed and shaped the other." Saul Bass

Print vs television design Art directing commercials is quite different than art directing ads or Web sites. For one thing, commercials are like mini movies and require a particular talent to tell a powerful story over ten to thirty seconds. For another, "spots" or TVCs ("*television commercials*") are almost exclusively imagery with a logo and a tagline as a super at the end. So is it design or movie direction? One thing is for certain: television is one sexy medium.

What TV and print have in common are the initial two or three seconds to try to get people to stop long enough to show them a reason to stay until the end. And of course, television and print are always parts of a unified campaign that must share visual traits for brand recognition.

The commercials shown here were chosen because they represent various ways in which type and image can interact on screen. Many more fine examples can be found in movie titles.

It's all done by pictures . . . Philco Television's Brilliant, Clear, Deep Dimension Picture advertised in LOOK — America's exciting picture magazine...to brighten up your sales picture

1

1 A 1954 direct mail piece for *Look* magazine uses television's influence on the new importance of visuals in magazines imposed by television. Seven years later, one presentation made at the Sixth Annual Visual Communications Conference of the Art Directors Club of New York was "The Role of the Creative Art Director in Television Commercials." William H. Schneider, the program director, said, "New concepts in visual communication are proliferating as never before... creative (people) in the field... find it increasingly difficult to keep up the flow of fresh creative ideas."

Design:
Print vs
Billboards,
TV, Web,
Interactive,
and Radio

Mini situation comedy *"The Dynamite One with Walter Chiari."* In 1958, at the dawn of the television age, there were no models for commercials to follow, so some copied the look of the programs, even having a title and the star's name. This evolved into "slice of life" commercials in the 1960s.

Using a security camera adds realism and immediacy. This campaign lets the viewer peek in where we aren't supposed to, so we can see how others shop. This :30 spot has two male voice overs describing the fitting as if it was a gymnastics routine: "She's about to start her routine... She starts off with a peck-and-tug, and moves right into a sleeve-shake... She nails it!"

Image and type shuffle like cards, showing and asking "Who do you love the least?" in this :60 spot. Art direction is evident in the monochromatic blue and the extreme close up camera work on "your" children and parents.

Note that the on-screen type is high contrast for increased legibility. Whether reversed or not, this is even more important than for printed type.

Split screen shows pairings of form to express the convergence of wants on one side and needs on the other for Target stores. The elegance of this spot conveys the store's attitude as a place to get well-designed objects at low prices. The simplicity of the campaign extends to billboards (*below*) and print ads, too.

  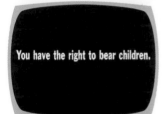 

Type and space About as simple as it gets. Space is used to indicate sides of the bed by positioning the two halves of the conversation on sides of the screen.

A time-based Ayers No.1 This TVC has a primary visual followed by a caption, both of which include motion. This is a very simple and effective way of showing something shocking, then explaining what is meant. Ironically, the baby would put the gun in her mouth for this filming only after maple syrup had been smeared on it.

A "normal" TVC uses type as a caption after a moving image because it's an approach that works. This British commercial makes its point simply and surprisingly: workers simultaneously hang a poster and wrap the pole. A passerby, taken with the low price of the car, walks into the pole, explaining for the viewer the purpose of the pole wrapping.

All type It doesn't get simpler or cheaper than this to introduce a new reservation number. Here's what the voice over adds: "Think of that as an 'I.' Then 'I ate.' And those look like two eggs. Now say you ate those two eggs for your cousin Moe. Then 'tell six people.' 'I ate two eggs for Moe, tell six.' Works for me."

Design:
Print vs
Billboards,
TV, Web,
Interactive,
and Radio

Characters interact with type on screen Letters come out of the telephone (reading, *Banco Crefisul fits completely in my telephone*) and across the screen (reading, *Banco Crefisul isn't complicated like other banks*) as a woman makes a paper airplane, and then sweeps the letters up and tosses them away.

Type superimposed on an image An immigrant talks about his love for the U.S. when a woman's voice suddenly begins to come out of his mouth with anti-immigrant content. The message: vote or someone else will speak for you.

Strong art direction without type Memorable styling of the set can brand a product. This Canadian commercial makes the point that the coffee is so good, if it hadn't been tied down during this commercial's shoot, even this mugworth would have been purloined and enjoyed.

Type, image, and space Very of-the-moment design applied to a TVC. This Toyota commercial was part of a brief, seasonal campaign that increased sales 30 percent.

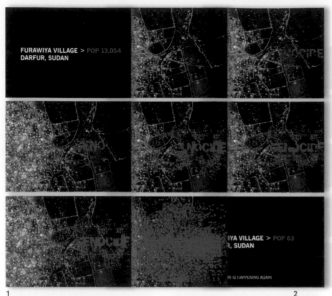

FURAWIYA VILLAGE > POP 13,054
DARFUR, SUDAN

...YA VILLAGE > POP 63
R, SUDAN

...N IS HAPPENING AGAIN

1

2

1 Dots represent deaths and displaced persons. Though this is a flipbook, it can easily be a series of stills from an interactive file.

2 Many banner ads have motion – spinning logos, flashing signs, and other gratuitous treatment – if only to catch attention in a "made-you-look"

kind of way, since motion is not inherent in the subject matter. This banner ad *uses* – not just *has* – motion to make its point for the São Paulo Eye Bank: as

you roll over the Braille characters, the arrow cursor becomes a hand, and the corresponding letter appears in the background.

Interactivity existed before the digital age, though obviously in a far more rudimentary way. Interaction is encouraged in this spread ad, even putting dashed cut-out lines around the life-size cookies. Designed by Seymour Chwast of Pushpin Studio in 1965.

Print vs Web* and interactive design Web and interactive design is all about participation, with every user's action tracked and scrutinized. "Impressions" is the exact number of people that see your ad (try doing that with a billboard), "click through" is how many people clicked on your ad and "conversion" is how many people actually did what you wanted them to do. If one banner in your campaign is not performing well, you can instantly replace it with a higher performer (again, try that with a billboard).

Motion has always had to be *implied* in print. Even a flip book or pop-up book can only *approximate* motion. Now the Web makes motion a normal characteristic of design.

The Web interrupts a viewer differently than a television spot: television is a passive medium. An online viewer is more engaged and is perhaps less likely to attend to advertising. On the other hand, Web ad-

Advertising
Design
and
Typography

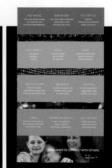

1

* This discussion is limited to Web *advertising* – not Web *site* –design. Many of the principles are the same but the terminology differs. For example, people seeing an *ad* are called "impressions"; people viewing a *site* are called "hits" or "visits."

1 Interaction on paper Paper has dimensionality and can be folded, which can be manipulated to arouse a reader's curiosity. This insert is printed

separately and bound into magazines. Its four perforated windows may be peeled up to reveal a succession of messages. The inclusion of the

sponsor on the front (*bottom right corners*) might detract from the sense of curiosity this expensive piece is supposed to engender. Does it cause some

browsers to skip peeling any panels to find out about "the internet we've all been waiting for," given that they already know who the sponsor is?

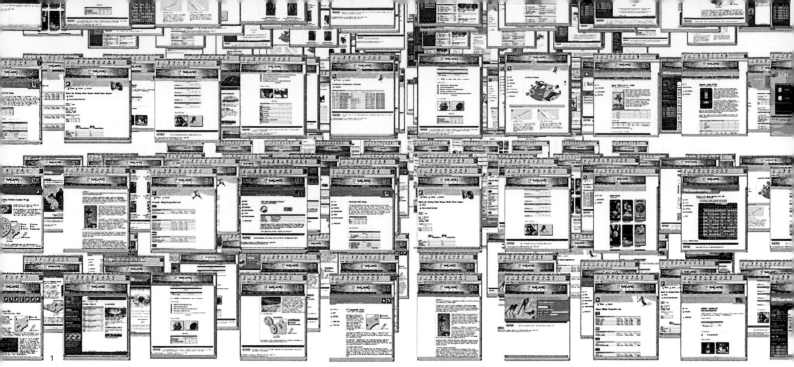

1

The Internet was born as the "ARPANet" in 1969. Sponsored by the U.S. Advanced Research Project Agency, it was a small network connecting four west coast universities.

1 Site architecture and visual design This is a sampling of the pages belonging to the site for the 1998 Nagano Winter Olympics. (The Adobe site has 6,000 pages.) Such sites are, in essence, magazines whose pages are constantly change-able by a league of designers. By using a grid and standardiz-ing elements, the site architec-ture must resolve enormous variety with making each page look like it belongs to the site. Yet enough flexibility must be given so the content of each page can be presented with utmost interest and clarity.

vertisers can target their audience more effectively than television, so the reluctance of viewers to pay attention is allayed by their likely interest in the product.

Web and interactive design differ from print in the area of typographic control: unless you are showing a *picture* of type, Web-safe fonts are necessary for all HTML-based designs. Like any restriction, this is an op-portunity for creativity by pushing the limits of what can be done. Some sites have a "type size" button, allowing the user to select from three or four sizes, each prefit to the layout. With Web-safe fonts, the user can alter the font and type size, typically through their preferences panel, adding a different meaning to "interactive design."

These are not mere technical differences. But from the user's perspec-tive, what works in print – contrast, emphasis, and space (principles based on familiarity) – are applicable to all media. Design is still design.

"Once people know how to appreciate excellence, they will not accept mediocrity. So it has been for centuries, and so it will always be for those who care." Aaron Burns, co-founder International Typeface Corporation

Design:
Print vs
Billboards,
TV, Web,
Interactive,
and Radio

i

3

1 Visual hierarchy is crucial, especially on retail sites, where the progression through find-ing and buying must be as invisible a process as possible. Scale, position, and weight are used to clarify relationships.
2 The placement of menu and submenus The top of the page is the expected place for menus. The user expects sub-menus to drop down from the primary listing.
3 The relationship of text and visuals They can either be side by side or overlap. Type over image is hard to read, so reduce contrast in the background, as this site has done with a trans-parent dark panel.

Design unity to integrate elements on each page and the overall feel of the site with the rest of the branding players. Some type choices, decisions, and spatial relationships will be inherited.

Divide information into equivalent chunks so each page offers about the same amount of content. Have a single focal point per page.

Lead the user to a precise piece of information or to a definite page. Make the "next" and "back" buttons prominent. Don't give the user unnecessary options.

Typefaces must be highly legible with large x-height and open counters. Add space for easier reading on screen. Use words rather than icons, which must be learned.

1 It isn't easy *showing* radio commercials. This German magazine campaign does a great job of *showing* sound clarity, using typeface choice and color to increase impact. **2** At right is a 60-second radio spot that is highly visual. Art directors are rarely credited for work on radio projects, and this is sadly no exception.

This is a postcard being sent from a Frenchman vacationing in Texas. First we hear him speaking in French as he writes, then we hear the translation:

Philippe Chers Jeanne et Ralph…
Translator *Dear Jane and Ralph…*
Philippe J'adore mes vacances ici au Texas.
Translator *I love my vacation here in Texas.*
Philippe Les gens sont très sympatiques.
Translator *The people are friendly.*
Philippe Les femmes sont adorables.
Translator *The women are lovely.*
Philippe Et même les chevaux sentent bons.
Translator *The horses even smell good.*
Philippe La semaine dernière, je suis allé faire des tonnes de courses sans égard.
Translator *Last week I went shopping with reckless abandon.*
Philippe Hier, j'ai mangé du barbeque Texan delicieux.
Translator *Yesterday I ate some delicious Texas barbeque.*
Philippe Ensuite je me suis promené sur la plage.
Translator *Then I walked on the beach.*
Philippe A pied nu… et nu aussi.
Translator *Barefoot and naked.*
Philippe Pour un instant je pensais être en France.
Translator *For a moment, I thought I was in France.*
Philippe S'il-vous plait envoyez-moi de l'argent sous caution.
Translator *Please send bail money.*
Philippe A bientôt, Philippe.
Translator *Regards, Philippe.*
Announcer Come to Texas for your next vacation, or just a weekend getaway. Call 1-800-8888-TEX for your free 264-page Texas Travel book. That's 1-800-8888 TEX. *Le Texas plus qu'un état c'est un pays á luis seul.* It's like a whole other country.
Brian Brooker, Copy; Guy Bommarito CD. Texas Department of Commerce

Print vs radio design Radio is communication without visuals and requires a special gift for creating a real world in the listener's mind's eye. It may be tempting to think radio is purely a copywriter's problem, but a gifted visual communicator is indispensable in developing good radio commercials. Besides, art directors can't help but bring their peculiar points of view to bear on any problem, and the job in radio – as in all advertising – is to interpret the business strategy in creative and memorable ways. It is also a lot of fun to work in another media; it uses a different part of the brain.

Even copywriters find it tough. Mark Gross, SVP, Group Creative Director at DDB Chicago and part of the team that created the "Real Men of Genius" award-winning radio spots for Budweiser Light, says, "Plain and simple, writing radio is brutally hard… It's hard to reinvent or approach radio from a different angle. That is until someone comes along and proves otherwise."

Design: Print vs Billboards, TV, Web, Interactive, and Radio

  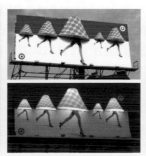 

1 Scale replicas of billboards are constructed and placed next to normal-sized posters to advertise childrens' shoes.

2 Billboards can change dramatically from day to night. The simplicity of this design adapts to both versions.

3 *Ambient advertising* is a category of marketing that is designed to be part of the surrounding environment. This example for a laundry cleaner was bleached directly on the cement wall alongside a roadway.

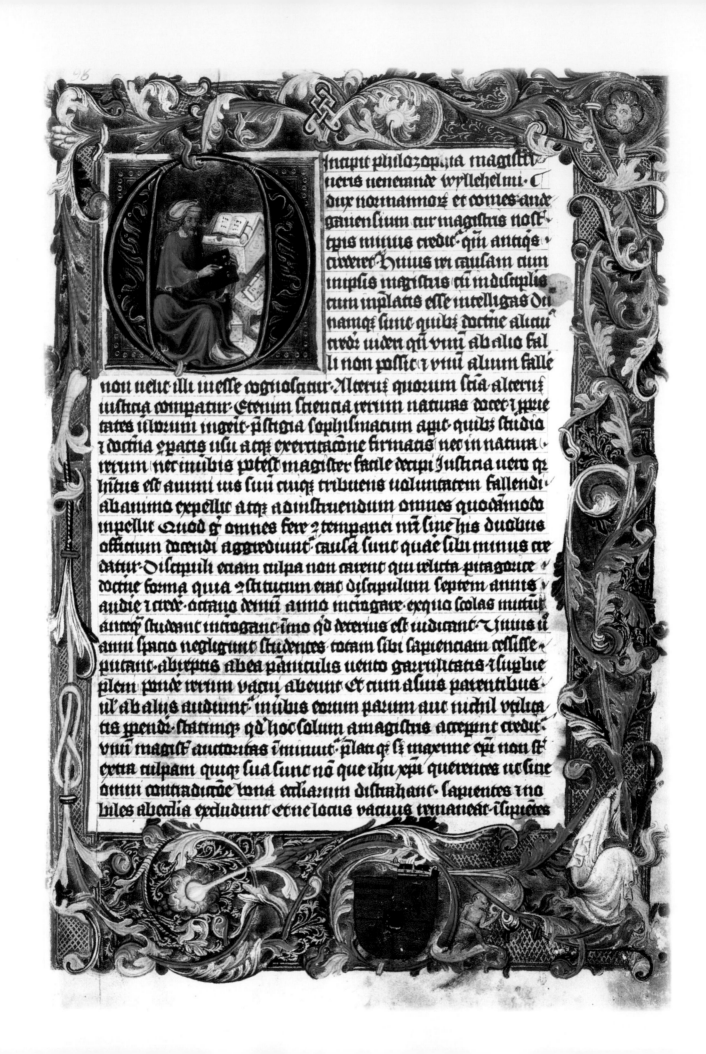

Incipit philozophia magistri
veneris venerande wyllehelmi . C
dux normannorum et comes aude
ganensium cur magistris nost
tris minus credit. qui antiqs
caverет. Huius rei causam cum
inipsis magistris cum indisciplis
cum inplatis esse intelligas du
namque sunt quibz doctrine alicui
credi: viden qui vnu ab alio fal
li non possit: et vnul aliuum falle
non velit illi inesse cognoscatur. Alterum quorum scia alterius
iusticia comparatur. Eternum sciencia rerum naturas docet: et proprie
tates illorum ingerit. psistigia sophismatum agit. quibz studio
et doctina exactis usu atque exercitacione firmatis nec in natura
rerum nec inuibis potest magister facile decipi Iusticia vero qz
habitus est animi ius suum cuique tribuens uoluntatem fallendi
ab animo expellit atque ad instruendum omnes quodammodo
impellit Quod si omnes fere et tempanei nu sine his duabus
officium docendi aggrediunt causa sunt quae sibi minus cre
datur. Discipuli etiam culpa non carent qui relicta pitagorice
doctine forma quia constitutum erat discipulum septem annis
audie et credere. octauo demum anno inciogare. ex quo scolas mutui
antequ studuint inciogant. imo qd deterius est iudicant: et huius ii
anni spacio negligunt studentes totam sibi sapienciam collisse
putant. abreptis abea panticulis vento garrulitatis et supbie
plem ponde rerum vacui abeunt Et cum aliuis parentibus
uel ab aliis audunt. inuibis eorum parum aut nichil vtiliga
tis pendi. statimque qd hoc solum a magistris acceperit credit:
vnui magisf auctoritas iminuit. placa qz si maxime qui non st
certa culpam quiqz sua sunt non que ihu xpi querentes uc sine
omni contradicione vona eccliarum distrahant. sapientes et no
biles abeccalia excludunt Et ne locus vacuus remaneat insipientes

Section 3
Executions: Typography

Long before there was advertising – because everything was locally produced – there was manuscript writing. Copies were written by hand, one page at a time. It could take a year of a scribe's time to copy one book, so every book was enormously valuable and highly treasured. This page is from a c1400 copy of *Dragmaticon philosophiae*, a scientific textbook written by William of Conches for his pupil, King Henry II of England, in about 1150. It shows William in a *historiated*, or *figured*, decorated initial Q (drawn backwards as was the style at the time).

It is easy to make a typographic *thing*, an ordinary piece of typesetting determined more by computer defaults than artistic vision, and craft. It is much more difficult to develop a type treatment that conducts information and personality like electricity through a wire.

While it is true that visuals get a reader to look, type delivers the message and the meaning, the tone of voice and feeling, and an explanation of the ad's importance. Type is the literal translation of spoken into visual information delivery. Pacing and visual tone of voice are essential considerations to its effectiveness.

Section 3 describes the development of type from written characters in 1450 and how technology has changed the way type is made and used since then. Spacing, the critical aspect of type that divides the plain from the fine, is given a thorough discussion. Lastly, the two kinds of type – display and text – and their distinctive handling, are examined.

1 Hand painting on cave walls in Borneo may be as old as 10,000BC. Some hand outlines found elsewhere (*inset*) have the addition of a series of lines and marks on the palms whose meaning is not yet known.

2 Egyptian hieratic script (*left side*) and hieroglyphics ("sacred writing," *right side*) on a papyrus scroll. Hieroglyphics were frequently placed near illustrations and served as captions, describing the imagery.

Chapter 8 **Type Knowledge**

As you have read elsewhere in this book, there are three ingredients that designers use: image, type, and space. It is important to have a thorough understanding of each to manipulate them in fresh, visible, message-compelling ways.

The study of type has two equally important areas:
- ☛ The design of letterforms and typefaces, and
- ☛ The use of type on the page.

This chapter has many examples of both, beginning with a brief history of type and its use. The examples throughout this book illustrate – in addition to the specific subject for which they are included – many other ways of using type. It is worthwhile revisiting the book in its entirety for these many other approaches to type's use.

Humans have been speaking for perhaps 500,000 years. The first markings date from 22,000 years ago as cave paintings, and the earliest proto-writing dates from 5,000 years ago. Writing grew into the area where verbal and visual languages overlap.

Advertising
Design
and
Typography

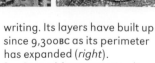

1 The walled Citadel of Erbil, in northern Iraq, may be the single oldest continuously lived-in city in the world – and it may be the birthplace of writing. Its layers have built up since 9,300BC as its perimeter has expanded (*right*).
2 c1800BC Mesopotamian livestock trader's notes on a small clay tablet.
3 c1200BC Sumerian cuneiform (from the Latin *cuneus*: "*wedge*") uses simplified pictures.
4 This 300BC Mayan sample discovered in Guatemala is the oldest writing found in the Americas. The Zapotec in southern Mexico may have preceded the Maya by about 300 years.

c3,000BC
Egyptian hieroglyphics

c3,000BC
Hittite hieroglyphics

c2,000BC
Babylonian cuneiform

c1,600BC
Cretan linear script

c1,100BC
Phoenician soundscript

c1,000BC
Cuneiform script

c1,000BC
Egyptian hieratic script

c1,000BC
Late Phoenician script

3

800BC   100BC

4

A B Γ Δ E F I Θ S K Λ M N O P Q R S T Y Ξ

5

A B Γ Δ E F Z H I K Λ M N O Π P S T Y X

A B C D E F H I K L M N O P Q R S T V X

A B C G D E B F H I K L M N O P Q R S T V Y Z

6

3 Verbal and written language begin merging as a single alphabet in which each spoken sound corresponds with a written symbol. The Phoenicians get credit for this invention.

4 The evolution of Greek (*left column*) to Roman, or Latin, letters between about 800BC and 100BC.

5 The Gospel According to St. John, handwritten on papyrus in 230AD. A similar document, the Gospel of Judas, has been found and its date authenticated.

6 Woodblock printing, in which art and lettering are carved together, is first used in 1423. Books made this way are the world's first mass-produced products.

What makes type knowledge important? Steve Jobs, co-founder of Apple Computers, makes an eloquent case for its impact on personal computers: "I dropped out of college after the first six months, but then stayed around as a drop-in for another 18 months… Because I didn't have to take the normal classes, I decided to take a calligraphy class. I learned about serif and sans serif types, about varying the space between letter combinations, about what makes great typography. It was beautiful, historical, artistically subtle in a way that science can't capture, and I found it fascinating… Ten years later, when we were designing the first Macintosh, it all came back to me… If I had not dropped into that single course in college, the Mac would never have had multiple typefaces or proportionally-spaced fonts… If I had not dropped out, I would have never dropped in on this calligraphy class, and personal computers might not have the wonderful typography that they do."

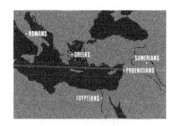

Sumeria (present-day Iraq) develops written system unrelated to speech. It spreads through trade to nearby civilizations and goes through many simultaneous changes. Phoenicians (present-day Syria and Lebanon) connect written symbols to spoken sounds. Greeks adopt Phoenician system, adding nine characters. Romans adopt Greek alphabet, adding seven characters.

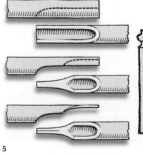

5 The edged pen, made from quill, reed, or cane, was the primary writing tool for centuries. It was cut in a simple three step process.

6 Monks hand-copy manuscripts making changes in letterforms to speed up the writing process. These *minuscules* become our lowercase letters.

7 Letters as mystical marks: geomancers write messages in the dirt to predict the future in this detail from a manuscript illustration, c1415.

8 German manuscript writing c1420 features blackletter in crudely justified columns. Gutenberg was to perfect his movable type within 30 years.

1 Erhard Ratdolt's types, reproduced actual size from 1476 (*top*) and 1496 (*top right*), showing two type styles during the *Incunabula*, the first fifty years of movable type printing from 1450-1500. These types were interpretations of regional manuscript writing, not merely artistic whim. Using regionalized writing styles made typeset material look familiar and accessible to its audience.

2 Johannes Gutenberg creates movable, reusable type in Mainz, Germany in 1450. His masterwork is the "42-line Bible," which looks much like a handcopied manuscript of the time and region.

1 William Caxton, the first printer in England and the first printer of English, produced this work in 1489. His books, notably Chaucer's *Canterbury Tales*, were instrumental in standardizing English usage. Caxton imported type from Belgium and Holland, which used "blackletter," and eventually began cutting his own types, which looked very much like those he'd bought. Early British printing therefore looked dark and northern European, rather than lighter, like that from Italy (*right*) and France. Caxton's types became known as "Old English."

The Incunabula Before type, there was lettering. *Lettering* is hand-drawn. *Type* is machine reproduced, whether by metal bits on a printing press or digital characters on screen. Lettering evolved over tens of thousands of years, primarily in what is now the Middle East. Type was invented in about 1450 (the year of Leonardo da Vinci's birth) by Johannes Gutenberg in western Germany. With this invention, information could be much more rapidly reproduced and knowledge and literacy spread to many more members of society. It is no coincidence that the Renaissance occurred as type dispersed knowledge throughout Europe.

The first fifty years of the printed word, from 1450 to 1500, is known as the Incunabula, or "cradle," because of the explosion of printed works in that period. How much information was available? Enough so that larger type was invented in about 1500 to answer the need for labelling books to make them identifiable in the fast growing abundance of printed works.

3 Italic type used by Christophe Plantin in Antwerp, 1557.
4 Type made by Paolo Manuzio in 1559 in Venice, shown actual size. The type is used here by Antonio Pinelli in his 700-page "Historia Veneta" in 1623.
5 Type made in 1574 in Cologne, though it is based on French characteristics; actual size.

Aldus Manutius, a Venetian printer, invented many typographic standards we use today (*shown above right much larger than actual size*). This is one of his inventions, *italic* type (1501), which was based on local writing. Note the use of roman initials: Manutius had not yet developed slanted capitals.

A a	A a	A a	A a
B b	B b	B b	B b
C c	C c	C c	C c
D d	D d	D d	D d
E e	E e	E e	E e
F f	F f	F f	F f
G g	G g	G g	G g
H h	H h	H h	H h
I i	I i	I i	I i
J j	J j	J j	J j
K k	K k	K k	K k

ABCDEF
LMNOPQ
VWXYZ
abcdefghij
rstuvwxyz

1 A comparison chart printed in 1693 showing the differences between Garamond's 1530 type and Grandjean's new "King's Type," made at the request of Louis XIV.

2 Grandjean bases his letters on a *geometrical ideal* rather than hand drawn forms, preceding Baskerville (*below*), Bodoni (*opposite*), and Didot (*opposite, below*) by decades.

3 William Caslon's types are popular in the Colonies for all sorts of uses and are chosen for the original setting of the Declaration of Independence in 1776.

III. *The Old English,* or BLACK *Alphabet.*

A	a	A	a
B	b	B	b
C	c	C	c
D	d	D	d
E	e	E	e
F	f	F	f
G	g	G	g
H	h	H	h
I	i	I	i
J	j	J	j
K	k	K	k
L	l	L	l
M	m	M	m
N	n	N	n
O	o	O	o

A 1787 comparison of Old English (blackletter) and roman type at actual size.

Advertising
Design
and
Typography

Rivieres de France. 3
LA MARNE.
Cette Riviere a sa source en Champagne, à une demie lieuë au-dessus de Langres, d'où coulant au Septentrion elle passe à Vitry-le-François & à Chaalons; passant à l'Occident par Château-Thierry & par Meaux, elle se rend enfin dans la Seine près & au-dessous de Charenton.
L'OISE.
Cette Riviere a sa source en Picardie, d'où coulant au couchant, & peu après vers le Midy, elle passe

P. VIRGILII MA

GEORGI

LIBER SECU

HACTENUS arvorum cultus, et
Nunc te, Bacche, canam, nec
Virgulta, et prolem tarde crescentis
Huc, pater o Lenæe; (tuis hic omni
5 Muneribus: tibi pampineo gravidu
Floret ager; spumat plenis vindem
Huc, pater o Lenæe, veni; nudata
Tinge novo mecum direptis crura
Principio arboribus varia est nat
10 Namque aliæ, nullis hominum cog

1 Typesetting and printing were the technological equivalent of computer literacy today. Children of means were encouraged to become familiar with the skills necessary to print. This page, from *Cours de principaux,* was set and printed by Louis XV in Paris as a child in 1718.

2 John Baskerville develops smoother paper in 1757. He is then able to design types (*above and right, all actual size*) with thinner strokes.

Tander
A B C
Baskerville's original type,
1777

Tande
A B C
Monotype's
Baskerville interpretation, 1923

Tande
A B C
URW's
Baskerville Old Face
digital interpretation, c1992

1 2 3 4 5 6 7 8 9 0

La pompa lugubre, il funeral mausoleo, i mesti cantici de' sacerdoti, e la numerosa frequenza di tutti gli ordini vi appalesan bensì, o Signori, ch'oggi tutto è qui sacro alla memoria ed al pianto d'un

4 Giambattista Bodoni (1740-1813), above, the head of the royal printing house in Parma, creates some of the most elegant, refined letterforms ever. His types introduce a new classification of type known as "Modern," identifiable for their hairline serifs and heavy vertical strokes. Bodoni made a series of type families, each very similar and, to some extent, interchangeable. These numerals, from 1788, show an exquisite balance of thick and thin (due in part to advances in making smoother paper). Proving their value, Bodoni's type designs were copied by seven foundries between 1909 and 1959, each of whom devoted significant money and personnel to satisfy the demand of their clients.

Printing types began as imposters of handwriting: they were made to imitate the styles that were written in the area where the printer (who was also his own typefounder) lived and worked. Typefaces designed in these early years, 1450 until about 1700, are called *Old Style*. As improvements were made in paper's smoothness so it could accommodate finer print quality, greater letterform contrast followed. These typefaces, made in the 1700s, are called *Transitional*, because they have attributes of both Old Style and Modern. Transitional typefaces led to *Modern* faces, forms that were based on geometry rather than handwriting. Didot and Bodoni pushed letterform design in the late 1700s and early 1800s to a level of detail never before attained. This was possible as much by continuing improvements in paper and inkmaking as by developments in culture and art. As in all other areas of creativity, typographic developments were a reflection of their times.

Some of Bodoni's hardened punches, used to make female molds for multiple copies.

EFGHIJKLMN
YZ&1234567890
nopqrstuvwxyz

4 Firmin Didot, a third-generation French printer and type founder, cuts type based on his father's designs in 1783. As a reflection of the times and technology – ever smoother paper and better inks – it shares many characteristics with Bodoni's types, which were made at about the same time.

5 Type is made from a letter "punch," a carved master version of the letterform. The punch is then hardened and "punched" into softer metal to make a female mold, into which molten lead is poured to make copies. **6** The copies are on blocks of metal so letters can be spaced and aligned.

ABCD
ABCD
ABCD
abcdef

ABCDEFG HIJKLMN
TO BE SOLD
LECTURES AT THE ANTIQUE
CANTER ROOM
Roses

ABCDEFGHI LMNOPQRS KLMN PQRS STUVWXYZ !12345678

1 The transition from bold type (*top*) to *really* bold type, called Fat Faces, was made by William Thorowgood in 1824.

2 The first sans serif (*top two lines*), called "grotesque" because it and subsequent versions were considered quite ugly. This type was made by William Caslon iv, descendant of the great English typefounder, in 1817. His font had only capital letters and appears never to have been used. Later versions of sans serifs are shown beneath.

3 Darius Wells invents a machine to produce wooden type in 1827, making large-scale type common. There are three styles: Roman, Antique (heavy serifs), and Gothic (sans serif).

ABCDEFG
HIJKLMN
OPQRST
UVWXYZ
1234567890

Though William Caslon iv was the first to make a sans serif type in 1817, it was Vincent Figgins who named the style and made his version marketable in 1847. Many founders were inspired by Figgins to make their own sans serifs.

The Industrial Revolution

Centralized machine-aided manufacturing takes over from localized craftsmanship in the nineteenth century. Products need introduction and promotion, so agents work with printers to get messages reproduced for mass marketing.

Until the industrial revolution, printers typically made their own type for their own use. (The first type foundry – a place where type is made and sold to others for their use – was Claude Garamond in 1535.) Hand typesetting a single letter at a time is replaced by line setting using molten lead forced into casts of each character, which, after printing, can be melted and reused. Manufacturers develop their own technologies – and typefaces – and compete in the marketplace. Typestyle offerings expand, serving the needs of the new and growing advertising business.

The design of objects and announcements about them is seen as a way of differentiating competing products in an industrialized world.

Advertising
Design
and
Typography

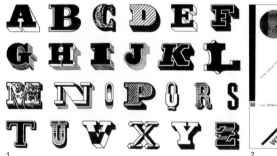

1 Some of the highly decorative fonts made in the mid-1800s. These display- size types used on posters were made of carved wood because metal would have been far too heavy.

2 Type becomes maleable. This brochure cover, designed in 1928 by Piet Zwart, is a Dutch de Stijl (The Style) experiment that explores 45° angularity and the contrast of the linearity of type and rules and roundness of both type and imagery.

3 Type samples, or "showings," from the 1929 D. Stempel catalog, a German type foundry that introduced many of the sans serif types we still use today, though as digital outlines.

4 | 5 | 6 | 7

4 Felix Vallotton's magazine covers integrate type and image in a new way that leads to Vienna's Art Nouveau movement.

5 The form of letters were explored in the Art Nouveau, Art Deco, and Futurist movements.
6 Two of H.N. Werkman's posters using found materials.

Making the most of random materials was a reflection of the upheaval of Europe between the world wars.
7 Futura – and the Bauhaus

discipline it represents – is designed by Paul Renner in 1928 for the Bauer Type Foundry. Its popularity leads to sans serif designs from other foundries.

In the search for speed and efficiency, the quality of type and printing suffers terribly. The American type manufacturing community decides to adopt a single measuring system. More than half the members join together and become the American Type Founders in 1893, which dominates the type design and manufacturing field for decades. They consolidate their individual libraries and have 750 typefaces for sale. They expand some faces into families. From that point on, all their new types are designed as families. By 1923, they offer more than 8,000 typefaces.

As the 20th century begins, a succession of avant garde art movements sweeps Europe. Each contributes to what becomes a vastly different way of seeing and communicating. Symmetry – centered balance – surrenders to asymmetry, a dynamic balance that takes emptiness into consideration. Graphic designers develop as separate contributors to the printing process.

Every typographic norm is the solution to a problem. For example, keyboards got the QWERTY layout because it kept typewriter keys from sticking. The typist would have to stop and release the jammed keys, then return to typing. In 1873, C.L. Sholes asked a mathematician to determine *the least efficient keyboard format* so fingers had to travel the farthest.

ABCDEFGHIJKLM
Memphis (Linotype)

ABCDEFGHIJKLM
Beton (Bauer)

ABCDEFGHIJKLM
Rockwell (Monotype)

ABCDEFGHIJKLM
Cairo (Intertype)

ABCDEFGHIJKL
Karnak (Ludlow)

a B C D E F G
H I J K L m
N O P Q R S T
U V W X Y Z

4 | 5 | 6 | 7

4 Slab serif types were popular in the 1930s, so every major foundry had one designed. That they looked a lot like Futura, which was introduced only a few

years earlier, with added serifs is not coincidental.
5 *"Our 4-cylinder small car. A surprise for you."* Tatra, a Czech

carmaker, ran this handlettered ad in 1934 by Emil Weiss.
6 Alexey Brodovitch's 1932 asymmetrical ad for the introduction of Beton ("concrete") type.

7 "alphabet 26," is a unicameral face proposed by Bradbury Thompson in 1950. (Black = uppercase forms; red = lowercase; and dark red = the same in both.)

BANKING
BANKI
BANKI

L-R: 1857, 1865, and 1913.

1 Handlettered panels in the Art Nouveau style, c1900 by Chicago sign painter and lettering artist Frank H. Atkinson.

2 A page from a 1929 type manufacturer's catalogue shows nine styles of faces and settings. These types were proprietary to the D. Stempel Foundry in Germany.

3 Four panels of sample lettering by an unknown artist, c1930 show a profusion of voices and flavors. Set type lacks this sense of spontaneity and craftsmanship.

Background: Type sample cards are used by art directors and designers to make comprehensive sketches, or "comps."

Lettering by sign painters developed quickly in the 1890s as street-car advertising was introduced with the replacement of horse-drawn vehicles by electric trams. This was a huge ___ for advertising as this new media was invented.

Because display lettering was hand drawn, a profusion of individual styles were introduced. Some of the best work of this period is today available as digital type, though the spark of custom lettering – each character having been uniquely drawn – is missing. (OpenType fonts can accommodate a hugely expanded character set, so some fonts of handlettered characters come with several alternates of each letter.)

After World War II, type begins another transition. Herb Lubalin says, "The realization came to many of us in the early '50s that type was not just a mechanical means of setting words on a page. It was, rather, a creative and expressive instrument."

Typesetting transitioned from one letter at a time (*top*) to one line at a time, as shown in this 1958 photo of "slug casting operators." A "slug" is a line of hot metal type.

1 Condensed sans serif display types – where more characters could be squeezed into the same space while maintaining a dark typographic "color" – became valuable in the early 20th century as sources of information proliferated. Demand from newspapers who were competing for visibility at street kiosks caused many type foundries to produce their own versions of such types. Shown above are several news bills from August 22, 1939. Opposite at actual size are, top to bottom, Stephenson Blake's Elongated Sans No.5, The Times of London wood type, and Stephenson Blake's Condensed Sans Serif No.1.

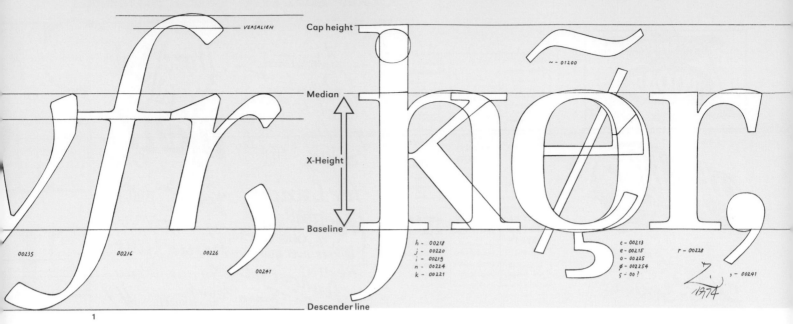

Cap height

~ - 01200

Median

X-Height

Baseline

00235   00216   00226
00241

h - 00218
j - 00220
i - 00219
n - 00224
k - 00221

c - 00213
e - 00215
o - 00215
ø - 002254
ς - 00 ?

r - 00228
, - 00241

Z
1774

Descender line

1

1 Type's *x-height*, the distance from the *baseline* to the *median*, determines its apparent size. The parts of lowercase letters that extend above the median are *ascenders*. The parts of lowercase letters that extend below the baseline are *descenders*. The figures being used here are two similar, though unrelated, typefaces (Aurelia Italic and Marconi) by Hermann Zapf. Zapf designed, among many other typefaces, Palatino, Melior, Optima, and a set of ornamental dingbats. All of his types are based on handwriting, and are therefore *humanist* faces.

REVIEW: Preparations=Bri
From our Special Correspon
=Epidemic=Russia-Special
Good Friday ⸬ Brother Ign
surings in which I
palities are kept. .
of the local Gover
has been holding

Capitals and lowercase letters are all designed to the same height, allowing lines of newspaper type to be more closely spaced in this c1885 typeface by Andrew Tuer. Earlier *unicase* experiments existed, but none resolved ascenders and descenders like this.

Type basics Type evolved over hundreds of years, since Gutenberg invented reusable metal "stamps" with letters copied from regional handwriting in the mid-1400s. From its very complex, labor-intensive beginnings, type has become so easy to use, even schoolchildren make type decisions when preparing their homework. This demystification has reduced the value of type knowledge and expertise to some extent.

Type treatments have an aspect of rightness or wrongness. This is determined by the message and the client, the medium, and the audience. These three areas must be given equal consideration, balanced with the art director's own intuitive sense of style and design. Much typography is determined only by the latter: what the art director likes or is motivated to copy. If a typographic solution has no more basis than having been pulled out of a hat, it's no wonder that clients and the public denigrate type's importance. But there is another way to think of type...

Advertising
Design
and
Typography

Hairline   Serif   Apex   Counter   Terminal   Ascender

Spine   Bar   Arm   X-Height   Shoulder   Ear

SHFARGxhgd

Junction   Stroke   Bowl

Tail   Descender

1

1 Knowing the parts of letters is necessary. The more you learn about type, the more equipped you are to make right design decisions and persuade others to the rightness of your opinion. This diagram identifies only the most important letter parts: there are more than three times as many, but they are essential only to those who actually design letterforms. The type used here is SG Nicolas Jenson, a splendidly quirky interpretation of Jenson's type. This is a "Venetian Old Style" face, a type originating around 1470 and based on the handwriting of scribes in Venice.

äpcfẽgȟksüyxzfi

&›?’;:!„ß1ß40786__

ÄBQDEĦMNRS

ÄBDEĦRMSTZQ

1ß4786*&?’;:!„ß

2

Weight variations
Light (Extra Light, Ultra Light, Thin)
Regular (Medium, Roman, Normal, Plain, Book)
Demi (Demi Book, Semi Bold)
Bold
Extra Bold (Super Bold, Ultra Bold, Heavy, Black, Fat)
Width variations
Compressed (Ultra Condensed, Extra Compressed, Narrow)
Condensed (Tall)
Extended (Expanded, Wide)
Style variations
Gothic, Grotesque
Antique, Old Style
Serif, Semi Serif
Slab Serif, Egyptian
Sans Serif, Semi Sans
Small Caps, Old Style Figures, Lining Figures, Initials, Swash
Mono, Monospaced
Stencil, Shadow, Rounded, Square, Unicase, Engraved, Inline
Outline, Open, Contour
Solid
Script, Italic, Oblique, Cursive, Chancery, Informal
Ornaments, Flourishes, Dingbats

3

2 Process renderings of the Biblica type family by Kurt Weidemann show letters and numerals with shared form. This family was developed specifically to resolve existing type problems in Bibles: characters that fill in with mediocre printing; too much contrast between thick and thin strokes makes reading difficult – and the thins can drop out; and bracketing serifs helps maintain superior character definition in printing. A slightly condensed letter shape allows a larger x-height for maximum legibility. Originals are drawn 4¾" tall.

3 Type weight and character fidelity is revealed by overlapping letters. Type design is the art of making changes in letterforms while retaining the type's fundamental characteristics.

	XXX Condensed	XX Condensed	X Condensed	Condensed	Regular	Extended
Roman	R	R	R	R	R	R
Antique	R	R	R	R	R	R
Gothic	R	R	R	R	R	R

Type began to be cut in *series* or families beginning in the 1830s. These large wood letters, used for posters, date from the 1880s and show three series that range in width and weight: Roman (serifed), Antique (slab serifed), and Gothic (sans serif).

ΚΝΡΕΡΑΤ SΡΙRΙΤ
Uncial c600

Interimperazzere
Carolingian Miniscule c800

MOTRIBP
Trajan Column c1200

ratur. Et nuchlomin
Germanic Blackletter c1250

Apud cognoſcat
Venetian Scribe c1400

Serif type development
Acegmorty
Venetian Old Style c1470

Acegmorty
Geralde Oldstyle c1500–1600s

Acegmorty
Transitional c1700s

Acegmorty
Modern late 1700s

Acegmorty
Egyptian (Slab Serif) c1800s

Sans serif type development
Acegmorty
Grotesque/Gothic c1900

Acegmorty
Geometric c1925

Acegmorty
Humanist c1930

Curved	Unbracketed	Bracketed
Latin	Hairline	Slab

Serifs were "invented" by Roman stone carvers either as an unintended result of the finishing at the end of strokes, or as a purposeful, æsthetic addition. There are six classifications of serifs (*above*), though the chunkier ones ought to be used only in display sizes.

GIRLS WERE MADE FOR "FLIRTY SKIRTS"

2 Numerals have existed longer than written language. One through nine have been used in India since c250BC. Zero was added in c400AD. Arabs brought numerals west while trading, so these came to be called "Arabic" numerals. Abstract machine-readable numbers were developed around 1960.

2

3 The serifs in this hand-lettered headline makes it visible. Mortimer Leach uses baroque styling for a lacy look, appropriate for a ladies' bathing suit ad.

3

We read not letter by letter, not even word by word, but in *sacadic jumps*, or clusters of words and word fragments. It is easier to read lowercase letters than capitals because word shapes are more distinctive: ascenders ⌐ descenders fall └ expected places, so └ pattern ⌐ shapes └ learned. ALL-CAPS ARE ALL BRICKS, IDENTICAL EXCEPT FOR LENGTH. Display type, though, must first attract attention, so limiting all-caps to a few words is preferred.

Good typography calls for typographic adjustments not only to the layout — to make a block of copy "look good," but to maximize the reader's comfort. You are reading 24-point Centaur, designed by Bruce Rogers in 1914 and based on Nicolas Jenson's *Eusebius* type from 1470, which is considered the first true roman (as compared to blackletter) type. It has been set here "solid," with no additional line spacing. Notice how reading each line seems a little more difficult than the 30-point type in the first paragraph. That's because there are about 56 characters per line here, seven more than the first paragraph. The optimal number is about 50-60 "CPL," so both are, in fact, within range.

It is even more pronounced in this paragraph, which is set 14/14, or 14-point type set solid. Here, the lines are so long relative to the type size that reading is seriously hindered. Having the optimal number of words per line is a guide, like all other typographic rules. And rules may be broken consciously by mitigating the transgression. When setting too many characters per line, usually to make the layout "look nice," it is essential that you throw the reader a life preserver by adding a lot of linespacing. If you don't make a correction, you might as well put up a sign saying "Don't bother reading this: it isn't important," because that is precisely the result you will get.

and in the of is

Type is meant to be read Our marketing efforts, on the other hand, are meant to be seen. So we must balance readability (visibility or the quality of attracting eyeballs) with legibility (the ease with which type can be read).

Characters-per-line is one measure of type's legibility. Others are the inherent legibility of the typeface, type size, letterspacing, word spacing, linespacing, and format. The legibility of a typeface is determined by whether the typeface draws attention to itself rather than simply and invisibly transmitting the information contained by the letterforms. Legibility is challenged by anything to which we are unaccustomed. Text is no place to compromise legibility, if your purpose is to communicate marketing information. If it is to amuse or entertain, that is a very different purpose and whomever is sponsoring your affected ad design should be forewarned. Sans serif types are mistakenly thought to be more difficult to read than serif types. That's because serif types have those little feet that help move the reader's eyes horizontally. But serifs also provide built-in space between letters which, in text settings, is very useful. Sans serif types are often set too tight in text settings, which does make them more difficult to read. So make sans serifs as easy to read as serif types by adding more *tracking*, or comprehensive paragraph spacing.

Italics are harder to read than roman types. Most italics are lighter in typographic "color" and thus have less contrast with the paper. We are also simply not used to reading italic type for long stretches, and not being used to a type treatment may be all that's necessary to repel readers. Use italics in short passages and for emphasis only.

Outline, shaded, and inline types are for display only. Their detail is lost at text sizes and they are simply too busy.

This column has been set in 12/14 across a column width of 20 picas. This is a comfortable setting with 56 characters per line. The additional 2 points of linespacing makes the text look a little lighter and more palatable. In real estate terminology, this is called "curb appeal," the attractiveness of a house as first seen by a prospective buyer. Text must have curb appeal, too.

90% of typography is managing the spaces around the letters, and letter-, word-, and linespacing are the areas that need tending. Each of these must be *optically consistent.* Software is improving, but defaults are never optimized and it is the AD's responsibility to know what to adjust. *Kern* between difficult pairings in display type. Word spacing is seen in proportion to letterspacing. There must be enough to separate words from each other, but not so much that the line of type is broken into bricks. Linespacing must be set for easy returns from right back to left.

This has been set in 12/14.7 across 30½ picas. It is not a comfortable setting, having 89 characters per line.

A contributor to type's legibility is type size, which is seen in proportion to column width. When type is too big there are too few characters per line, which interrupts sacadic jumps and slows down reading speed. This paragraph is set with type identical to the column at left, but here it is too big because the column has been narrowed: you are aware of the work of reading.

The rule for type size is simple: the longer the line, the larger the type must be. The optimal number of characters per line is an average of 50-60, unless adjustments are made on behalf of the reader's comfort. Display settings in headlines or captions, for example, may be much shorter than this.

Type's perceived size is determined by its *x-height*, the distance from baseline to median.

Text ought not be very small, regardless of column width. But what's too small? Kids and the middle-aged and elderly need somewhat larger type for different reasons. Kids are still learning letter shapes, so making them larger helps. Middle-aged and elderly have decreasing eyesight, so making type larger – and increasing letter-, word-, and linespacing is a thoughtful and correct decision.

This column has been set in 12/14 across 9½ picas. It is not a comfortable setting, having only 26 characters per line.

Type's format affects its legibility. Formatting includes column alignment, which is typically either flush left (even on the left, or leading edge, of the column) or justified (even on the left and right edges of the column). Less frequently used formats are flush right (even on the right and uneven on the left edge), centered (equally uneven on the left and right edges), and asymmetrical alignment (unequally uneven on the left and right edges).

Readers want an even left edge because it is much easier to find the beginning of the next line. Having to consciously locate the beginning of each line is visual static and may be the difference between type that is read and type that is ignored. Of course, there are reasons to set type this way: captions relate to their images with a clean shared edge, and poetry can be enhanced by less structured typography. Justified type gets that way by distributing the space normally left at the right end of each line into the wordspaces throughout the line. As this example shows, it is easy to have inconsistent wordspaces distributed in default justified settings. There is craft and artistry to good typography, and uneven wordspaces reveal your level of craft. Don't set justified type across a too-narrow measure where space distribution can't be adequately adjusted. Familiarize yourself with the Hyphenation and Justification (H&J) settings in your programs.

Formatting also includes paragraph indentions (*set your default to the size of type being used*), punctuation (*display type's punctuation looks too big: use a smaller size*), space between paragraphs and columns (*proportional to linespacing: add a half linespace*), position on the page (top is perceived as more valuable), and type set in shapes to wrap around images (*intensely self-conscious*).

This column has been set in 9/12 across a column width of 9½ picas. It is a reasonably comfortable setting, though on the short side, having 33 characters per line.

Type
Knowledge

Th

Normal settings	With ligatures
affect	affect
fiery	fiery
flinch	flinch
piffle	piffle
ruffian	ruffian

1

2

3

1 Character spacing is supposed to look even, but some character pairs are tougher than the rest: fl and fi are two examples. **2** *Ligatures* are joined letters that resolve the awkwardness of these pairs. A cartoony all-caps typeface by Ed Benguiat requires many more ligatures than usual to make each setting look handlettered. This font has programming that evaluates neighboring ligatures before replacing character pairs with an unused alternate. **3** Gutenberg's first type had about 160 ligatured pairings, of which half are shown here, to accurately emulate manuscript writing.

These examples of early punctuation, dots to separate words aiding oratory, are from a 200BC Roman tomb, Roman capitals from the Arch of Titus (72AD), and Rustic Capitals (c300AD).

Until the 1400s, writing as a way to record ideas and as a visual form were generally done by the same person. With the invention of movable type, the printer took over the responsibility for the presentation of others' words. Many early printers were highly cultured, but as decades and centuries passed, and printing technology became more and more complex, printers became more technicians and less writers. Conversely, authors began to care less and less about the form of their manuscripts since a printer would take it and convert it to type. Yet the task of today's printers and designers remains the same as ever: to present information as efficiently and as memorably as possible.

Typography is a living art form. It changes as technology and readers' needs evolve. The Bible, the first book set in type, has been translated into text messages. Typical passages read, "In da bginnin God cre8ed da heaven & da earth," and "U, Lord, r my shepherd. I will neva be in need."

1

2

Like every aspect of written language, punctuation is an evolving process. Punctuation was introduced about 260BC to help moderate reading speed for public delivery. Authors had their own idiosyncratic systems until printing helped standardize regional punctuation.

1 Shakespeare's use of punctuation is like stage direction: it indicates the length of pauses, even using a period in the middle of a sentence (1623 edition).

2 Artists use punctuation abstractly, showing its potential beyond its everyday purpose and mining it as raw material for creative ends.

4 Being unfamiliar to western readers, Cyrillic letterforms can be more easily seen as abstract characters. These recently designed versions, for display use only, show the same variety of personality and shape as our more familiar roman characters.

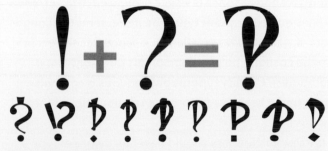

The *interrobang* expresses both surprise and incredulity. Invented in 1962, it is the newest punctuation mark. It is also the only one designed by an American, Martin Speckter, an advertising executive. He almost called it an "exclamaquest." The first font to include the interrobang was Richard Isbell's *Americana* in 1967 (*top*). It fell out of favor, partly because it is considered bombastic. It has recently surfaced as a trademark for a non-profit organization.

The Partnership **P** for a Drug-Free America®

3 Spelling counts – or you lose the potential of *misspelling on purpose*, as in this hand-painted protest sign against Britain's Prime Minister, Tony Blair, and this sendup of the similarities of the names of two neighboring mid-east countries.

Display typefaces

ABCDEFGHIJKLabcdefghijklmnnop
Letter Gothic Bold IE Drawn

ABCDEFGHIJKLabcdefghijklmnnopa
Moon

ABCDEFGHIJKLabcdefghijklmnnopqrstuv
Hair

Script typefaces

ABCDEFGHIJKabcdefghijklmnopqrstuvwxyz
Sign Painter House Script

ABCDEFGHIJKabcdefghijklmnopqrstu
Mercurius

ABCDEFGHIJK abcdefghijklmnopqrstuv
Pepina

Glyphic typefaces

ABCDEFGHIJKLMNOPQRSTUVWX
Ephesus

ABCDEFGHIJKLMNOPQRSTUVWXY
Penumbra

ABCDEFGHIJKLMNOPQRSTUVWX
Delphian

Blackletter typefaces

ABCDEFGHIJKLabcdefghijklmnopqrstuvw
Goudy Text

ABCDEFGHIJKLabcdefghijklmnopqrstuu
Totally Gothic

ABCDEFGHIJKLabcdefghijklmnopqrst
Blackmoor

Symbol typefaces

Geornaments

Golden Cockerel Ornaments

Call Yes! AMAZING! FREE Sale! SPECIAL ONLY! and... Quality NEW! CHEAP! th
Ad Art

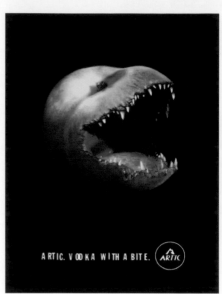

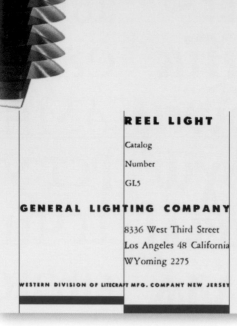

1 Letterspacing can be manipulated to create a sense of
roughness and disjointedness.

2 It is said that 90 percent of
typography is managing the
space between the letters and
only 10 percent is managing
the letters themselves. This

example from the 1950s manages the indention and halved
column width to create emphasis while maintaining order. It
uses only two type sizes (really

only one size except for the
small "mouse type" to define
the column width at the bottom), and contrasts of weight,
capitalization, and linespacing.

*"When a good ad is set right,
no one notices the letters –
they're too busy reading the
words."* Herb Lubalin

Typographic spacing Negative space is visible around each letter, each
word, and between lines and columns of type. The management of negative space is the heart of typographic excellence: it separates the professional designer from the casual type user (and an art director from a
copywriter with a computer). Quality typography requires a compulsion
for attending to details and a keen eye for precise relationships of form
at the near-granular level.

  The best spacing is invisible. Readers should never be aware of type's
spacing unless the s t a c c a t o or speededup reading process illustrates
itself. Default attributes in page makeup programs are for text-size settings. While these defaults may be more or less reliable, I don't know a
single type-loving designer who would ever allow their program's defaults
to be the last word on any text setting. Defaults are adequate to not make
egregious mistakes, but they are not adequate to make fine typography.

1 Letterspacing may make this
newspaper ad (announcing an
upcoming redesign or "face-
lift") harder to read. But it contributes the only personality to

an otherwise ordinary design.
2 Space between letters can be
used to enhance identity. It is
shown here in three quantities:
completely removed, normal,

and very open. The BLEU example,
a 1921 magazine logo, trades
individual character legibility
for overall unity as a shape.
3 Word spacing that is greater

than linespacing becomes unavoidably visible.
4 Word spacing condensed letterforms must be tight to preserve the integrity of each line.

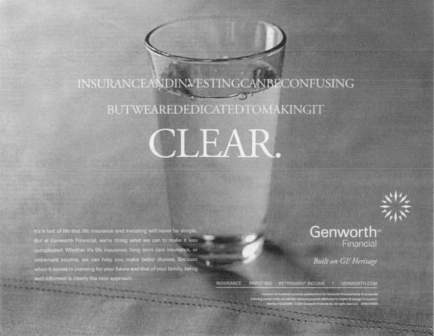

3 Word spacing used to typo-graphically illustrate a service provided by a film and video production company.

4 Ideal word spacing should be invisible. But it can be purpose-fully used to illustrate meaning. Here it is removed – creating two long words – to contrast verbal cloudiness with clarity. Scribes in Medieval Europe wrote exactly as this headline looks (all *majuscules* with no wordspacing) as they devel-oped *minuscule* (eventually called *lowercase*) letters be-tween the 4th and 8th centu-ries and introduced wordspac-ing to speed reading aloud.

Go to the Preferences panels and tweak them for optimal spacing based on the typeface, size, and line measure. It takes a little experimentation to get the hang of it, but the time you invest will be repaid many times over. You are training your eyes to see type and space. Regardless of using de-fault attributes in text settings, they cannot be used for display type for one reason: display is not merely big text type. It requires much greater letter-to-letter attention than that. Convert display type to paths and space the individual characters as discrete shapes.

Word spacing can affect meaning. Here is a bit from the comedy duo Bob and Ray: *"This is a supplementary bulletin from the office of Fluctu-ation Control, Bureau of Indigestible Fats and Glutinous Derivatives, Washington, DC: Correction of Directive 9924326-198B, recently issued, concerning the fixed price of groundhog meat. In the directive above named, the quotation on groundhog meat should read* ground hogmeat.*"*

An extreme example of word spacing is married to a splitscreen image that illus-trates the two half words.

"Some designers approach typography intuitively, emotionally, and playfully, while others are the opposite: controlled, rational, and objective." Jan Conradi

5 Linespacing is used to great illustrative effect in this po-litical poster from the 1970s. Note also the copywriting to get perfect line breaks.

6 One of Herbert Bayer's out-standing mid-1950s posters for the CCA uses open linespac-ing to relate the text to the arrows.

7 Asymmetrical display type gives this mid-60s ad a casual, familiar tone, appropriate for such a friendly pose and topic of conversation.

8 Paragraph indents show a new idea is coming. These indents are *noticeably deep*. But with short paragraphs, does this technique clarify or confuse?

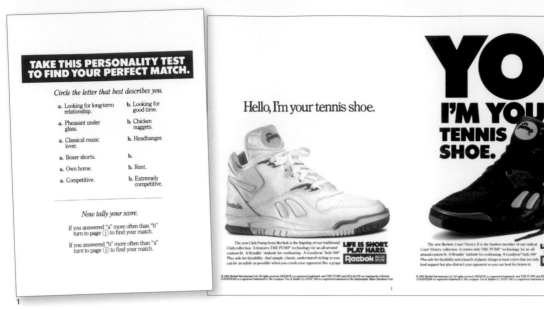

1 Type has exploitable personality, as shown in this 1991 three-page ad that equates type treatments with either shy or extraverted footwear – and tennis players. Interpreting verbal language into type lets readers "listen to type." The translation from oral to visual delivery is a one-to-one ratio: be literal in your interpretation of volume, intonation, and pauses.

Blackletter characters from the 1400s and Didot from 1815 are abstracted in a student exercise. The purpose is to explore the form of letters, their inherent legibility, and their plasticity – even to the point of converting type into imagery.

Tone of voice, contrast, repetition, balance, dominance, and unity
Visuals get you to look, but *type* delivers the message and meaning, tone of voice and feeling, hierarchy and importance, explanation and clarity. Type is an integral part of the best designs. If it is altered or removed, the piece falls apart.

Type added to a visual message is the equivalent of what sound adds to a silent movie or to the performance of a mime. Type is *frozen sound* and should be handled as an actor handles volume, pitch, and tone in the delivery of a role to add emotion, attitude, character, and quality.

Type strategy includes a size and weight sequence for the headline, subhead, captions, and text so each is distinctive and easy to recognize while sharing design characteristics to create design unity. The purpose of art direction is, in part, to create a smooth and effortless reading (or "visual information absorption system") experience.

1 Saul Steinberg treats letters as objects in one of his type and image explorations. Designers must remember and use the "object-ness" of letters.

2 Psychedelic posters, originating in San Francisco in the mid-1960s, were drawn to express both a new artistic vision and to replicate the acid-tripping experience of the concerts they advertised. Legibility was not a concern.

3 Advertising must get attention before it can be absorbed, so in this car ad, legibility is sacrificed for readability, the quality of attracting and holding attention.

2 *"Overwhelmed?"* Type has visual weight, as illustrated in this 1966 German ad.
3 Actual handlettering, not a script typeface, gives this campaign a personal feel. The type's counters filled with white add to the casual attitude.
4 Mixing typefaces in a headline can add confusion and visual clutter *unless it makes a point*. This point-of-purchase poster for a local coffee company uses eclectic types and monochromatic imagery to invoke old fashioned qualities.

There are four tools used for type sequencing: contrast, repetition, balance, and dominance. They should work together to make a single overall impression for design unity, which was named *gestalt* by Bauhaus practitioners in the early 1900s. Each of these attributes should be used to create an environment of similarity so that a focal point can be perceived by having it contrast with the system in which it is seen.

Naturally, one more element acts on quality typography: talent. It's what you bring to the problem. Daniel Friedman, a particularly well-informed practitioner, said in 1973, "Existing teaching methods for typographic order, harmony, and proportion... (rely) heavily upon an education in technical competence, historical preservation, and commercial simulation. They do not rely upon the exploration of an open-ended, creative, new vision... Any really new typography will be derived from a truly artistic energy..."

Graffiti abstracts letterforms to make them nearly illegible, but here stylization is the point.

4 Type is frozen sound: letterforms and their presentation stand in for a speaker's tone of voice. This billboard is a literal interpretation.
5 Abstracting type as leaves, snowflakes, or raindrops in a German poster.
6 Russell's Reserve uses obviously, almost maximally, contrasting types in its headline.
7 Flying Pig Marathon uses a variety of type sizes in the headline to convey the ebb and flow in the way runners feel – at times strong and able and at times lethargic and exhausted – as they run a marathon.

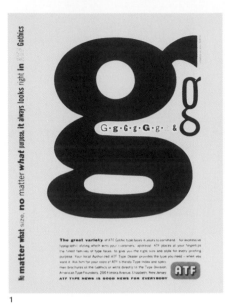

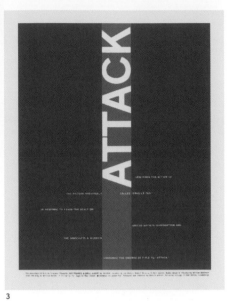

1

2

3

1 Contrast of size Will Burtin's magazine ad for the American Type Founders.
2 Contrast of color John Massey's magazine cover.

3 Contrast of direction Saul Bass' magazine ad.
4 Contrast of space George Tscherny's direct mail piece for an art school.

5 Contrast of type form Bob Gill's poster for an art gallery show.
6 Contrast of tone or value Ivan Chermayeff's poster.

These six examples are winners in the Type Directors Club Third Annual competition held in 1956. This was a simpler, possibly more elegant time for

"Ds are just Bs without their belts on." Dennis Miller, referring to school grades

It takes more than one "voice" to get a message across. The fullest conversation includes one voice to stop the browser, one to fill in the informational gaps and make a mini-pitch, one to explain the visuals, another to announce the sponsor, yet another to leave a lasting message, and the last voice, often the quietest on the page, to give the sales message. Often, these voices are reduced to just four, perceived in this order: a headline, logo, tagline, and text.

The fun of designing is to define these voices distinctly, that is, make them visually contrast, and at the same time corral them into a unified whole. The process starts by making them all agree: choose one typeface and one size. Then add contrasts *one at a time* to make each voice look different, because consciously allocating contrasts is the best way to retain unity. Ours is a balancing act between contrast and similarity, and it is always easier to add more contrast than to put back similarity.

Advertising
Design
and
Typography

1

2

3

4

Contrasts are rarely found one at a time. There are usually more than one so the focal point gets maximum visibility. These examples each have a

predominant contrast, though others can be identified.
1 Size Very large (and dark, condensed, and damaged) headline contrasts with very small

and horizontal text in this newspaper ad.
2 Color Complementary colors unify these designs.
3 Direction The vertical base-

line implies gravity, aided by the "collapsing" text.
4 Space Scale, rotation, and density are used to create a three-dimensional image.

4   5   6

typography, caused partly by the limiting use of hot metal type. Commercial phototypesetting was just being introduced. Incidentally, *type directors*

worked at ad agencies alongside art directors to ensure quality type use. This position became obsolete in the late 1980s as art directors became

responsible for typesetting (and comprehensive type knowledge *and* typesetting quality control) with the advent of digital typesetting.

There are six typographic contrasts. Each requires a proportion of at least 75% "normal" to 25% "contrasting" to look purposefully applied:

☛ **Contrast of size** Bigger is perceived as more important. Extreme size contrast is visually dynamic.

☛ **Contrast of color** Use color to guide and emphasize the most important element. Don't use it as decoration.

☛ **Contrast of direction** Horizontal is normal. Vertical is dynamic. Diagonal is very hard to reconcile with the rest of a design: great contrast, but lousy unity.

☛ **Contrast of space** Fullness contrasted with emptiness.

☛ **Contrast of type form** Bold roman sans serif is quite different than flowing script. But how to reconcile such contrasts with design unity?

☛ **Contrast of tone or value** Dark or colorful is perceived as more important. Extreme contrast is visually dynamic.

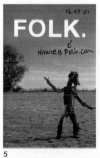

5   6   7

5 Type form Handlettering contrasts with set type. It works because the lettering agrees with the image's roughness.
6 Type form Various versions

of a lowercase *g* are cropped and composed as mosaic tiles into a new g. This combines contrast and similarity in an interesting way.

7 Tone/Value Similar to the handling of color, lightness and darkness is used as a tool to both differentiate parts and unify the whole of these posters.

How do I choose a typeface?

Type choice is more than a whim. There are several legitimate and defendable considerations: What is appropriate for the message, the audience, and the client? What is timely? What is appropriate historically or locationally?

1 What is the tone of your message? Though it may be fun for you to use the newest, craziest font, it may not represent the tone of voice of the message. Typography is called "frozen sound," and some fonts whisper while others S H O U T. Choose a shouting font only if that helps reveal the content. Rather than outrageous, illegible display typography, rely on imaginative word choice to lure readers.

2 What is the ad's purpose? How much text is there? How many visuals are there?

3 How is the ad to be read? In an easy chair with lots of light or on the side of a passing bus? In a low contrast newspaper or in a four color magazine?

4 Who is your audience? What are they used to reading? Younger readers are more comfortable with familiar typefaces, but comfort is essential to all readers.

5 What typefaces are available to you? It is possible none lead to a look your client can *own*. When you purchase a new font or family, consider how it expands your entire font menu.

Aside from these five guidelines, which are based on common sense and make the design work as communication, there is the issue of the designer's good taste. Good taste is formidably subjective. Good taste can improve with time and experience, but fundamentally, it takes talent to be a good designer. Talent is largely a function of good taste. But there is an out:

6 Reconsider the five issues described above. *After they have been addressed,* after the sensible issues have been resolved, your own taste can be applied to the choicemaking process. This puts taste into a more appropriate, lessened, role of importance.

The Natural Wonders

Oxida™ *Paul & Koziupa* 2 faces (incl. alternates) *Umbrella* **$79** NEW A Veer Exclusive

SilkyMax™

Breathable... Comfortable!

Kari™ **Complete** *Neil Summerour* 8 faces *Umbrella* **$240** NEW

Hot Summer Kisses

Ministry Script™ *Alejandro Paul* 1 face (w. extensive alternates and ligatures) *Umbrella* **$99** NEW A Veer Exclusive

Herb Encrusted

Chocolate™ *Paul & Koziupa* 3 faces *Umbrella* **$79** A Veer Exclusive

Surf Hawaii

Luvbug™ *Miles Newlyn* 5 faces *Umbrella* **$79** NEW

Zerah Colburn

Dear Sarah™ *Christian Robertson* 5 faces *Umbrella* **$79** A Veer Exclusive

I'M SO GREEDY

Tourette™ 2 faces *Virus* **$99** A Veer Exclusive

Plastic Craftsmen

Wesley™ 2 faces *Jukebox* **$79** NEW A Veer Exclusive

The Spanish Main

Koziupack™ *Paul & Koziupa* 1 face *Umbrella* **$45** A Veer Exclusive

Stars of 1972

Ink Gothic™ **A** *Bonislawsky & Jaramillo* 4 faces *Umbrella* **$119** A Veer Exclusive

Lucy & Louis®

Olduvai™ *Randy Jones* 4 faces *Umbrella* **$119** A Veer Exclusive

LUXURIOUS

Incognito™ 10 faces *Fountain* **$179** A Veer Exclusive

Wedding Day

Mrs Blackfort™ *Bluemlein & Paul* 1 face *Umbrella* **$45** A Veer Exclusive

The Last Snowfall

Gizmo™ 1 face *G-Type* **$60**

Conquistador

Lisboa™ 30 faces *Fountain* **$399** A Veer Exclusive

Zanzibar™ 3 fa

Mostra Compl

Happy Hour™

Mr Lackbough

Libris™ *Jonat*

Cocktail Shak

Farao™ *Peter*

Kon Tiki Trac

JEEN'S PARK RD.

wk™ 1 face *Device* **$39** A Veer Exclusive

The North & West

5

ÔTE D'AZUR

RIS – MÉDITERRANÉE

son 15 faces *Umbrella* **$89**

ation Hall "B"

49 A Veer Exclusive

Ribbons, Etc.

Miss Packgope™ *Bluemlein & Paul* 1 face **$45** *Umbrella* A Veer Exclusive

itality Room

Paul 1 face *Umbrella* **$45** A Veer Exclusive

WOODPIGEON

Bello™ Pro *Underware* 4 faces *Umbrella* **$90** A Veer Exclusive

ED·BUTTER

ce *Umbrella* **$39**

The Mild Bunch

Stephanie Marie™ 1 face *Jukebox* **$49** A Veer Exclusive

ble Coupons!

r 1 face *Umbrella* **$39** A Veer Exclusive

New Dimension

Fenway Park™ 1 face *Jukebox* **$49** A Veer Exclusive

IRON.

untain **$89**

Mr. Knightsbridge

Brioso™ Pro Poster 2 faces *Adobe* **$65**

grounders

ox **$49** A Veer Exclusive

Company Founder

Mr Stalwart™ *Bluemlein & Paul* 1 face   *Umbrella* **$45** A Veer Exclusive

Like clients and products, type comes in many, many flavors. Each has its own personality and feel. Matching type to message gives the client a look they can own, which is an essential part of the art director's responsibilities. Despite the wealth of typeface alternatives, typeface *selection* is still less important than typeface *manipulation* – unless you want the star of your design to be that other guy who designed the typeface. Always consider the difference in legibility between attention-getting display faces (shown in these examples) and information-conveying text types. Design accordingly. These samples are from the veer.com catalogue, one of many digital type foundries that have emerged since the early 1990s.

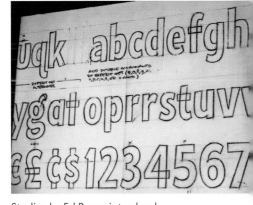

Studies by Ed Benguiat, a leading type designer throughout the 1960s, '70s, and '80s, for a humanistic sans serif display face. Such studies are made to ensure consistent type color and proportion among characters. Benguiat was a partner in Photo-Lettering, the leading developer of display faces in the '60s, and '70s. The introduction to their 1971 catalogue, which contains over 6,000 typefaces, reads in part, *"(This manual) is replete with style, the kind of style that comes from many different people dreaming individually, competing with one another, and trying not to be trapped by anybody who does their dreaming for them."*

ESPERIENZA

Del follevamento de' fluidi nel vano de' cannellini fotti-lissimi dentr' al voto.

Opinione d'al- cuni, che il fol levarfi quafi tutti i liquori ne' cänelli ftret tissimi di vano fia effetto del- la natural preffione dell' aria.
Come fegua, fecondo loro, tal folleva- mento.

TRAGLI altri effetti della preffione dell' aria è ftato da alcuni annoverato anche quello del follevarfi, che fanno quafi tutti i fluidi dentro a' can- nelli ftrettiffimi, che in effi s'immergono. Dubitano quefti, che quel fottiliffimo cilindro d' aria, che giù pel cannello preme, verbigrazia, in full'acqua, operi più debolmente la fua preffione, per lo contrafto, che gli fa nel difcendere il gran toccamento ch' egli è col

1

1 Roman and italic types in five sizes used to express inherent differences in content. This was a complex printing job and stylistically forward-thinking for its time. Setting the small italic type at far left justified across a narrow measure causes uneven word spacing. This is crude typesetting by today's standards, but was an achievement in its day. Note also the insertion of a space both in front of and after punc- tuation: styles change over time. Giovanni Filippo Cecchi, Florence, Italy 1691. Shown actual size.

Hierarchy the simplest way: descending importances in which what is above is more important than what is below. Note that color is present as a confusing rather than a clarify- ing agent. This typography is a result of either necessity or ignorance. Either way, it does not speak well for the quality of the detailing service being offered, even at 99¢ – or is it $99?

Hierarchy: three levels of type Have you noticed how one television newsreader often introduces a story, then hands it off to a co-anchor for illumination, who then passes the story on to an on-site colleague for additional reporting? They know something about the best method to get and hold a viewer's attention. That one-two-three delivery is similar to the way a headline/deck/text progression works for readers. Readers like to be given information in a predigested form: intrigue (headline or caption), explanation (subhead), story (text).

Browsers respond to information that has a clear type progression. The natural order a browser, or uncommitted reader, will follow is pic- ture-caption-headline-deck (the decision point to enter the text) and then, maybe, if the story as presented in the display type seems interesting, the first paragraph of text. A balance must be achieved between visual similarity, to unify various bits of type, and contrast, to make hierarchy

Advertising
Design
and
Typography

1   2

An editorial technique to draw readers in is to create exactly three levels of importance. The first level gets attention and stops the browser: it is okay to use the most abstraction here. The second level buttresses the first point and completes the message for those who don't stick around for the rest of the message. The third level is the text, or the copy that makes the sales pitch. The first two examples have success- ful three-level hierarchy. The other three examples may be fine designs, but not because of their typographic hierarchy: each specifically avoids such structured order.

2

3

2 Hierarchy and order were specifically rejected in the Dada movement, which flourished between 1915 and 1925.

As a result of the societal disintegration and physical devastation of World War I, artists found it necessary to use whatever materials and paper could be rummaged. This 1922 example is from Zagreb.

3 The best way to determine type complexity is to count the number of type "flavors." This spread ad has six type styles, but only #3 is out of order.

clear. Too much similarity and type will look dull and skippable. Too much contrast and a page will look noisy and repellant.

The design process should start with all elements alike, then introduce the fewest contrasts necessary to make distinctions between *kinds* of information. Starting a design with various contrasts at the outset encourages dissimilarity. It is easier to see lack of contrast than to recognize when you have too much, and it is much easier to know where to add contrast than where to reduce it.

More than three levels of type is counterproductive: the most important and the least important will be visible, but distinctions between middling content which is more or less equivalent just adds noisiness and visual clutter. Unless you are being very purposeful, don't present messages so complex that readers must decipher them. They won't: they'll turn the page. After all, isn't that exactly what you do?

> "A typographer can get away with anything so long as it looks like it was done on purpose."
> Unknown

3

TOURIST INFORMATION

NEW ZEALANDERS STAY CLEAR OF TWICKENHAM ON SATURDAY

4

The Now Taste of Tab.

5

3 Breaking for sense emphasizes the natural sound bites of a headline or sentence, regardless of line length or the type's shape.

4 The best way to determine natural segments is to read a headline out loud. Breaking for sense makes a headline read as powerfully as possible.

5 This 1965 soft drink ad emphasizes the phrase "The Now Taste," but other line breaks are available, each deserving consideration. The alternatives suggest the original break is, in fact, the best. By the way, why does the model look like she's curling her lip at the prospect of drinking a Tab?

"Careless Talk – Enemy's Help!" Three elements in a 1954 poster by Viktor B. Koretskii – drawing, primary and secondary type – share a horizontal space in which nothing is *wrong*, but in which relationships can be made to work much better with the inherent spatial division of the image. The two parts of the headline are, at best, *approximately aligned* with the two heads while ignoring the much more distinctive bright/shadow partition. *Enemy's Help* has been moved over to align with the corresponding portion of the art and *Careless Talk* has been enlarged to fill the "non-Enemy" space.

The copy from Herb Lubalin's ad opposite top reads:
"Let's talk type *Some ads must whisper, some must shout. But whatever the tone of voice, creative typography speaks with a distinction that sets your advertising above the clamor of competing messages. If you share our interest in good typography, and the other creative tools that work with it, we would welcome the opportunity to show you how we at Sudler & Hennessey...* **let type talk"**

Advertising
Design
and
Typography

1   2   3   4

1 Make alignments obvious: they clean up the design and make it look like a "solution" for the reader, not a problem.
2 Standardize design and type placement to build consistency and familiarity over time.
3 Infuse your type with one distinctive attribute. The reader and the client (and your portfolio) deserve it. This example shows a *lack* of distinction: it is mere typesetting. The text is also set across a much-too-wide column for easy reading.
4 Relating image and type is the best way to make type speak. Here, the inside/outside feature of a convertible is interpreted in letterforms.

1 Herb Lubalin adjusted every letter pairing to make this look simply and perfectly spaced.
2 The right edges of each letter extend beyond a vertical line defined by the stroke of the *t*. This creates *optical alignment*, which is far more important than digital alignment, particularly in display type.
3 The display type is set flush right and has punctuation "hung," or set outside the right edge for optical alignment. Optical alignment in text, because it is smaller type, is generally seen in both hung punctuation and all-caps settings, where letter shapes are most visible.

Typographic craftsmanship The level of craftsmanship is magnified in display type, since it is the primary type and intended as the first type to be seen and – at least subconbsciously – evaluated as an attractant. Mistakes or "errors of default" are simply more visible in the biggest type. Text mistakes are just as bad, but at least they are small, and computer defaults are generally set to text sizes so text will look okay (if not great). Merely okay is not adequate for display type.

If you only use ready-made materials, you are sure to have results that look like everyone else's. It is like cooking with prepared, frozen food: How special can your cooked results be? Possibly good, but certainly limited by the ingredients you use. Make your design elements from scratch and you will surely have distinctive results.

The last word on type craftsmanship is this: If, after careful consideration and thoughtful adjustment, it *looks* right, it is.

(212) 121-2121
Classic, dull, typewriter-like

212-121-2121
Dashes

212.121.2121
Periods

212◦121◦2121
Dingbats

212|121|2121
Vertical rules

212 121 2121
Spaces

212 121 2121
Italics contrast

212 121 2121
Size contrast

212 121 2121
Weight contrast

212 121 2121
Typeface contrast

5 Dare to solve a problem with your own hand-drawn type. Throughout type's 550-year history, artists have invented new shapes to solve emerging problems. For example, the ampersand as crafted by Gabriel Giolito in 1556; a digital screen version (superimposed on its outline or "printer" version) from the mid-1980s; and a handdrawn character from 1995.
6 There are always alternative ways to organize type. Even a phone number can use specific contrasts to differentiate *kinds* of information. Use this list of type contrasts as a reference for your own exploration.

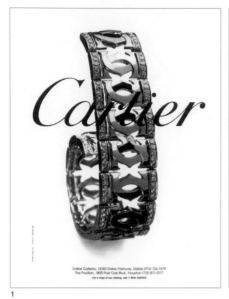

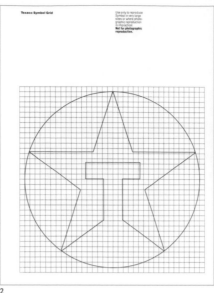

1 2 3

1 A corporate logo is a valuable asset that must be protected or its value is diminished.
2 A *standards manual* is pre-pared by the identity design team that describes what may and may not be done with the logo. But standards, developed to ensure a consistent brand and identity, are only as useful as the level of compliance with which they are followed.

3 Marilyn Monroe's renowned beauty mark has been re-placed by the Mercedes logo in this 1997 corporate ad.

1500BC
Mycenæ

1300BC
Mycenæ

600BC
Mesopotamia

A logo is a mark that identifies an individual or business entity. The first identifiers were stamp seals and appeared in 6000BC in Iran (*top left*), marking the invention of private property. Later stamps told stories des-scribing the individual, acting like signatures.

Chapter 9 **Display Type**

Display type is the (usually) big type meant to be read first. It is crafted to attract attention and, second only to the image, gives a large degree of "style" to an ad. The one piece of display type that appears everywhere in a campaign is the company's logo. More than any other typographic ele-ment, it represents the product in the marketplace.

Logo is Greek for "*word.*" It is a term that is applied to any trademark, though it is properly used only for marks with a written name, like "*Nike,*" but not ✔, which is a *symbol*. Marks have been around for about 17,000 years, since humans have been leaving records of their existence. Personal identifying marks appeared in 6,000BC (*left*), preceding written language by about 3,000 years. They were invented just after the twin

Advertising
Design
and
Typography

1 2 3 4

1 Art Kane mixes up-to-the-minute scientific developments with teenage beauty in his 1955 x-ray inspired image for a few-year-old *Seventeen* magazine.

2 Powerful illustrations of a ben-efit need no more than a brand, as in these two ads for a Ger-man steel-toed safety boot manufacturer.

3 Similarly, a powerful head-line needs nothing but an identifying sponsor, as in this poster by Nancy Rice.
4 The more familiar a mark is to its audience, like this one for the *New York Times*, the more it can be abstracted. Such familiarity often takes years to develop.

1 No name, not even a logo in Helmut Krone's 1961 ad for a recently imported German car.

2 The logo – trashed, scratched, and beat up – can be the primary typographic element, as in this moody spread for fishing equipment marketed to unreasonable fishermen.

ideas of "mine" and "yours" were realized. Merchants marks became common about 800 years ago and identified their products as distribution gradually grew from local to regional enterprises. Farmers burned marks into their livestock, and, in 1282, the first papermaker identified his wares with a watermark embedded into the paper fibers. Logos used as marketing tools in the modern sense were invented in the late 1800s during the Industrial Revolution when sales of centrally produced goods became widespread.

All logos are symbolic and abstract to some degree. Abstract marks must be learned through repeated contact, which is an investment in time and money just for recognition. Smaller, local businesses tend to have less abstract, more literal, marks. Companies whose businesses can't be easily illustrated benefit from more abstract marks, as do conglomerates and global entities.

Handlettered logos by Alan Peckolick and his partners are well beyond the possibilities of set type. The craftsmanship shown in these letter combinations is as rare today as it ever was – and just as satisfying.

1 A product shot replaces a logo, effective when they are similar.
2 A Canadian ad challenges the reader to *imagine* owning this car. *"Created by Nissan"* in the lower right corner – an explanation or an apology – is peculiarly where a logo is expected.
3 The (uninteresting) logo is the primary type. Note the very small headline that packs a punch despite its size.
4 The logo is the headline. This provocative visual, which may be intentionally mistaken as vomit, illustrates the fact that these candies contain fruit pulp.
5 All logo in an all-type poster has specially drawn letters that feel like numbers.

1

2

1 The only copy in these two ads for a mountain bike is the logo. When the imagery is as clear as this (bike plus outdoors or nature), and the surroundings are as spacious as this, perhaps it's all that's needed.

2 The wool mark is given "supergraphic" treatment as a background in this c1968 ad. Supergraphics, shapes, and colors taken to an unprecedented large scale, were a rage in design at the time.

Logos are given prominence in a 1955 black and white Bank of America television spot. Color and illustrative style make them stand out.

Consider these questions as you develop a logo:

☛ **What marks are currently being used by the client?** A new logo may be an update, a unification of two or more marks, or it may be a completely new design.

☛ **What marks are the direct competition using?** Will yours be similar or contrasting? An identifying mark must be, by definition, sufficiently different to stand out. Both shape and color are aspects of competitors' marks that must be considered.

☛ **What is the current universe of marks?** Know *all* marks. A mark is going to be seen in a larger context than just your client's specific business category (*opposite*). Ovals, circles, and swooping shapes were wildly popular during the dot-com boom in the 1990s. To be *hip* was to follow the crowd, but to be *visible* was to design against the trend. It is not good practice to design a logo that, unbeknownst to you, already exists: NBC

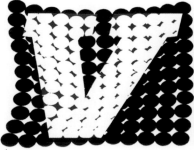
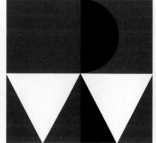

1

2

3

4

1 Lettermarks can be very abstract and remain legible.
2 This is a mark combining *W* and *R*. Distilling letterforms to their geometric bases is a productive way to interpret letterforms.
3 Simple contrasts are the best in designing logos because marks must work at very small and very large scales. Hermann Eidenbenz designed this motion-filled logo in 1948. In addition to advertising work, Eidenbenz designed German and Swiss bank notes.
4 This seven-letter combination was drawn in 1526 by Giovanni Baptista Verini as a exploration of formal beauty.

Representational signs
Realistic pictures of objects

Ideograms
Pictures of nonrepresentational objects

Logos (words)

Pictograms
Iconic, or descriptive, pictures of objects

Diagrammatic signs
Nonrepresentational and arbitrary

Lettermarks

Combination marks

Symbolic signs
Pictograms altered to have a new meaning

Synonimic signs
Images of the same referent

Symbols

1

Semiotics is the study and codification of signs and their meanings.
1 Having an understanding of these categories will give you control over abstraction. As in any area of art, overlap exists between categories: some

determinations are simply a matter of degree.
Logos come in four versions.
2 Words, Lettermarks (combi-

2

nation of letters not spelling a word), Combination marks (symbols and type together), and Symbols (marks without type).

---

hired a prominent New York design firm to develop a new logo for its network. Many hundreds of thousands of dollars were spent. One design was chosen and implemented. Then it was discovered that a fellow in the midwest had designed and had been using that exact lettermark for a modest local television station.

☞ **Who is the audience for the mark?** Because of cultural and language differences, global audiences may need a more abstract mark than local or national audiences.

☞ **Will the mark be part of a series of related marks?** Some products are perceived as part of a family. Global campaigns often use variations of a mark to make it accepted regionally.

☞ **Will the mark have additional elements?** Taglines and promotional materials may be known or should be planned for.

☞ **In what media will the mark be seen?** Sketches should be developed

Logos are seen in the context of all logos, not just those of a client's direct competitors.

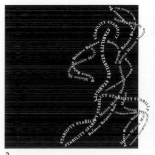

1   2   3   4

1 Some logos must be alterable into other languages for global applications. The Nickelodeon logo is in English and Chinese and in its previous 1903 version.

2 Simple letterforms work better than complex ones for abstraction. This is Franklin Gothic Bold Condensed.
3 Multiple words can be used

in logos with the caveat that small size will aggressively affect such designs.
4 Futura was used for this mark because it was designed

during the period in which this museum specializes. The vertical rules and the letterspacing are used throughout the identity program.

CITY COLLEGE OF NEW YORK

CITY COLLEGE OF NEW YORK

CITY COLLEGE OF NEW YORK

1

2

3

1 The final studies for CCNY's University Student Government captures a sense of active city life and the nontraditional, multi-tasking student body who attend this Manhattan university. It uses the shape of the University's seal, the school color, and the feeling of the stained glass University seal.
2 The grayscale version had the contrast increased slightly.
3 The bitmap version had lines thickened to the weight of the type to ensure that it held up at smaller reproduction sizes.

City College's seal shown in stained glass. The circular shape and shading were kept in these studies.

simultaneously in full-color, grayscale, and black-and-white versions, so the mark can be applied to any message in any media with optimized resolution and character.

☞ **Are there legal requirements?** For example, the FDA requires pharma logos to conform to a particular size relationship between the brand and generic names.

Logos are ordinarily the last part of a message. Steve Cosmopulos says "a logo can upstage an ad quickly if it grabs the audience's attention *out of sequence*. A logo does not have to be large and conspicuous to do its job. If a client says, 'Let's make the logo a little bigger in case they don't read the ad,' I say scrap the ad and just run the logo."

Logos are flags representing the sponsor. They promise the advertiser approved the ad, that it gives an accurate presence of the company, and that the advertiser stands by what the ad says.

Advertising
Design
and
Typography

UG CCNY   UG CCNY   UG CITY COLLEGE OF NEW YORK

USG   USG   *USG*

CITY COLLEGE OF NEW YORK

1

2

CITY COLLEGE OF NEW YORK

3

CITY COLLEGE OF NEW YORK

4

Background The City College of New York, located in upper Manhattan, has the most diverse student body and produced the most CEOs of any university in the world. It is a singularly dynamic academic institution. It needed a new logo for its University Student Government.

1 Basic letterform explorations of a geometric sans serif face.
2 Maximum letterform overlap and busyness, representing the activity of the New York City environment.
3 Type placed below mark for greater economy of space.
4 Application of the school color.

ADVERTISING DESIGN
Logo Development Exercise

PURPOSE
To gain mastery over typographic abstraction by developing a unique logo.

BACKGROUND
Every client who gives you a logo or identity project expects a unique treatment that will make them look good in the marketplace. A logo is their most important design element, the one that gives a company its public presence. It is their suit of clothes. | A logo cannot be merely typeset letters or words. That is not nearly distinctive enough, even if you select an uncommon typeface. Besides, as the logo's designer, why would you let the typeface designer get all the credit? | Abstracted type is the path to distinctive logos just as mastery over abstraction is the path to design excellence. This exercise will cause you to gain some mastery over abstraction.

PROCESS, PART 1
"Logo" is Greek for "word." Technically, the only business mark that is really a logo is a mark that is a readable word, like The Smoking Gun, YouTube, Method, and iRobot. Your logotype in this exercise must be of a readable word. | To save you the trouble of choosing your "client," and wasting time when brilliant solutions don't immediately materialize, choose from the terms at right for the name of your client. | To determine your product, Google the name of the street you lived on in, say, sixth grade. Choose the sixth listing. Choose something at that site as your business' product.

PROCESS, PART 2
You now have the company name and the product or business. Now you need the process. The logos at far right are from a special section of a single issue of a magazine. Each logo has a group of design attributes that has to be defined and applied to your client's logo. The translation and interpretation of the design attributes is what is interesting

and worthwhile. Simply copying the logo and changing the name from, say, *Galveston* to *Nainsook* is not useful. | Choose one logo and prepare a document describing the design attributes of your selected source logo.

PROCESS, PART 3
Apply those attributes in various ways to bring out the meaning of your client's business (*right*). All studies must be output at 7" longest dimension optically centered on 8½" x 11" vertical bright white sheets. | Experiment with various typefaces and treatments, but remember that it isn't the choice of font that will make a logo succeed, it is *what you do with the font.* | Pay particular attention to the negative space between and around letterforms in your logotype studies. | The success with which you interpret the list of design attributes of your source logo will determine the quality of your effort. This process does not limit your *creativity*; it expands it by limiting some of your *choices.* | When you have selected a single direction, develop it in three versions: RGB, grayscale, and bitmap. Output each of these final logos centered on its own 8½" x 11" vertical sheet in three sizes (nine pages total): 7", 3", and 1" longest dimension.

Source logo attributes
Square format
Box rule
Type at top and bottom of square
Bold condensed type at top, bold below
All-caps throughout
Bottom type letterspaced with diamonds
Space above and on sides of top type equal
Illustration is black with white lines covering ±½ the square
Strong black and white contrast

Reinterpreted logo attributes*
Square shape is negative space
Line from drawing surrounds square
Type above and below
Type is larger at top
All caps throughout
Letterspacing added in bottom type
Strong black and white contrast
*Example by Kyle Nelson

Company names These words all happen to be fabrics. The names can be applied to whatever business you select:

Aralac	Huckaback
Astrakhan	Lastex
Axminster	Maline
Batiste	Mousseline
Brocatel	Nainsook
Buckram	Panne
Byssus	Pongee
Cambric	Qiana
Casheen	Rugging
Cheviot	Samite
Covert	Sarcenet
Crash	Shaloon
Dimity	Shot Silk
Drap d'Or	Stamin
Drugget	Swansdown
Duvetyn	Tricotine
Faille	Tussah
Fustian	Vicara
Grogram	Vinyon

1 | 2 | 3

1 The primary type is an artistic interpretation of the brand name in the visual of this 1961 newspaper ad.

2 A primary type can be gibberish and still communicate, as in this 1950 Cuban self promotion for an ad agency. The asterisk leads to a caption that reads *"It's not Greek, it's very easy to understand."* Then the headline translates as "Good Advertising Is Remembered By Everybody."

3 Primary type is simply typeset, yet has personality by virtue of its asymmetrical alignment and lack of capitals.

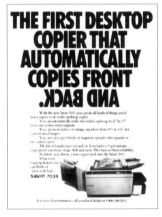

Primary type can be abstracted (its legibility can be compromised) to make a point, as in this 1985 Canadian ad.

Primary type City residents are hailed by all sorts of sidewalk salespeople wanting to give out flyers that advertise businesses, getting signatures on petitions, or giving out free samples. But regardless of their purpose, sidewalk salespeople can't communicate further without making an initial contact. The way they look and the first few words they say make all the difference in whether passersby will pause long enough for their pitches. After all, no one walks around looking for interruptions. Most city residents are trying *not* to be accosted.

Take away the live salesperson and you have a print or media ad. Everything about it must be chosen with initial contact – stopping the passerby – in mind. The overall *gestalt*, a German word meaning *wholeness*, of a design is the most important facet of presentation. Then the first words lure the reader into engaging with your ad. If you don't catch a reader, you don't communicate.

9 **176**

Advertising
Design
and
Typography

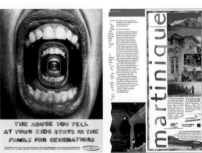

1 | 2 | 3 | 4

1 Damaged type Three sizes of damaged type clustered in a unit give this headline character.

2 Type dusted with car crash fallout makes it as visually interesting as the image.

3 An indistinct rotten, rusting, metallic dimensionality is applied to this headline with great craft.

4 This sideways headline has been hand drawn in patches of color that give it a festive, relaxed feel: just the thing for a resort destination.

1

2

1 The headline draws you in deeper because it is repeated in variations of one typeface. This ensures unity while infusing variety by using two

weights, three sizes, and in both all caps and all lower case, all at 45° angles, which contrasts with the vertical cookie package.

2 If all type in an ad is display type, is it one long headline or just big text? This calligraphy is purposefully sloppy (abstract-

ed), representing the way the art director imagines the fish's voice would sound.

Display type has traditionally been defined as type over 18 points in size. But typographic developments through the second half of the twentieth century have changed the definition to any type whose purpose is to be seen first. It is therefore properly called *primary type*, which removes size from its definition. In advertising, there is often little or no text, and when that happens, all type is display type.

In editorial design, the purpose of primary type is to move the reader on to secondary type, whose job it is to move the reader on to the text, where the story is. In advertising design, the purpose of primary type is to stop the uncommitted browser or passerby by saying something they cannot help but let through their message-bombardment filtering systems. In advertising, the idea is paramount, but the presentation is nearly as critical because it is the message lubricant that allows the idea to get through the tiny cracks in the consumer's armor.

The Hero Club
For Type O donors only

THE HERO CLUB
FOR TYPE O DONORS ONLY

THE HERO CLUB
FOR TYPE O DONORS ONLY

THE HERO CLUB
FOR TYPE O DONORS ONLY

THE HERO CLUB
FOR TYPE O DONORS ONLY

Five settings of the same content provide five different identities. Legibility is one consideration, audience is another. Personal preference is the third, and least important.

Display
Type

1

2

3

4

5

1 A rectangular area of type contrasts with the organic outline of figures in this 1913 poster. A lettering artist made four lines of type look perfectly justified.

2 Centered type separated into color fields echo trends in art in this 1927 travel poster.
3 The lamp's globe shape is repeated in the geometric sans

serif letters of a 1936 Dutch poster.
4 Another interpretation of repeated headline in the Pavesi campaign (*top left*).

5 A campaign against buying "dirty gold" uses the Periodic symbol for gold set within SLAUGHTER, referring to the regular loss of miners' lives.

1

2

1 The varying sizes of type are not for logical emphasis, which is the most defendable design decision, but they are adjusted to fill the available space. Pity the *i*'s are all identical: it's a giveaway that this is a font, not a custom-damaged headline.
2 The *i*'s are similarly set in lowercase in this early 1970s spread for a then little-known German car. The art director, Helmut Krone, used Herb Lubalin's new and soon-to-be-very-popular Avant Garde typeface. It is letterspaced tightly to overlap, which suited Lubalin's original intention of reducing the individuality of letterforms.

A page of type samples is distributed and used in an exercise that explores type abstraction and its malleability.

Content and form Type has two properties: content and form. Content is the message it contains. Form is the way it looks. Pure legibility (which doesn't really exist – legibility is a relative idea, not an absolute idea) may communicate most cleanly, but it won't make people look and it won't build brand identity. Pure form flirts with illegibility, but it does make people look. Art direction, particularly typography, is finding a balance between these two properties.

Twenty-five years ago, before the invention of the personal computer, the copy produced on a typewriter was considered "unadorned" written language. It was the manuscript that was sent to be typeset. Today, the computer is the typesetter: there is no such thing as unadorned copy. Except for pens and pencils on paper, all written language is designed, so *everyone* today is a designer. As an art director, your typographic decisions must be acute and defendable to your colleagues and clients.

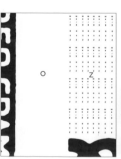

1

2

3

4

5

Typographic abstraction must be learned. These studies are the result of a first-year exercise I give. Students receive a one page assortment of type, including several historical samples (*above left*). These are treated as pure form and adapted to several design principles.

1 A grid helps draw background space to the front.
2 Baseline contrast and size create the focal point.
3 Letterspacing is the subject of this study.
4 Sans serif types and angled baselines.
5 Type structure and organic/geometric contrasts.

1

2

3

1 Primary type does not need to be large to be seen. The sponsor's name is the headline, but the illustration by Jerome Snyder is the focal point in this 1943 institutional ad. Charles Coiner art directed many avant garde artists in this campaign. The client, Walter Paepke, was a remarkable corporate leader and a man of vision. His drive for quality art and noble ex-

pression helped CCA, a cardboard box maker, increase their sales six-fold between 1936 and 1948.
2 Space makes this modestly sized headline visible in a 1955 ad for a typesetter.
3 If the visual is provocative, readers will seek out the caption for explanation. This one reads, *"Corolla. For overprotective parents."*

A little history Prior to movable type printing in 1450, only a very small elite group could read. Everything was handwritten which took time and money and limited the quantity of reading material. Consequently, everything written was valuable. With movable type printing came the democratization of information and knowledge. Suddenly, there were many books and there came a need to differentiate them. Erhard Ratdolt, a printer in Venice, invented the ornamented title page in 1476, which was immediately copied by other printers and evolved into book covers (*see page 144, far left*). Describing the content of a thing with a brief, large title is actually the invention of display type. Until the early 20th century, display type was set in capital letters and generally centered at the top of the page. The purpose of display type today is largely the same as it ever was. What it describes, though, has changed from mostly text to mostly imagery. This is particularly true in advertising.

Rhythmic interaction of lines of primary type and image emphasizes that these are pre-sliced strips of meat in this 1955 magazine ad.

Display
Type

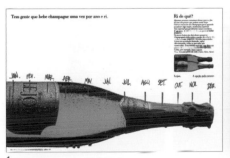

1

2

3

1 *"There are people who drink champagne only once a year and they laugh. About what?"* Head and subhead are widely separated but they are base aligned. Despite their small size, space makes them visible.
2 *"With Macintosh it's easier to be a Leonardo da Vinci today than it was 500 years ago."* A 1984 introductory ad for Apple shows *Hello* backwards in blackletter, as if printed with movable type, a reference to Gutenberg's 1450 invention, not da Vinci.
3 *"Let's Reconstruct!"* The headline is drawn from wood shavings coming from the planing tool.

1

2

1 Stacked lines of handlettered type allow for subtle adjustments in form and spacing to *appear* even (multiple characters are shown at far right for comparison). Spacing inconsistencies would have added visual noise to an already explosive marquee-inspired treatment.

2 Film Iris uses a spiralling headline to indicate reel of film, c1964. Hewlett-Packard uses a spiralling headline to a much less discernable effect. The headline reads: *"Compliance without chaos."* Is it a random design treatment that is eye catching? Nothing in the ad suggests otherwise.

Color is integral to the lettering treatment on this 1936 British poster. Removing the red and white shows its essential role.

Read by shape Reading is a learned skill. Listen to a child read out loud and you will hear her speaking words, even syllables, one at a time. Phrases and sentences come with practice. Our ability to read increases with familiarity of word shapes. After a while, we no longer have to actually read each letter of words we've seen many times before. Subconsciously, our brains recognize *familiar shapes* and the meaning they convey is processed much faster than if read as strings of letters. To try this for yourself, read a word with which you are unfamiliar. How about *dihydropyridine* or *phenylalkylamine*? To be able to speak these words out loud, you have to parse them into syllables, repeatedly, until you can string the syllables together into the complete words.

Be aware of the usefulness of the shape of words, especially in display type. Each word's distinctive shape helps readers absorb effortlessly. They may be enhanced or degraded, but they should always be considered.

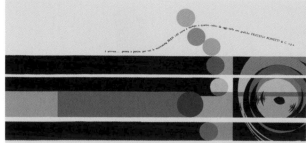

1

2

3

1 Type is bent to look like a sheet of paper being fed through a press for the Fratelli Brothers Printery, c1965.

2 *"Cross section"* in German. Display type can be abstracted to reveal meaning and still retain reasonable legibility.

3 A 1993 anti-drug poster by Pierre Mendel puts all the abstraction into the visual and lets the type be the foil. Nevertheless, the vertical baseline adds a slight sense of unexpectedness to the typeset treatment.

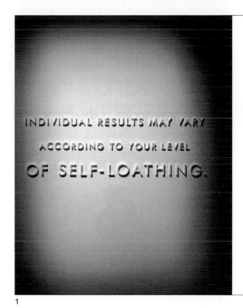

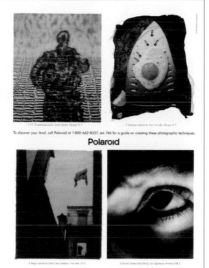

1

1 The dimensionality of these letters adds to the starkness and drama of the copy. This is an effective counterpoint to the four images, which is what is being advertised.

2

2 Nauseatingly hyperactive lettering is just right for this statement against driving with one's family. Like a full car, there is absolutely no empty space in this ad.

Typographic elegance Elegance is tastefulness, refinement, and panache. In design terms, it is having all necessary information with nothing extra. Elegance is a lack of complexity. It is, in other words, *expressive clarity*. Complexity won't help get messages across because, though it may be interesting to see, the message is obscured. Simplicity won't get the message across because, though it may be easy to read, it's importance and value won't be recognized. Only expressiveness combined with lack of compexity makes the message both interesting and legible. Contrast type style, size, weight, position, color, or treatment to show hierarchy (that makes the message clear) and value to the reader.

What is *right* with your type? It is not enough to simply have nothing wrong with it. There should be something definably right with whatever treatment you give it. Discover what is unique and express it.

Elegance is the lack of complexity. The design decisions in this spread all further the message: tough pants made for years of wear. The style of the figure, the monochromatic images, and the antique washboard are simplicity itself. The all-caps headline is placed through the center of the spread, in front of the images. There is nothing that can be taken away without damaging the message itself.

9 **181**

Display
Type

1

1 Handlettered type conveys a hand-crafted, personal feeling to this event. It does not appear to be a corporate-sponsored festival.

2

2 Will Burtin uses a child's (his daughter's) lettering to imply innocence in a 1948 ad. This is one of a series for Upjohn Pharmaceuticals in which

3

Burtin explored representation of scientific content.
3 "*Industrial Design Exhibition, Odessa,*" 1910. The headline is drawn as if it was tiled.

4

4 Use history for inspiration. The type for a poster for an artist active in the late 1800s is based on the work of William Morris, c1885.

This is a forty-eight point headline set in News Gothic Bold

This is twenty-four point News Gothic Demi which uses the weight and typeface of the head

This is 11-point Nueva Standard text set across a twenty-pica measure. This is the width that contains fifty to sixty characters per line, the number for optimal reading ease. This is 11-point Nueva Standard text set across a twenty-pica measure. This is the width that contains fifty to sixty characters per line, the number for optimal reading ease.

1

This is a forty-eight point headline set in News Gothic Bold

This is twenty-four point Nueva Standard Bold which uses the weight of the head and the face of the text

This is 11-point Nueva Standard text set across a twenty-pica measure. This is the width that contains fifty to sixty characters per line, the number for optimal reading ease. This is 11-point Nueva Standard text set across a twenty-pica measure. This is the width that contains fifty to sixty characters per line, the number for optimal reading ease.

2

This is a forty-eight point headline set in News Gothic Bold

This is twenty-four point Nueva Standard Regular which uses the weight and face of the text

This is 11-point Nueva Standard text set across a twenty-pica measure. This is the width that contains fifty to sixty characters per line, the number for optimal reading ease. This is 11-point Nueva Standard text set across a twenty-pica measure. This is the width that contains fifty to sixty characters per line, the number for optimal reading ease.

3

A subhead must be read in sequence: after the headline and before the text. Assigning attributes makes it a more or less effective bridge that moves readers effortlessly. These three subheads share the same point size, which is about halfway between the headline and text, so it can't be mistaken for either.
1 This subhead retains all the attributes of the headline except for typesize. It has very little in common with the text. **2** This subhead's attributes are about evenly split between the headline and text. **3** This subhead is more like the text than the headline.

"There are three kinds of letters: Uppercase, lowercase, and varsity." ESPN ad in the New York *Times*

Secondary type Having stopped a reader with primary type, some ads have more to say: an explanation, details, or facts about the product. The next level of information can be a subhead, or text, or the logo. What makes these different kinds of type similar is their position in the order of perception.

Subheads A subhead bridges the headline and the text. It completes the idea begun in the primary type so a browser will get the gist of the sales message even without reading the text. A subhead must appear in its correct order and contribute to design unity. Without being dogmatic about it, there are worse ways of doing this than by choosing a variation of one of the two typefaces being used and mathematically dividing the type sizes between headline and text. For example, if the primary type is 48 points and the text is 11 points, the subhead will be distinguishable

1

2

3

1 Profoundly damaged type Photoshopped onto a rusty steel sign suggests "the old days." **2** Secondary type is mingled with the text causing stream–of–consciousness expression. Handlettering gives a quirky, personal, autobiographical feel, linking the copy to the athlete on the right. **3** Despite the crisp alignment and purposeful white space, the order of the type and the application of color confuses rather than lubricates this message. In fact, given that green is used to define the primary type, which is the secondary type: the black text or the green type beneath the logo?

This is a forty-eight point headline set in News Gothic Bold

This is fourteen point Nueva Standard Bold whose size is close to the text

This is 11-point Nueva Standard text set across a twenty-pica measure. This is the width that contains fifty to sixty characters per line, the number for optimal reading ease. This is 11-point Nueva Standard text across a twenty-pica measure. This is the width that contains fifty to sixty characters per line, the number for optimal reading ease.

This is a forty-eight point headline set in News Gothic Bold

This is thirty-six point Nueva Standard Bold (close to the headline)

This is 11-point Nueva Standard text set across a twenty-pica measure. This is the width that contains fifty to sixty characters per line, the number for optimal reading ease. This is 11-point Nueva Standard text across a twenty-pica measure. This is the width that contains fifty to sixty characters per line, the number for optimal reading ease.

This is a forty-eight point headline set in News Gothic Bold

This is thirty point Nueva Standard Bold which tends toward the headline size

This is 11-point Nueva Standard text set across a twenty-pica measure. This is the width that contains fifty to sixty characters per line, the number for optimal reading ease. This is 11-point Nueva Standard text across a twenty-pica measure. This is the width that contains fifty to sixty characters per line, the number for optimal reading ease.

4 I have chosen the subhead that is visually halfway between the headline and text (*Fig. 2 opposite*) because it is the one that most acts as a bridge. It

shares their attributes equally, lending type unity, without accidentally looking like either one.
4 The size similarity makes this subhead look like the headline,

but the typeface contrast is too great. The huge size does not bridge with the text.
5 I prefer the twenty-four point (*Fig. 2 opposite*), but either of

these two work best of these six samples.
6 This subhead has too little in common with the headline to be an effective bridge.

set in 24-point type. A subhead should bridge the headline and text and look halfway between the two in size and weight, as shown in the examples above.

Text A headline often leads directly to text in advertising. Editorial typography often offers up one or two additional opportunities (like breakouts and quotes) for the browser to become engaged with a story before entering the longer text. That is an idea that should be applied to ads with text long enough to be a "considered avoidance."

Logos Some ads say the equivalent of "Drink up! Brand identity." The product's mark is the secondary type. Not much of a compelling reason to try a product, but maybe the visual shows happy people. Or a frosty glass or mountain stream. Very subconscious conditioning.

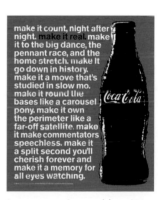

Long text or long subhead? It doesn't matter. It's long secondary type.

1 Dimensional letters are used in the photo for the primary type. Secondary type is at right angles in the upper left corner, interspersed with secondary

images and aligned with the flying *R*.
2 How do you use type to show an electric car is quiet and loves nature? No shouting. No

big type. No straight lines. Asymmetry brings poetry and aesthetics to mind – even if only subconsciously.
3 This headline is spaced so

the transition to text is automatic. Fullness contrasts with emptiness, and secondary visuals help define the product's foreign character.

1

2

1 Captions guide the reader to the correct interpretation of the imagery. This half magazine spread bank ad uses captions

to illustrate opposing ways of perceiving value.
2 A brief extract of text, or "breakout," is literally ripped

from a story and used as a large caption. This is part of a campaign that shows how this particular magazine looks at

familiar subjects with breadth and understanding. This example also shows how a caption can itself have a caption.

This visual, an excellent *use* of blurriness, requires a caption to lead the reader to the point: a free eye examination. Note how this mortise makes the caption float in the foreground.

Captions serve three functions: they explain images, they encourage the reader to continue into the message, and they help create the design personality (i.e., branding) of the product. If you observe your own reading habits, you will see that you look at captions before you read text. Any type read before text is the definition of display type. Captions are actually small-sized headlines. They are there to intrigue, explain, and sell. They are *not* there to just say what can obviously be seen in an image. They should add to and explain the significance of the image.

Captions have two relationships that need expression: caption/image and caption/type.

The caption/image relationship Type and image are different from each other, so our job is to find a way for them to achieve design unity. There are three fundamental ways to do this, but each of the three is interpretable in infinite ways:

1

2

3

4

5

1 **Position** The caption surrounds the image along the top and right edges.
2 A caption-as-headline is above and bigger than the image.

3 Captions are labels glued beneath parts of a visual.
4 What could be more solid than a concrete dam? This 1960 ad in which the caption is

the primary type, tells us this car is for "people who want to be boss." Boss of the road, driving in a concrete colossus.
5 The caption spotlights the

story within the story in this modified Ayers No.1 layout that looks fresh and up to date because of line spacing and flush left alignment.

1

2

1 Layering Type enclosed in a box is a *mortise*. A mortise allows type to be layered over image and retain its legibility, but it does so by distinctly segregating the two. This design would be better if there were greater relationship between the mortise and the background image. Captions explain: without this one, you wouldn't know what an elevator had to do with phones.
2 Captions can be layered by sprinkling them throughout an image.

☛ **Relate by position or alignment** Captions belong with pictures. Proximity is the best way to unify them. Having them share width, height, or vertical axis are additional connections.

☛ **Relate by layering** The ultimate nearness is *on top of*, so this is in a way a subset of the preceding category. Put the caption – or perhaps just the first word made large to preserve legibility – on top of the image and they are unified. This is even stronger when the image is not full bleed: the caption has an alternative to be off-image.

☛ **Relate by treatment** This can be a shape, direction, angle, color, or texture. Extracting one of these from the image and bestowing it on the caption will unify them.

The caption/type relationship Captions are part of a typographic hierarchy. They can be seen first, as a caption-as-headline; they can be seen

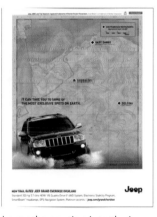

Layer the caption into the image by making it the key to a map (*top right*).

1

2

3

4

1 Layering Each caption (dialogue, identifying characters) is surprinted on lime-green polka dots. These are a design treatment of the times, the mid-60s, and an interpretation of the daughter's concern that "we might all be blasted off the face of the earth" by, presumably, a nuclear war.
2 Multiple captions are doodled on the image, calling attention to various parts of it.
3 The caption is superimposed into the image, inspired by a television's video adjustment.
4 To ensure legibility, layered type is on a lightened area of the image. The band's edges are softened, but quite visible.

Captions serve as headlines far more in advertising than in editorial design because a lone piece of explanatory type communicates fastest.

1 Treatment Embedding the caption into the image itself creates design unity. The rightness of its size, in this case, is a little arbitrary.

2 "Damaging" the type so it looks like the image unifies the design. Be sure the treatment is not gratuitous. It must be extracted from or inspired by the image.

Structure contrast Captions that are not supposed to be read *with translations*. It is possible to use captions that really can't be read, yet have them serve the message. Of course, each caption in Japanese is also provided in English. Or is it the other way around?

second, as a caption-as-subhead; and they can be seen third, which is their typical, misguided ranking. They should never be seen after the text, because they have no value at that level of insignificance.

Because captions are part of the typographic hierarchy, they must relate stylistically to the other type elements to define a personality for the product. There are a finite number of typographic contrasts and similarities that can be exploited for a relationship. They are:

Size Large and small. Larger type must be visibly larger. A point or two difference is insignificant and is useless at display sizes. A difference of 25 percent to 30 percent is meaningful, so a caption set in 13-point type, for example, will be visibly larger than text set in 10-point type.

Structure Serif and sans serif. A common contrast is sans serif for display because it fits closer and is darker, and serif for text because it is easier to read at length. So a bold lead-in for both caption and text could be set

1 Size contrast The caption (just below the period of the headline) of this 1969 diet meal replacement ad reads: *About this picture: Our photog-rapher said, "Since Metrecal's a complete meal, let's shoot it like one."*

2 Just because it's big doesn't mean it's a headline. Note, too, that this 1960 caption-as-head-line is closer to the image than to the text, strengthening its role as a descriptor.

3 Size and space are used in a risqué statement that passing fashion is not what this retailer is about.

4 Two sizes emphasize "organic," all rotated ninety degrees.

1

2

1 Form contrast Contrasting all caps with lowercase while keeping all other attributes the same creates type distinctions while maintaining type unity. In this ad, the caption headline is the lone element set in all caps. The other copy is set in lowercase of a lighter weight of the the same type family. Does the period at the end of the headline add anything but a reason to stop the reader from continuing? And does one out of three type segments in blue deemphasize it, or make it more noticeable because of its specialness?
2 *"No size limits."* Lowercase contrasts with the all-caps mark.

in a sans serif with a similarly shaped serif for the balance of the type.

Weight Heavy and light. Depending on family, skip two weights to make the bolder face look purposefully chosen. For example, book to **regular** isn't sufficient contrast, but book to **bold** is.

Form Caps and lowercase. Set a phrase or lead-in in all caps to make it stand out in a lowercase caption. All caps are harder to read when more than three lines deep (a quantity that separates perception of "few" from "many"), so keep all-caps settings short.

Width Regular and condensed or expanded. Regular is far easier to read than condensed or expanded, so use the latter for display and attraction only. Never, never digitally expand or contract typeforms: it is amateurish and it makes the type ugly by forcing it out of proportion. Instead, use authentic condensed or expanded fonts that have been proportionally altered by letterform experts.

Structure contrast Letter structure of roman serif and script logo (along with letter shape, –spacing, –size, capitalization, and color) are contrasted to make the caption look planned.

Display
Type

1

2

3

1 Weight contrast Bold lead-ins announce the beginnings of individual caption in this 1967 fashion ad.

2 Four weights are used in the caption at the left side of this half spread horizontal ad for a furniture retailer. This might be one weight too many in other designs, but the steady decrease in weight makes it look purposeful here.

3 Sufficient boldness makes type visible, even when surprinted on a busy all-type background. Size and color contrasts help, too.

1

1 When you care enough to send the very best® Mortimer Leech handlettered this tagline for the Hallmark campaign, originally written by Foote,

Cone & Belding in the 1930s. A funny story about taglines is from the mid-1950s, when Tampax tampons began their marketing in earnest (though

they'd been around for about twenty years). The leading product in the category then was Modess pads, whose tagline was, "Modess...because,"

a fairly indefinite phrase. Copywriter Julian Pace proposed that the Tampax tagline should therefore be another conjunction, "Tampax... insofar as."

1917   2006

Maxwell House coffee's *"Good to the last drop®"* tagline has been around since 1907. It was written not by an ad agency, but by President Theodore Roosevelt, who regularly drank coffee under his doctor's orders to check asthma attacks. TR said it with great enthusiasm after a cup of Cheek-Neal Coffee at the Maxwell House Hotel in Nashville. General Foods bought the rights from Joel Cheek and changed the name of the brand.

Taglines A tagline is "a sentence or phrase used to summarize a market position," according to the AIGA's *Dictionary of Brand*. In turn, this is part of "the process of differentiating a product, service, or company in a customer's mind to obtain a strategic competitive advantage; the first step in building a brand." Other names for *tagline* are *slogan* and *why-to-buy message*: the most compelling reason to buy a product.

A tagline has an important persuasive role to play in a campaign if it is well written. Here are a few that are of very questionable value to a company's marketing: *A company of uncommon enterprise; We're involved; We help make it happen; We understand how important it is to listen; A company worth looking at; We're basic to success; The company.* These serve the ego-centered needs of the company's executives, but say nothing about the consumer. Indeed, they may only add an additional splotch of ink at the bottom of the page. A good tagline must describe a market

Advertising
Design
and
Typography

1   2   3   4

1 A diamond is forever™ One of the greatest and longest lasting advertising campaigns of all time. Diamonds are rocks, literally. That they have

become synonymous with love is not "just the way things are." It is the result of eloquent and continuous advertising begun in 1948 by N.W. Ayer & Son.

2 Live richly™ Set in an optical recognition font, to emphasize efficient financial processing. **3 Insurance. In-synch.**™ Why that width? To align with the *R*

– much less apparent than if it had been the *T* – of Travelers? **4 Design for all**℠ The largest type and only slightly smaller than Target's mark.

ough
est

Match the tagline with its owner (turn the page for answers)

1 Better sound through research®
2 Close to home. Far from expected.
3 Direct from Freeport, Maine™
4 Done.®
5 Gain from our perspective®
6 Going your way
7 i'm lovin' it™
8 Living. Improved daily.™
9 Reach out and touch someone.®
10 Smart service. Great ideas.™
11 The right technology. Right away.™
12 The signature of American style
13 The ultimate driving machine.™
14 This is SportsCenter.®
15 Way to shop®
16 We like you, too.
17 We'll leave a light on for you®
18 We never stop working for you®
19 We've got a check for you®
20 With you all the way

☐ AT&T
☐ BMW
☐ Bose
☐ Cayman Islands
☐ CDW
☐ Dow
☐ ESPN Sports
☐ Franklin Templeton Investments
☐ jetBlue
☐ L.L. Bean
☐ Long Island Rail Road
☐ Lord & Taylor
☐ Macy's
☐ McDonald's
☐ Mitchum
☐ Motel 6
☐ Nextel
☐ SellJewelry
☐ UnumProvident
☐ Verizon Wireless

What is *right* with the design of these taglines? As you look through the tagline samples on pages 188-191 and read my comments on their design, you will notice that most have very poor relationship with their logos and other typographic elements. If design is "to plan," are these taglines in fact designed? Or are they inherited? Or are they the result of a committee? They appear to say, "this company is not well organized," which is the shared responsi bility of the art director, the ad agency, and the client. These taglines mostly refute that *design matters* in advertising. What missed opportunities.

position and be ownable, that is, not interchangeable with any other company. Here are few of the best, selected from the Advertising Age Top 100 Advertising Campaigns: *A different kind of company, a different kind of car; Breakfast of champions; Does she... or doesn't she?; Have it your way; Just do it; Let your fingers do the walking; Melts in your mouth, not in your hands; 99 and 44/100% pure; Tastes great, less filling; The un-cola; We bring good things to life; We try harder; When it rains it pours; Where's the beef?;* and *You deserve a break today.*

The importance of the tagline's consistent use is superseded only by that of the company's logo, which is why you will almost always see the logo and tagline in a specific and regular relationship. The tagline and logo should be designed as a single entity and saved as "standing art," an out-line EPS file, as opposed to live type, which varies   even slightly   with every setting.

You're in baseball country now® A subway placard that encourages civic responsibility while defining a team's terri-tory. Team colors; centered beneath the logo; no apparent size relationship.

Display Type

1 **Create your space®** Sized to match width of *Trex* logo.
2 **Let's build something to-gether**™ Too wide for the logo; has to fight with the additional – and temporary – 60th anni-versary mark; contrasting font doesn't agree with any other type on this ad; maybe it's here by mistake.

3 **Get the good stuff®** Too wide for the logo; wrong font doesn't match the logo, headline, or text.
4 **Starring in over 170 coun-tries®** The tagline's cap height matches the x-height of the *Heineken* logo.
5 **Perfection has its price**™ Too wide for the logo and mis-matched font.

A mind is a terrible to waste

1

1 A tagline running since the late-1960s for the United Negro College Fund. Often lampooned ("A mind is a waste of a terri-ble thing," "A waste is a terrible thing to mind"), even badly misquoted by Vice President Dan Quayle, this tagline has become part of the U.S.'s cultural fabric, recognized by over 80% of the American public. Its strength comes from em-phasizing the potential of the African American community. The UNCF has helped tens of thousands pay for college.

1　　　　　　　　　　　　**2**　　　　　　　　　　　　**3**

1 Go beyond™ Type size and setting matches the headline; width matches the logo.

2 Born from jets™ Upper right corner is unexpected; matches typeface throughout ad, ex-cept for the logo.

3 Let's motor® Design disci-pline is one of the certainties of this campaign. One typeface, two weights, always all caps.

The Web site listing, tagline, and logo are all horizontally aligned through their mid-points.

Advertising
Design
and
Typography

1　　　　　　　　　**2**　　　　　　　　　**3**　　　　　　　　　**4**

1 Drivers wanted® Horizontal alignment through the mid-point. The visual is left to speak for itself.
2 Think. Feel. Drive.™ There are four unrelated sans serif faces in this ad: logo, tagline, head-line, and text. This would be a more unified design if, say, two could be made to conform. My choices would be the logo/tag-line, and the headline/text.
3 The brilliance of common sense® Taglines do not have to be near the logo; all type gets the same distressed treatment.
4 Moving forward® Good relationship with the logo; ob-vious unity with the headline and secondary type.

hing

9
13
1
2
11
8
14
5
16
3
6
12
15
7
20
17
4
19
10
18

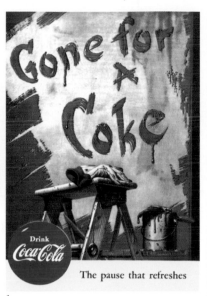

1

2

1 The pause that refreshes® Coca-Cola's most famous line, introduced in 1929. Note the wordspacing in this 1953 ad is quite open by today's standards.

The words are four bricks as much as one line of type.
2 The curiously strong mints® One typeface, all caps, centered. This ad is from 1998.

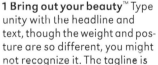

1

2

3

1 Bring out your beauty™ Type unity with the headline and text, though the weight and posture are so different, you might not recognize it. The tagline is

centered beneath the right edge of the image and is only casually proximate to the logo.
2 A sweeter look at yourself™ Only one typeface is used in

this ad, all heavily manipulated. The oddest thing here is the Brazilian artificial sweetener's package design, which is much less hip than the ad. *Finn* is an

impression of *fino,* "elegant/ fine/thin" in Portuguese.
3 Stay smart.® Three lines of type, three typefaces. But they *are* centered.

9 **191**

Display Type

1

2

3

4

5

1 The fastest way to receive money worldwide™ The same width and colors as the logo. This is an ultimate tagline/logo connection: they have been

made into a single entity.
2 Pressure's off™ One type family for the tagline, subhead, and text.
3 Goodnites mean good morn-

ings® Letterspacing seems whimsical, though a little *more* would get it the width of the text column.
4 Makeup so pure you can

sleep in it™ All lowercase; matches mouse type at bottom, but neither on jar lid.
5 The best a man can get™ All one clean, masculine typeface.

1

2

3

Two examples from 1924 show vastly different styles and the transition to modern asymmetrical, sans serif design.
1 This award-winning ad has

the era's typically long text: this is *everything* you would possibly need to know to agree to receive a free month's supply of hot cereal.

2 In contrast, Kurt Schwitters' all-type ad is set with text in the shape of a rectangle. Relationships abound: the black rectangle equals the height of the

text block, and line lengths are precise. Shown scaled to the size of the cereal ad (1).
3 Text *primarily* as form, Piet Zwart, 1928.

Chapter 10 **Text Type**

Setting text is different than setting display type. Display type's purpose is to be noticed and to convey its meaning in a way that makes you want to continue on to the next "type opportunity," whether a subhead or caption. The ultimate destination of all multilevel display type is the text, where additional copy points are and the sales pitch is.

Having invested so much in getting the reader to the pitch, text is no place to be unneccesarily creative. Though text deserves as much craftsmanship as any other part of an ad, make it as effortless to read as possible: set it perfectly by knowing what makes small type invisible as a *content delivery system*. Don't impede the copy in its job of conveying the pitch.

Art directing is like catching a fish: prepare bait that will attract read-

1

2

3

4

5

1 Headline/subhead/text hierarchy is made by value, or grayness, not type weight or size, the traditional means. 1963.
2 Purposeful monotony in claims

by hundreds of unrelated products of being "the Swiss Army Knife" of their fields, i.e., extremely versatile and useful.
3 Extra-long line length in all

caps is not easy to read. But the "error" is mitigated by plenty of additional line spacing.
4 Equally long lines in lower case are maybe a tiny bit more

legible. Space (the deep indents) relate text to headline.
5 These are long lines, too, but the larger type size reduces the *characters per line* to 55.

1 Getting readers into the text is like fishing: prepare a message that will attract readers both in its strategy and in its words and pictures;

2 Make readers stop long enough to see the visual and headline;
3 Get readers to continue on to a secondary type opportunity;

4 and finally "land them" by getting them to read the text. If this step doesn't happen, readers will have only tasted the bait (the display type). It

is vital that even a taste of the message – what might be considered an ad which is at least a partial failure – makes a lasting impression.

ers; make them stop and take in the headline; get them to continue on to a secondary type opportunity; and finally land them by getting them to read the text. Without getting them to the text, you may have caused them to have had an adventure, but you didn't "land the reader."

I had a misadventure deep sea fishing with my brothers. Aside from discovering that I am intolerant of Atlantic swells, I learned that fishing for sailfish has four distinct parts:

🐟 Setting the hook with live "goggle eyes" bait that sailfish like to eat;

🐟 Presentation of the bait to hook the sailfish (a true fisherman "lives for the top-water strike," a bait presentation so adept that the sailfish attacks the bait at the surface, in view of the fisherman);

🐟 Reeling the fish in as it fights (hopefully with a tail-walk); and

🐟 Landing the sailfish (actually getting the angry so-and-so close enough to admire him, snap a photo, and let him go without serious injury). If you

"If you have something of importance to say, for God's sake start at the end." Sarah Jeannette Duncan

"Writing is equivalent to power... Legibility is of the essence. The layout (i.e., the planning) is far more important than letterforms. Too much attention to letterforms distracts from the planning which is the heart of writing... If anything goes wrong, readers may lay a piece of writing aside after a mere glance." Ferdinand Baudin, 1977

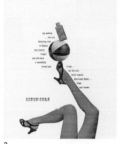

1 Idiosyncratic text oozes personality. Many random substitutions to make it look handcrafted and old fashioned.
2 Text is given a playful arrange-

ment in relationship to the image in Paul Rand's 1944 cosmetics ad. This was quite forward-thinking at the time
3 Asymmetrical text says "fun"

in the company of pink bubbles and barrel-tub, c1967.
4 Text is broken for sense and reversed from mortised bars.
5 Interrupting text with images

succeeds when their scale is in balance. Centered design (stability) and historically accurate types are properly used for the Library of Congress.

1 | 2 | 3

1 Individual event listings for a conference look like bits of "frozen sound" coming from an impassioned speaker in Alan Fletcher's 1996 poster.

2 The text begins as an element of the artwork, curving under the guitar before changing to a justified five-line column. Saying "exotic romance" in what was then a new way, this 1938 ad by Charles Coiner and A.M. Cassandre is an early use of abstract art in advertising.

3 Text set in a single line and shaped to the curve of the road creates design unity. I wonder whether the "7" is intended.

Text is not always necessary. Nothing more needs to be said besides giraffe, long brush, and "Reach." The two additional copy points are buried in verbiage.

miss the last step by, for example, letting the fish escape from the hook – a so-called "Palm Beach Release" – you aren't considered to have actually caught the fish.

Text is the test of a reader's commitment. It takes time and energy to read it. So the biggest design challenge is to get readers into the text. It takes a message crafted so it appeals to them, a design on which they can get snagged, and absolute effortlessness to read once they get there. Text is no place to challenge readers to decipher text or make the least effort to read.

How to make text type inviting Set it a point size larger than you "should."
- Make it legible: choose a medium weight of a quality typeface.
- Make it legible: give it a comfortable size and column width.
- Make it legible: give it invisible (unselfconscious) spacing attributes.

Advertising
Design
and
Typography

1 | 2 | 3 | 4

1 Because of its even tone, text *is* gray. Here its grayness is used. Is this an interpretation of the padding of an assigned paper for parent-aged prospects?

2 Light bulbs aren't as significant to consumers as "light." This message is that light affects the kitchen. The text arrangement suggests light rays.

3 The dynamic text shape of a business-to-business printing ad from 1946. It is hard to read without becoming aware of the extremely wide word spacing.

4 The flopped question and answer format – of precisely equal length – makes this 1963 Lotus ad. This is exceptional text craftsmanship.

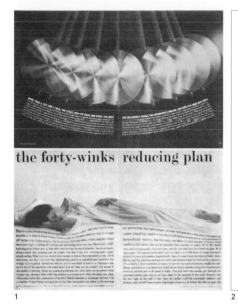

the forty-winks reducing plan

1   2

Text, like all type, is really much more about managing the spaces between the characters, words, and lines than about manipulating the letterforms

themselves. These are extreme examples of space manipulation, but their lesson is applicable to more sedate, usual type treatments.

1 Text manipulations like this were very difficult to produce in 1962. Otto Storch cut apart printed type proofs with horizontal baselines and pasted

the words (and individual letters) in position to achieve the curved baselines in these ads.
2 The faux text is from the facing "unrelated" editorial page.

Space and text Typography is space management. It is balancing space as a separator and space as a connector. It is highly visual and computer defaults cannot be relied on for fine spacing craftsmanship. Space in text appears in five places: between characters, between words, between lines, between paragraphs, and between columns.

👈 **Character spacing** is achieved in two ways. *Tracking* is setting paragraph-wide spacing attributes. In contrast to display type, tracking in text should tend more toward open spacing rather than tight spacing to compensate for text's smaller size. This extra bit of space, an addition of perhaps five to ten percent, helps letterforms stand apart. *Kerning* is adjusting space between specific pairs of letters, which is less significant than in display type, where individual characters can be readily seen. Kerning text is generally unnecessary because we read text by word shapes, not one or two characters at a time.

"Tradition is what you resort to when you don't have the time or the money to do it right." Kurt Herbert Adler

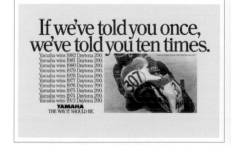

If we've told you once, we've told you ten times.

1   2   3

1 This text, nearly the same sentence repeated over and over, looks like "dummy type," used on preliminary ad roughs before actual copy is written.

2 Text set in three very, very long lines (perhaps to provoke the feeling of long-distance running) reinforces the adidas three-stripe mark.

3 The image is framed by three groups of words, with the text and tagline placed sideways at the left. Sideways text will certainly reduce readership, but

the benefit may be in being the crazy, devil-may-care brand that sets text sideways. Their target audience may well respond to that attitude.

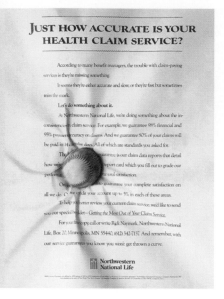

1 Text as verbiage – fresh, plentiful, and backed up – is used to illustrate the effect of inhibited freedom of expression.

2 Obscuring text is a risky move: a great investment has been made to lure a reader to that part of the message. It must be done to make a valuable point. Text can be obscured without loss of communication at the primary (headline) and secondary (caption, deck or subhead) levels. In this case, the text is written so the area hidden by the ball is missable.

"If the tastefulness required to produce fine typography is absent, then fine typography will not be possible under any conditions using any technology." Aaron Burns

◆ **Word spacing** is perceived in proportion to character- and linespacing. Word spacing should be "invisible," or just enough to separate words without looking either too tight or too open. Good word spacing maintains the integrity of the line so it doesn't break into individual word chunks.

◆ **Linespacing** must be larger than wordspacing, so the eye reads across a line rather than downwards. It should be increased as line length expands beyond the optimal 52-60 characters per line to ease returns to the leading edge of the next line. And, while "minus leading" is recommended for display type to darken it, minus linespacing should be used only with great care at text sizes because it makes small type harder to read.

◆ **Paragraph spacing** separates one idea from the next. Paragraphing may be achieved by indenting the first line, by indenting all but the first line (a "hanging indent"), or by adding a half or full line space between paragraphs. ◪ Another method of paragraphing, and the first to be

Advertising
Design
and
Typography

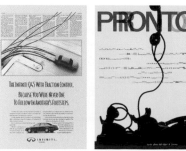

1 Faux text is violated in this full-page newspaper ad. The treatment is a visible focal point *and* it illustrates the road-holding ability of the car.

2 *"Hello..."* Text as gibberish and set to look like a conversation in this 1959 self-promotion poster for an ad agency in Milan.

3 Hand lettering was interpreted by the first printers, which led to today's typographic principles. Word spacing seems very narrow in this 1440 personal prayer book. This emphasizes the line over the word. Of course, the purpose of this book is to be read slowly and contemplatively.

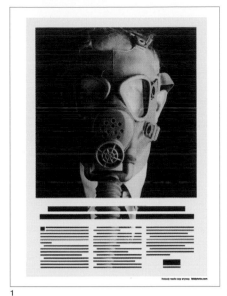

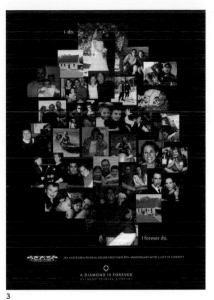

1 What if text is replaced by an image? Does a picture literally equal a thousand words? A stock photo enterprise inserts a single image behind the headline and text of a mock ad. The cynical tagline states "Nobody reads copy anyway."

2 A harsh text treatment combining lettering and set type adds value to a harsh message about suicide.

3 The long story between "I do" and an eighth wedding anniversary is told emotionally with pictures rather than text.

---

invented, is to use a dingbat or paragraph symbol (¶). This classic style gives text an uninterrupted shape for text wraps. Never indent the first paragraph of text: it is an obvious beginning and the indent is a typographic redundancy, which makes the designer look poorly informed.

☛ **Column spacing** should be at least twice as large as word spacing, so readers don't accidentally "jump a gutter," or read across to a neighboring column rather than drop down to the next line. A pica space (⅙ of an inch) is usually an adequate distance.

Text abstraction Don't do anything to text that will repel readers. You've led them to the goodies, now let them sup on the sales message in peace. Using abstraction to catch an already caught reader is wasteful and risky. But this isn't to say you can't reveal meaning through *modest* abstraction. Just pay extra attention to the fragile balance of small size and legibility.

Four basic ways to paragraph:
1 Hard return, no indent
2 Skip a half-line space
3 Indent
4 Hang the indent

1 Calligraphic handlettering is used as text to make a half-page ad's point that flying in this aircraft is smooth. This is a print version of a *demonstration ad*, an approach often used on television where motion and time reveal before and after proof.
2 Lengthy display type and image have been damaged, as if letterpress printed or photocopied repeatedly, in contrast with the sharp caption, product shot, and logo in the bottom right corner of this Swiss campaign. Art lives in the same area as sharp polarity. Cover the bottom right corner to see how the message changes without the contrast.

Garamond
Century
Caecilia
Fairfield
Didot
Neuva
Menhart

⇕ LESS LEGIBLE | MORE LEGIBLE ⇕
but MORE CHARACTER | *but LESS CHARACTER*

Legible text faces Some text types are inherently more legible than others; balance simplicity with a style that contributes to brand identity. A large x-height increases legibility.

A great concept is not merely a different shade of blue. It is red.

A great concept is not merely a different shade of blue. It is red.

A great concept is not merely a different shade of blue. It is red.

Serif vs Sans serif Serifs put space between characters (*top*), making it easier to read at text sizes. Sans serif types (*middle*) can be made equally legible by opening their letterspacing a bit (*bottom*).

Line length is optimal at an average of 50 to 60 characters per line (*top*). Add linespacing for lines with more than 60 characters per line (*above*) and for typefaces with large x-height.

Great ideas feel foreign
A pretty good idea is a concept that is *different* from what has been done before. A pretty good idea is *creative* because it does something in a different way. But a pretty good idea lies within what might be expected of an intelligent person given the right information.
A great idea transcends *different* and *creative*. A great idea is **surprising**. It requires a new conceptual framework, not just another idea within a pre-existing framework.
A great idea FEELS FOREIGN. It will feel strange. It will feel as if there has never been anything like it. If everything that has come before is "blue," a great concept is not merely a different or better shade of blue. It is "red."
Identify which direction the category is moving and go in the opposite direction. That's the easy part. Making that counter direction *work for the message* is the hard part.

Consistent spacing is how text type is judged. This example is inconsistent. Any spacing decision in text should be to make it look even, including decisions that would be "textbook wrong." If it *looks* right, it *is* right.

Justified vs flush left Justifying text across a too-narrow measure will produce uneven word spacing (*left*). Manually hyphenate for even color. Flush left/ ragged right always has even word spacing (*right*).

Don't indent the first paragraph of text.

Justified type can produce uneven word spacing. Check for and rebreak these lines.

Underlining is amateurish and far too visible a contrast in text.

Use true small caps, which are drawn for equal body weight. Downsizing capitals look too light.

Setting defaults Spend an hour defining and perfecting *paragraph styles* in your software for each client so you don't have to think so much about it thereafter. This ensures immediate quality and long-term consistency.

Do not use a straight apostrophe for an apostrophe. It should look like a 9.

10 **198**

Advertising
Design
and
Typography

Great ideas feel foreign[*]

A pretty good idea is a concept that is *different* from what has been done before. A pretty good idea is *creative* because it does something in a different way. But a pretty good idea lies within what might be expected of an intelligent person given the right information.

A great idea transcends *different* and *creative*. A great idea is <u>surprising</u>. It requires a new conceptual framework, not just another idea within a pre-existing framework.

A great idea FEELS FOREIGN. It will feel strange. It will feel as if there has never been anything like it. If everything that has come before is "blue," a great concept is not merely a different or better shade of blue. It is "red."

Identify which direction the category is moving and go in the opposite direction. That's the easy part. Making that counter direction *work for the message* is the hard part.

[*] Based on an article by Nkiruka "Kiki" Nwasokwa, AD at Cline Davis & Mann, Princeton, NJ

How to set perfect text Text has to be handled a little differently than display type. Spacing attributes generally have to be more open than display type so each character can be more easily read. Text's quality is determined by its overall color, or evenness of tone. Good text setting is more than mere data entry: if you are not overriding or changing the defaults, you are just entering data and you are not adding typographic value.

Widows (very short lines) and orphans (widows at the tops of columns) are not acceptable. Use real fractions ($\frac{1}{4}$, $\frac{1}{2}$, $\frac{3}{4}$) found in the Glyphs chart, not

A great idea transcends different and creative. A great idea is *surprising*. It requires a new conceptual framework, not just **another idea** within a pre-existing framework. A great idea feels foreign or <u>strange</u>. It will feel as if there has

Type on top of image is decorative, but it is a surefire way to create visual static for the reader. That is the antithesis of what designers do. If reading this disturbs you, "pretty" doesn't much matter.

Great ideas
☑ Transcend *different* and *creative*
☑ Are surprising and require a new conceptual framework

Great ideas
☑ Feel foreign and/or strange
☑ Feel as if there has never been anything like it. If everything

Italic/Bold/Underline are three ways of showing emphasis in text. Italic is for use within a text block. Bold breaks up text and should be used in headings only. Underlining is not professional. Ever.

Type on top of image is decorative, but it is a surefire way to create visual static for the reader. That is the antithesis of what designers do. Which of these two text settings did you read? The end.

Turnovers occur when copy runs longer than a single line. In bulleted lists, turnovers may be left at full measure to fit more copy (*top*), or indented to show the beginnings better.

Punctuation indicates thought groupings. The rules for its use have evolved since the first type in 1450 and can be interpreted. *Hang punctuation* to create a visually smooth column edge.

Well set text

Great ideas feel foreign

A pretty good idea is a concept that is *different* from what has been done before. A pretty good idea is *creative* because it does something in a different way. But a pretty good idea lies within what might be expected of an intelligent person given the right information.

A great idea transcends *different* and *creative*. A great idea is *surprising*. It requires a new conceptual framework, not just another idea within a pre-existing framework.

A great idea FEELS FOREIGN. It will feel strange. It will feel as if there has never been anything like it. If everything that has come before is "blue," a great concept is not merely a different or better shade of blue. It is "red."

Identify which direction the category is moving and go in the opposite direction. That's the easy part. Making that counter direction *work for the message* is the hard part.

Don't digitally angle letterforms for italics, which are properly redrawn and look more fluid. Some sans serifs have oblique versions rather than drawn italics.

Word spacing is always even in flush left type.

Make indentions deep enough to be visible.

Real quote marks look like 66 and 99.

Ligatures were invented as a way to coerce type into justified lines. There were at one time about 300, of which these three (*bottom row*) are about all that commonly remain. They sustain even type color.

Quotes and apostrophes It's been decades since desktop publishing forced designers to pay attention to "curly" or "smart" quotes. The rule is simple: Foot and inch marks (*top*) are not acceptable sustitutes for "66/99" single and double quotes (*above*). The keystrokes for the Mac are shown.

ad hoc versions made with the slash (1/4, 1/2, 3/4) – unless you need unavailable numbers. Then, in Preferences, set the super/subscript size at 60

percent, the superscript position at 28 percent, and the subscript position at 0 percent. Instead of a slash, use option-shift-1.

Don't use the space bar to set indents or spaces that separate: the distance varies with the type size. Set a tab. Text's overall color, or evenness

of tone, is the goal of fine text typography. The craftsmanship revealed in type's details separates the great from the good enough.

Glossary

Abstract mark A logo or symbol that has no obvious visual relationship to the object it represents. Also called *arbitrary mark*.

ADDY An award for outstanding advertising presented by the American Advertising Federation.

Advertising The use of paid media to sell products or communicate ideas by a sponsor.

Advertising quarangle The four elements of communication: the sender; the message; the medium; and the receiver.

Alignment Having elements' edge placement agree. Optical alignment is always more important than measurable alignment.

Allusion An indirect reference to a known figure.

Art A design, drawing, photo, or other visual material.

Art director One who creates and executes the visual presentation of advertising ideas.

Ascender The part of lowercase letters that extend above the median in *b, d, f, h, k, l, t*. See *Descender*.

Audience The group to which a product is aimed.

Avatar A brand icon designed for use across various media.

Ayers No.1 A classic layout consisting of, in order: a picture, a headline, a copy block, and the advertiser's name.

Baseline Invisible line on which letterforms sit.

Basis weight The weight in pounds of a ream (500 sheets) of paper cut to its basic size.

Benefit A perceived advantage derived from a feature or attribute.

Binding Attaching sheets of paper together for ease of use and protection. There are four methods of binding: edition, mechanical, perfect, saddle- and side-stitched.

Bitmap A character image represented as a pattern of dots on a screen. See *Outline*.

Blackletter Heavy, angular types based on medieval script writing.

Bleed Imagery or letterforms that run off the trimmed edge of a page. See *Full bleed*.

Body copy The primary text of an ad. Usually identified by a medium weight and a body size of 8 to 12 points.

Bold A typeface style that is heavier and wider than the roman style of the same typeface.

Brand A person's perception of a product.

Brand agency A strategic firm that creates or manages brand building services.

Brand asset Any aspect of the brand that has strategic value: attributes, associations, loyalty, etc.

Brand equity The accumulated financial and strategic value of a brand.

Brand essence The distillation of a brand's promise into the simplest, shortest possible terms.

Branding The art and science of building a brand.

Brandmark A symbol of a brand; a trademark.

Burst A graphic element like a circle or star with the words "New!" or "Improved!" interrupting a layout; to be avoided.

Cap height The height of capital letters, measured from baseline to top of the letterforms.

Category The arena in which a brand competes.

Centered Alignment in which the midpoints of each element are positioned on a central axis. The left and right edges of such a column are mirror images.

Character set The letters, figures, punctuation marks, and symbols that can be displayed on a monitor or output by a printer.

Cliché A trite or overused idea or expression; *to be avoided like the plague*.

Coated paper Paper with a layer of matte, dull, or gloss coating applied; keeps ink from absorbing into the paper, making images crisp.

Color, typographic The lightness or darkness of gray that a type area creates. Typographic color is affected by the type's size, posture, linespacing, weight, and tracking.

Commercial A paid message that is transmitted by television or radio.

Communication The transmission or exchange of information.

Comparison advertising The practice of comparing brands and naming names.

Concept The basic idea of an ad or campaign.

Condensed A narrow version of a typeface.

Contrast The degree of difference between light and dark areas in an image. Extreme lights and darks are high contrast; medium grays are low contrast.

Contrast, typographic The amount of variation between thick and thin strokes of a letter.

Corporate identity The brand identity of a company; its trade dress.

Counter The space, either completely or only partially closed, in letterforms like a, e, u and A, B, S.

Creative Having imaginative effort; a person paid to produce same.

Creative brief A document that sets parameters for a project.

Creative strategy An outline of a strategy including its objective, audience, premise, and theme.

Crop marks Thin lines added to the perimeter of a design showing where to trim the printed piece.

Cuffo Work without payment; speculative; off the cuff.

Cursive Typefaces with fluid strokes that look like handwriting.

Deadline The latest time a project can be delivered. The term's origin is the line drawn around a prison, beyond which inmates would be shot.

Descender The part of lowercase letters that extend below the baseline in *g, j, p, q, y*.

Design To plan; to organize with purposeful intent.

Dingbat Illustrative characters in a typeface.

Display type Letterforms that are supposed to be read first. Usually identified by a large body size and bold weight.

Double page spread See *Spread*.

dpi Abbreviation for dots per inch; a measure of resolution.

Drop cap A large initial set into the top left corner of body copy. A dropcap's baseline must

align with a text's baseline.

Duotone A two-color halftone, usually black and a second ink color. The result is an image with more richness and depth than a one-color halftone.

Ellipsis A single character of three dots indicating an ommission. The spacing of an ellipsis (…) is distinct from three periods in a row (...).

Em dash The longest dash in a typeface. An em dash is the same width as the type size being used: 10-point type, which is measured vertically, has a 10-point wide em-dash. Usually too wide for practical use. See *En dash*.

En dash The second-longest dash in a typeface. An en dash is half the width of the type size being used: 10-point type, measured vertically, has a 5-point wide en dash. Used in place of a hyphen for compound words. See *Em dash*.

Feature Any aspect of a product that delivers a benefit.

Flush A typographic term meaning aligned or even. Type can be set flush left, even on the left and ragged on the right; flush right, even on the right and ragged on the left; or flush left

and right, more properly called justified.

Folio A page number.

Font A set of characters that share common characteristics. Also called *typeface*.

Foot margin The space at the bottom of a page.

Foundry The place where type is manufactured. A foundry was originally a placed for metalwork; modern type foundries are digital.

Four-color process A printing process that uses magenta (red), cyan (blue), yellow, and black inks to simulate the continuous tones and variety of colors in a color image.

Full bleed Imagery or letterforms that run off all four edges of a page. See *Bleed*.

Grain The direction that most fibers lie in a sheet of paper. This is important in folding and tearing.

Grotesque Sans serif type; so called because it was considered ugly when it was introduced in the mid-1800s.

Gutter The space between columns of type and between facing pages of a book or magazine.

Hairline The thinnest line which a device can output, usually ¼-point.

Halftone A printed image in which continuous tone is reproduced as dots of varying sizes.

Hanging indent A paragraphing style in which the first line pokes out to the left. Sometimes called an *outdent* or *flush and hung*.

Hanging initial An initial letter placed in the margin next to body copy.

Hanging punctuation Allowing lines that begin or end with punctuation to extend a bit beyond the paragraph width for optical alignment. A certain indicator of typographic sensitivity and craftsmanship.

Head margin The space at the top of a page.

Hot metal Typesetting and the printing process that involves casting type from molten lead.

Humanist Letterforms that look a bit like handwriting, or at least don't look too mechanical or geometric. Identifiable by having a humanist axis, or angled emphasis related to handwriting.

Icon The visual symbol of a brand; a trademark.

Incunabula "Cradle"; describes the first 50 years of printing with movable type, from 1450-1500.

Italic Types that slant to the right. Must have letters that are distinctly different from roman version of the typeface, like a and *a*, or it is probably an oblique version.

Justification Aligning

both the left and right sides of a column of type.

Kern Removing space between specific letter pairs in order to achieve optically consistent letter spacing. See *Tracking*.

Leaders A line of dots that lead the eye across a wide space.

Leading Space between lines of type that appears between the descenders of one line and the ascenders of the next. Leading is added above a given line of type. The name comes from hot metal type when actual strips of lead were inserted between lines of type.

Lead-in The first few words of a paragraph set to attract attention.

Legibility The ability to distinguish between letterforms or to be read easily. See *Readability*.

Letterspacing A term used to describe general spacing between letters.

Ligature Joined pairs or trios of characters into one, as in fi and ffl, for optical consistency.

Light or **lightface** A lighter variation of a typeface.

Line spacing See *Leading*.

Lining figures Numerals that are equivalent to the cap height of the typeface; to be used in charts and in all-caps settings. Also called *ranging figures*. See *Old style figures*.

Logo A wordmark, often

misused to mean any trademark.

Margin The space at the inside and outside of a page. Also called side margin. See *Foot margin* and *Head margin*.

Marketing The process of developing, selling, and distributing a product.

Match color A custom-blended ink that matches a specified color exactly. There are several systems, including Pantone Matching System and Toyo.

Media advertising One-way messages designed to persuade or create awareness of a brand.

Median The invisible line that defines the top of lowercase letters that have no ascender. Also called *mean line* and *waist line*.

Minus leading Removing space between lines of type to give it a more unified and darker look. Should always be used with all caps display type and with great care on U/lc display type to keep ascenders and descenders from overlapping. See *Leading*.

Moiré (*mwah-RAY*) A pattern created by rescreening a halftone.

Monospace Typefaces in which each character occupies the same horizontal space. See *Variable space*.

Neologism An invented

word or phrase that can serve as a brand name.

NFNT Abbreviation for Macintosh font numbering system which assigns numbers to screen fonts.

Oblique An angled version of a roman typeface in which the same characters have been slanted to the right, not redrawn. See *Italic*.

Octothorp The number or pound sign (#). So named because it indicates eight farms surrounding a town square.

Old style figures Numerals that vary in height so they blend into a paragraph of text. Sometimes mistakenly called "lowercase figures." See *Lining figures*.

Optical alignment Adjusting elements or letterforms so they appear aligned, which is more important than actually being aligned.

Orphan A word or word fragment at the top of a column. A sign of ultimate carelessness. See *Widow*.

Outline The mathematical representation of a character that can be scaled to any size and resolution.

Phototypesetting Type set by light exposed through a film negative of characters onto light-sensitive paper. Introduced in the 1960s and replaced by digital typesetting in the 1980s.

Pica One sixth of an inch, or 12 points. Because it is divisible by points, and thus accommodates type measurement, use the pica for planning design space. See *Point*.

Point One seventy-second of an inch, or one twelfth of a pica. The basic unit of measurement of type. See *Pica*.

Point size The size of a typeface measured from just above the top of the ascenders to just beneath the bottom of the descenders. Also called *body size* and *type size*.

Positioning The brand-building process of differentiating a product to gain a competitive advantage.

Posture The angle of stress of a typeface. There are generally three postures: roman; italic or oblique; and backslant.

Product placement Paid advertising in which products or trademarks are put into nonadvertising media.

Readability The quality of attraction and visibility. See *Legibility*.

Rebus A pictorial representation of a word or a part of a word.

Recto The right hand page of a spread. Always odd numbered. See *Verso*.

Resolution The number

of dots per inch (dpi) displayed on a screen or by a printer, which determines how smooth the curves and angles of characters appear. Higher resolution yields smoother characters.

Rocket head A type treatment in which the first few words are set large, as a headline, and subsequent lines decrease in size until standard text size is reached.

Roman An upright, medium-weight typeface.

Rough rag Type set without hyphenation, causing a pronounced variation in line length. See *Tight rag*.

Rule A typeset line.

Runaround Type set around an element. The ideal distance is 1 pica, or enough space to separate, but not enough to dissociate the type and image from each other.

Sans serif Type without cross strokes at the ends of their limbs. Usually have consistent stroke weight. See *Serif*.

Segment A group of people who are likely to respond to a marketing effort in a similar way.

Serif Type whose limbs end in cross strokes. Usually have variation in main character stroke weight. See *Verso*.

Slab serif Type with especially thick serifs. All "Egyptian" typefaces are slab serifs.

Slogan A catchphrase or tagline.

Small caps Capital letters that are about the size of lowercase letters of the same typeface. Unlike using capital letters set a few points smaller, true small caps are the same weight beside their full-size capitals.

Solid Type set without additional linespacing.

Spread Two facing pages. It is redundant to call it a *double-page spread*.

Strategy A set of tactics to achieve a business goal.

Style Variations of a typeface, including roman, italic, bold, condensed, extended, and combinations of these.

Subhead Secondary type that explains the headline and leads to the text.

Symbol An icon or trademark that represents a brand.

Tagline A phrase that summarizes a market position. See *Slogan*.

Target market The group of customers a company has selected to serve.

Tight rag Type set with a small hyphenation zone, causing minimal variation in line length. See *Rough rag*.

Tissue A rough sketch; a preliminary study.

Tracking Adjusting space in a line or paragraph. See *Kern*.

Trade dress The colors, shapes, typefaces, and design treatments that create a public persona for a company.

Trademark A legally-protectable name or symbol of a company.

Trim size The final size of a printed piece after excess paper has been cut off.

Turnovers Type that continues on a subsequent line.

Typeface A set of characters of a unified design and bearing its own name, like Minion or Loire.

Type family All styles and variations of a single typeface. May include italic, bold, small caps, old style figures, etc.

Typographer Historically, one who sets type. In modern usage, one who practices the craft and art of designing letterforms and designing with letterforms.

Typography The craft and art of designing with type.

Type size See *Point size*.

U/lc Type setting using upper and lowercase letters.

Uncoated paper Paper without a surface coating.

Unicameral An alphabet with only one case in which capitals and lowercase are mixed.

USP Unique Selling Proposition: an impression that separates a product from its competitors.

Variable space Type in which each character is assigned its own width as determined by the characters' inherent widths. See *Monospace*.

Verso The left hand page of a spread; always even numbered. See *Recto*.

Weight The darkness of a typeface.

Why-to-buy message The most compelling reason to try a product; a tagline.

Widow A word or word fragment at the end of a paragraph. Words are okay, but word fragments are careless. See *Orphan*.

Word space Space between words. Proportional to letterspacing being used; if one is open, both must be open. If one is tight, both must be tight. "Correct" word spacing is that which is invisible: just enough to separate words but not enough to break a line of type into separate word chunks.

Wordmark A trademark that is a readable word; a logotype.

X-height The distance from the baseline to the median in lowercase letters. So named because it is the height of a lowercase *x*, which has neither an ascender nor a descender.

Bibliography

Adams James L. *Conceptual Block-busting.* New York: W.W. Norton, 1976.

Adams Richard. *www.advertising.* New York: Watson-Guptill Publishers, 2003.

Advertising Age periodical: Chicago.

Adweek periodical: New York.

Aitchison Jim. *Cutting Edge Advertising.* New York: Prentice Hall Publishers, 1999.

Art Directors Club annual: New York.

Art Directors Club of Europe annual: London.

Berger Warren. *Advertising Today.* London: Phaidon Press Ltd, 2001.

Bernbach Bill. *Bill Bernbach Said...* New York: DDB Needham Worldwide, 1989.

Blackwell Lewis. *20th Century Type Remix.* Corte Madera CA: Gingko Press Inc., 1998.

Blakeman Robyn. *The Bare Bones of Advertising Print Design.* Lanham MD: Rowman & Littlefield, 2004.

Bringhurst Robert. *The Elements of Typographic Style, Third Ed.* Vancouver: Hartley & Marks, 2005.

Byrne Robert. *The 2,548 Best Things Anybody Ever Said.* New York: Galahad Books, 1996.

Cheng Karen. *Designing Type.* New Haven: Yale University Press, 2005.

Chermayeff Ivan, Tom Geismar, and Steff Geissbuhler. *Trademarks Designed by Chermayeff and Geismar.* Basel: Lars Muller Publishers, 2000.

Communication Arts Advertising Annual Palo Alto CA.

Critique: The Magazine of Graphic Design Thinking Palo Alto CA.

D&AD Mastercraft *The Art Direction Book.* London: Rotovision, 2002.

Della Famina Jerry. *From Those Wonderful Folks Who Gave You Pearl Harbor.* New York: Simon & Schuster, 1970.

Debrow Larry. *When Advertising Tried Harder: The Sixties.* New York: Friendly Press, 1984.

Dwiggins William Addison. *Layout in Advertising.* New York: Harper & Bros., 1928. (The first book written on ad design.)

Dzamic Lazar. *No Copy Advertising.* Gloucester MA: Rockport Publishers, 2003.

Friedl Friedrich, Nicolaus Ott, and Bernard Stein. *Typography: An Encyclopedic Survey of Type Design and Techniques Throughout History.* Köln: Black Dog & Leventhal Publishers, Inc., 1998.

Gill Bob. *Forget All the Rules About Graphic Design. Including the Ones in This Book.* New York: Watson-Guptill Publications, 1981.

Ginger E.M., Editor. *Branding with Type: How Type Sells.* Mountain View: Adobe Press, 1995.

Heimann Jim, Editor. *All American Ads of the 40s, 50s, and 60s.* Köln: Taschen GmbH, 2003.

Heller Steven. *Paul Rand.* New York: Phaidon Press, Inc., 1999.

Heller Steven, ed. *The Education of a Typographer.* New York: Allworth Press, 2004.

Hickey Lisa. *Design Secrets: Advertising: 50 Real Life Projects Uncovered.* Gloucester MA: Rockport Publishers, 2005.

Hill Sam and Chris Lederer. *The Infinite Asset: Managing Brands to Build New Value.* Cambridge: The Harvard Business School Press, 2001.

Hinrichs Kit. *Typewise.* Cincinnati: F&W Publications, 1990.

King Emily. *Robert Brownjohn: Sex and Typography.* New York: Princeton Architectural Press, 2005.

Kurlansky Mervyn. *Masters of the 20th Century.* New York: Graphis Inc., 2001.

Landa Robyn. *Advertising by Design: Creating Visual Communication with Graphic Impact.* New York: John Wiley & Sons, 2004.

Levenson Bob. *Bill Bernbach's Book: A History of the Advertising That Changed the History of Advertising.* New York: Villard Books, 1987.

Lois George. *What's the Big Idea?* New York: Plume, 1991.

Loxley Simon. *Type: The Secret History of Letters.* London: I.B. Taurus, 2004.

Lupton Ellen, and J. Abbott Miller. *Design Writing Research.* New York: Princeton Architectural Press, 1996.

Lürzer's Int'l Archive periodical: Frankfurt.

Macmillan Neil. *An A–Z of Type Designers.* New Haven: Yale University Press, 2006.

McDonough John, Karen Egolf, and Jacqueline V. Reid. *The Advertising Age Encyclopedia of Advertising (3 volumes).* New York: Routledge, 2002.

Meggs Philip B. *Meggs' History of Graphic Design, 4th Ed.* New York: John Wiley & Sons, 2006.

Myers Jeremy. *Rewind: Forty Years of Design and Advertising.* London: Phaidon Press Ltd, 2002.

Negroponte Nicholas. *Being Digital.* New York: Basic Books, 1995.

Neumeier Marty, ed. *The Dictionary of Brand.* New York: AIGA, 2004.

Neumeier Marty. *The Brand Gap: How to Bridge the Distance Between Business Strategy and Design.* Berkeley: New Riders/AIGA, 2003.

Ogilvy David. *Confessions of an Advertising Man.* New York: Atheneum, 1962.

Ogilvy David. *Ogilvy on Advertising.* New York: Vintage Books, 1985.

The One Club Annual New York.

Peckolick Alan. *Herb Lubalin: Art Director, Graphic Designer, and Typographer.* New York: American Showcase, Inc., 1985.

Peters Tom. *Design: Innovate, Differentiate, Communicate.* London: Dorling Kindersley Limited, 2005.

Postman Neil. *Amusing Ourselves to Death: Public Discourse in the Age of Show Business.* New York: Viking Penguin, 1985.

Pricken Mario. *Creative Advertising: Ideas and Techniques.* London: Thames & Hudson, 2004.

Pricken Mario. *Visual Creativity.* London: Thames & Hudson, 2004.

Reeves Rosser. *Reality in Advertising.* New York: Knopf, 1961.

Reis Al, and Jack Trout. *Positioning: The Battle for Your Mind.* New York: Warner Books, Inc., 1986.

Roman Kenneth & Jane Maas. *How to Advertise.* New York: St. Martin's Press, 1976.

Scher Paula. *Make It Bigger.* New York: Princeton Architectural Press, 2005.

Seiden Hank. *Advertising Pure and Simple.* New York, AMACOM, 1976.

Silviera Mark. *Ordinary Advertising. And how to avoid it like the plague.* Xlibris Corporation, 2005.

Spencer Herbert. *Pioneers of Modern Typography, 2nd Ed.* Cambridge: The MIT Press, 1983.

Sullivan Luke. *Hey Whipple, Squeeze This: A Guide to Creating Great Ads.* New York: John Wiley & Sons, 1998.

Tschichold Jan. *The New Typography.* Berkeley: University of California Press, 1998.

Von Oech Roger. *A Whack on the Side of the Head.* New York: Warner Business Books, 1998.

Wheeler Alina. *Designing Brand Identity.* New York: John Wiley & Sons, 2003.

Williams Gareth. *Branded?* London: V&A Publications, 2000.

Wurman Richard Saul. *Information Anxiety.* New York: Doubleday, 1989.

The Type Directors Club is an organization founded in 1946 by a group of passionate "type directors," nearly-extinct specialists who encourage and oversee the informed use of type in an ad agency.

The TDC began a competition in 1953 to identify the year's best typography. These annual competitions are a who's who of more than fifty years of advertising design history.

The simple one-color booklets printed as keepsakes showing the winners have evolved into 320-page full-color catalogs that are recognized as the most valuable design annuals in the world. Why? Because imagery and graphic trickery isn't rewarded: outstanding typography is. And typography is where the most profound design thinking is expressed.

The Type Directors Club is based in New York City and offers a variety of programs to encourage informed type use. Some are free, some have a modest entry fee. All are unique.

Membership comes with the Annual; *Letterspace*, the Club's newsletter; and access to parts of the Club's Web site not available to the public. For more information, visit tdc.org.

Appendix

The Résumé

The function of your résumé is to get your portfolio seen.

What makes your résumé stand out in the stack it will be in?

If it is pretentious – or inoffensive with no reason to follow up – it will be thrown away. They are *looking for reasons* to throw some of these things away.

Make such a strong case on paper for your candidacy that your résumé has to go on the short stack.

No gimmicks.

No humor. (Humor is so subjective. It is unlikely that your idea of funny is the same as the recipient's.)

No peculiar formats that force the browser to search out your data: they won't.

No hobbies unless they are directly related to excellence in job performance.

No minor academic honors. Dean's List is simply not that impressive, and including it devalues the other achievements on your résumé.

Leave out any personal data that will not help you get a job but may help you lose it. No home address or other identifying data that can be stolen.

No embellishment of your education or past jobs. Verification is increasing annually and getting caught is deadly.

Never put "References upon request." It is an idiotic convention: obviously you will provide references. Not so obviously, you appear not to think for yourself.

The Portfolio

The function of your portfolio is to get an interview.

Your portfolio is seen as an indication of what you will do, not just what you have done.

Your portfolio reveals your intelligence, talent, and individuality.

Show the unpredictable. Have some pieces that say you are an individual who can really think.

Don't put in any more than your very best and most distinctive pieces. If that's three samples, so be it. The optimal number of pieces is 15. A series counts as a single sample and should be shown that way.

The first piece you show is your best piece. It sets the mood. The last piece is your second-best piece and it leaves a great impression. Be consistent.

Thinking is more important than execution. Craftsmanship should be impeccable regardless of your other abilities.

If explanation is necessary for a sample, you have failed as a designer. Each sample should demonstrate understanding of design principles and usefulness in the world.

The work you show should be related to the job for which you are applying. Ads for advertising, editorial for magazines, book covers and spreads for publishers. Off-target samples should be put in the pocket in the back, indicating you understand what is appropriate for this job and what is less so.

An outstanding comp is better than a mediocre printed sample.

Avoid dummy text: it is a necessary element that reveals your skill and understanding of where the message really is. Dummy text indicates you think it might as well be oatmeal.

Some creative directors and art directors care deeply about typography; they will evaluate your spacing attributes. Spacing reveals your innate talent.

Buy a simple, handsome, black box and a carrying bag. Put a distinctive tag on the outside with your name and phone.

Your portfolio is never finished. Like a garden, it is always a work in progress. Tend it constantly and lovingly.

The Job Search

Begin your job search by being organized. Go online and learn all you can about likely prospects. Keep a list of whom you've contacted and when, and notes about materials they've seen.

Use the power of numbers: contact as many people as possible. One may lead to something. Selectivity is a luxury you can afford once you have a first job.

Originality is essential in creative businesses. But don't show your natural peculiarity until you've gotten a job, and then let it out in measured amounts.

Perseverance separates the successful from the failures. It will probably take more than three months of continuous looking to get a job. If you have to take a lowly earn-some-money job to get through this period, be careful you use it only as a stepping stone to better things. It is a dead end for some.

Never show up unexpectedly. The person you want to see is working and will resent your surprise appearance.

No one is going to call you, so you have to be very proactive and aggressive in finding leads.

Don't alter your book after each interview. Everyone has an opinion and in the end yours is the one that counts. On the other hand, if you get repeated negative comments on some pieces, you should consider reworking them to make them less universally disliked.

Send a thank you postcard or email to the person whose time you took. Many candidates won't do this: it's an easy way to stand out in the crowd. It is polite and good business to thank people who have helped you.

If, after seeing every creative director in town, you don't have a job offer, it means you aren't good enough. Rework your book. Improve and replace. If that doesn't work, do it again.

Begin phone calls by identifying yourself immediately. It puts the recipient on equal footing.

The Interview

The function of the interview is to get a job offer.

Be prepared to answer some standard questions:

Why did you leave your last job or why are you considering leaving your present job?

What did you like most about your last job? What did you like least?

What are your strong points? What are your weak points?

Why do you want to work at this particular company? Or why this particular field?

How did you contribute to improved work procedures at your last job? Or how would you have if you could have?

What is the most interesting project you have worked on?

Provide references and credentials. You must assume these will be checked, so don't stretch the truth.

After you have been interviewed, you may receive an offer. Negotiate your salary, starting date, vacation, and benefits. Ask for 48 hours to consider their offer.

On the Job with Copywriters and Account Executives

They probably think design is art or cake decoration. Help them learn that design is, by defini-tion, essential to visual communication. Teach them the principles of design and typography. Show them how distinctive design treatments give your clients a recognizable personality and a boost in branding.

They must be helped to develop an informed opinion about design, just as you – as a designer – must have an informed opinion about writing.

Be sure you and your writer have a clearly-stated plan so the concept and design can be objectively evaluated.

Your job is to complement and extend the thinking of the writer.

Keep your supervisor informed of your work. Show her, tell her, hang your best somewhere where it will be seen. Toot your own horn just enough to be recognized but not so much that you are an egomaniac.

Prove your reliability by being early (or, at worst) on time with preliminary studies.

Actively create an environment in which art direction is perceived as equally important as concept development and writing. Failure in this area means you will be treated as an underling. The best way to do this is through partnership and cooperation.

If you don't understand the goal, you will be dancing alone in the dark: little chance for success and great likelihood of frustration. Ask questions.

Don't expect much encouragement in the workplace. You are receiving the company's highest compliment by receiving their paycheck.

Whether you work full time for a company or not, you are essentially a career freelancer: an employer can fire you anytime they want. There is a huge gap between what is legal and what is right. Count on companies to stay legal, but not always to be nice or fair. You must be prepared to move on at a moment's notice. Update your résumé and portfolio quarterly.

Being fired can be a doorway to a much better opportunity.

Design

Subscribe to at least one design magazine.

Become a member of at least one professional organization.

Use rules to clarify and organize, not decorate.

Use only enough type contrast to enliven and clarify.

ADVERTISING DESIGN
How to make an art director's résumé

PURPOSE
To apply typographic ideas to a revealing self-promotional document.

BACKGROUND
Getting a full-time job or an assignment as a freelancer usually follows a three-step process: résumé, portfolio, interview. This system provides the hirer with an efficient process of winnowing out the candidates that *appear* unsuitable. So it is essential for the prospective hiree (that's you) to present her- or himself in as positive and flattering light as possible at each of these three steps. | The purpose of your résumé is to intrigue a hirer into wanting to take the next step, whether to call/email a meet or to call/email and *see your portfolio*. The portfolio's purpose, by comparison, is to get the hirer to call/email and *meet you*. Finally, the meeting or interview's purpose is to *make the hirer fall in love with you* so you might then get to negotiate an offer. | The first step in this process, though, is the résumé. In its most basic form, a résumé is a simple listing of accomplishments and responsibilities. It is content-driven. | For art directors, however, a résumé is much more. It is a statement and a teaser — often the only sample a hirer is likely to see — of the kinds of work that may be seen in your portfolio. Showing your design personality is necessary to subtly indicate your vision as a typographer. Too little personality and your self-advertisement will not reveal you as a design thinker. Too much personality and you will turn off those hirers who don't like your style, or you may appear to be an egomaniac whose favorite subject is your own self.

PROCESS, PART 1
The Design-Neutral Résumé. Compile the data for your résumé. Apply it to a one-page 8½x11" vertical design-neutral document. Write all information in a way that reveals and clarifies your value to the hirer. Use action verbs like *created*, *designed*, *achieved*, and *caused*. | Make the type consistent by creating paragraph styles. Use a sans serif (less clutter in information graphics, which is what a résumé is) with an italic and a bold for two "flavors" of emphasis. Set everything in flush left 10/12 with no hyphenation, limiting yourself to spatial alignments and bold type for categorization and titling. Use the italic type for emphasis within the text settings. | Put your name and contact information (email and phone) at or near the top. | Use linespacing attributes to connect related sections of text and to separate unrelated sections of text. Be sure you are using spacing clearly and consistently. A half linespace to connect and a full linespace to separate work well. | Every line must be broken for sense. Quote marks must be 66/99. Double check your grammar and triple check for spelling and typographic errors. If all a hirer has seen of you is your résumé, they don't care about *you* yet so they have no reason to overlook your mistakes. With dozens, even hundreds, of résumés swamping their desks, they are *looking for a reason to reduce the clutter*. They'll toss your sheet in the garbage if they detect any errors. | Print on paper that furthers your cause. Paper makes an impression.

PROCESS, PART 2
Your Résumé. Having made a perfect design-neutral résumé, begin now to make your résumé your own. Any design decisions must *improve* the communicative and distinctive quality of your data so hirers are more inclined to want to see your samples. | Your final résumé study should rival your other portfolio samples as an expression of your understanding of spatial and typographic relationships and visual communication in general. | Provide a final print of the design-neutral document and your final "self-expressive" iteration. Résumés are emailed as attachments. Convert both your documents into separate pdf files and burn on a beautifully labelled cd. Be sure the fonts are embedded so your digital résumés don't come up in Courier on the recipient's screen. It would be wise to email them to a friend for certification before finalizing them.

ADDITIONAL TIPS
Some tips from recent articles on résumé preparation:

🐒 Do create a special job-seeking Internet address that doesn't have a silly name.

🐒 Do put a paragraph at the top detailing your leadership and problem-solving skills. This is no time for modesty: you only get thirty seconds, maximum.

🐒 Do include only information that tells a company why it should hire you on the spot. Everything else detracts.

🐒 Do mimic the language used by the company itself in its job listing, Web site, and its annual report.

🐒 Do use bold and italics only as warranted by the content itself, not for decoration.

🐒 Do create a text version (which will look a lot like your Design-Neutral Résumé) that can be pasted directly into an email: virus filters often kick out attachments.

🐒 Don't start sentences with "I" and "My."

🐒 Don't use clichés.

🐒 Don't include personal information like your social security number, home address, or date of birth on your résumé. Be wary of additional information requests over the phone or online, especially if you post your résumé on a job-seeking Web site. Assume you are stapling your résumé to a telephone pole where the world can see it. Identity theft can happen anywhere. The information on your résumé has a "street value."

Index

Colophon

This is 36-point UF
Grotesk Light desi
ed in 1985 by He
mann Zapf for i
maximum legil
ility. This is 36-

Advertising Design and Typography is set in URW Grotesk (*top, shown in four weights*). URW Grotesk was designed by Hermann Zapf in 1985 for use by a German newspaper publishing group. The newspaper project died, but URW (Untternehmensberatung Rubow Weber, based in Hamburg) continued producing the type family and released it shortly thereafter.

Zapf designed URW Grotesk by following classical proportions for increased legibility. Its open counters make it particularly suitable for long text settings in books, magazines, newspapers, and onscreen design. It has a twin serif type family, URW Antiqua (*above*).

Images were scanned at 600dpi and 1200dpi and processed in Photoshop CS2. Every effort was made to use the best sample available.

Advertising Design and Typography was designed and typeset by Alex W. White. It was composed on a Mac in InDesign CS2 and printed on 130gsm Thai Matte Coat by Sirivatana Interprint Public Company Ltd. in Bangpakong, Thailand.

Credits

My thanks to each and every art director whose work is in this book. Listed in clockwise order beginning from upper left corner of each spread: **10-11** *Penn: Arty Tan AD; Sales/Marketing: Alex Bogusky AD; Business Card: Bob Gill AD; Keith Richards: Philippe Taroux AD* **12-13** *Miller: Jeff Williams AD; 20% Off: Bob Gill AD* **14-15** *Fart!: Gabi Schnauder AD* **16-17** *Mr Clean: Lars Riebartsch AD; Tattoos: Åsk Wäppling & David Bell ADs* **26-27** *Lassa: Ali Bati AD; Oreo: Gints Bruveris & Larry Ioannou ADs; Aeroxon: Gerrit Henschel AD* **28-29** *Amtrak: Sissy Estes AD; F Studies: John Leung, City College of New York* **30-31** *Dewar's: Whit Friese & Steve Haack ADs; Playground: Christie Birsa AD; Underwear: Goldsmith/Jeffrey AD; Redbook: Irwin Goldberg AD; Pepe's: Mike Rylander AD* **32-33** *Lead Out: Herb Lubalin AD; Air Canada: D.J. Parnell AD; Organ Donor: Bob Marberry AD* **34-35** *Hot Dogs: Graham Lee AD; Pepsi: Christina Yu AD* **36-37** *Redbook: M. Pennette AD; Bic Marker: Nick Hine AD* **38-39** *Siré: José Luis Pintos AD* **40-41** *Sic Glasses: D. Bighi AD; Alvin Ailey Dance: Oberlander Group AD* **42-43** *Stomil-Olsztyn: Raymond Knox AD; Timberland: Dennis D'Amico AD* **44-45** *Il Giorno: Savignac AD; Crime: Gary Alfredson AD; Lexus: John Figone AD; Time Warner: Stefan Geissbuhler AD; Vinopolis: Mary Lewis AD* **48-49** *Steele Technologies: Doug Pederson AD; Levitra: Virgilio Neves & Tatiana Voivodic ADs* **50-51** *MDCCX: Joseph Friderich Gleditsch; Warner Bros: Aziz Cami AD; McCalls: Howard Stabin AD; Bull: Urs Frick & Victor Gómez ADs* **54-55** *Sopranos: Frank Anselmo, Jayson Atienza & Chris Maiorino ADs; Reebok: Simon Morris & Geoff Smith ADs; Quaker State: Ralph Jeanes AD* **56-57** *Quarantine: Markham Cronin AD* **62-63** *Dove: Britta Adaschkiewitz AD; Video: Cosmic Barcelona AD; fnac: Bernard Guillon AD; Nagano-Wagner: Volkmar Weiß AD* **64-65** *El Mundo: Rodrigo Sanchez AD; Dos Equis: Andrew Golomb AD; Target spread: Target AD; Hen Shoes: Jolyon Finch AD; Nylon magazine: Lena Kutsovskaya AD; Canned Wine: Richard Walker AD; Mo Better: Gilberto Mejia AD; Shop Composition: Ian Coyle AD; Independent Magazine: Vince Frost AD; Condé Nast Traveler: Kerry Robertson AD; LaSalle Bank: Bryan Dixon AD; MoMA/Whitney: Warren Corbitt, Lee Misenheimer, & Matt Owens ADs* **66-67** *Art Affranchise: Tien Kuei Huang AD; London Buses: Neil Dawson AD; Afasia: Cosmic Barcelona AD; VW 0-60: Lance Paull AD; Financial Times: Pedro Sydow AD; Loterj: Cláudio Gatão & Carlos André Eyer ADs* **68-69** *Humalog: Ken DeLor AD* **72-73** *DR TV: Per Mollerup; Novell: Logo designed by Frankfurt Balkind, Brochure developed by Hornall Anderson; Coke Can: Primo Angelli AD* **74-75** *Emphysema: Asher & Partners AD* **76-77** *Rheingold: Powell/New York; Snow Car: Dana Wirz AD* **78-79** *Ridazin: H.J. Rau AD; UN: Rich Buceta AD; 1928 Russian Poster: V. & G. Stenberg ADs; 1954 NH Logo: Herbert Matter AD; All: Amee Shah AD; Drink & Drive: Thierry Verbeek AD; Saccaro: João Pedro Vargas AD* **80-81** *Michelle Amini, Ines Atienza, Un Jeong Kim, Joanna Noh, Scott Vadas; Ribo Azumaya, Jonathan Fouabi, Ju Hyun Lee, Samantha Li, Christina Lopez, Kathy Urvalek; Ines Atienza, Ingrid Carozzi, Un Jeong Kim, Jeff Kurtz, Caroline Mitchell, Joanna Noh, Scott Vadas, Lauren Wickware, Junzo Yambe at Parsons School of Design; FT Magazine: Javier Talavera & Ednaldo Fernandes ADs; Apple: Marten Tonnis AD; Necchi: F. Grignani AD* **82-83** *Russian Cigarettes: From the collection of Maria Shkolnik; Ouch: Tom Ewart AD; Bank: Hans Tanner AD; Calf: Samporn Laokittichoke AD; Chart: Bill Sweeney AD; Karriere: David Mously & Christian Bobst ADs; Mule: Toby Talbot & Steve Hough ADs* **84-85** *Schubert/Abend: H. Buschfeld, S. Himmer, W. Holtz, H. Lippert ADs; BBQ: P. Scott Flemming AD; Bank of The Manhattan: Howard Wilcox AD; LL Bean: Greg Bokor AD* **86-87** *Xs: Brett Gerstenblatt AD; Languages: Andreas Leithäuser AD; Clarica: Craig Brownrigg AD; Poster: Green & K. O'Connor ADs; DIY: Thomas Kerk AD; Fiat: George Travelini AD; Cuba: Esteban Seyler AD; Masterfile: Diti Katona & John Pylypczak ADs* **88-89** *Isuzu: David Page AD; Rams: Luke Partridge AD; Yamaha Guitar: Ivan Horvath AD; Honda: Gary Yoshida AD* **90-91** *Cinequest: Mr Rick Tharp AD; Crocodile Poster: From the collection of Maria Shkolnik; Neocid: I.U. Pippa AD; Asics: Anna-Clea Skoluda & Danny Baarz ADs; Boxes: Sanjay Sure AD; Elektronik: Erhard Löblein AD* **92-93** *Alexander M. Rodchenko & Vladimir V. Mayakovskii, 1923: From the collection of Maria Shkolnik; Reptile Kingdom: John Boone AD; Tacoma: Steven Rudasics AD* **94-95** *The News: Worth Briggs AD; Merrydown: Dave Dye AD;* Apple teacher: Tony Kerr AD; Smirnoff: *Hershel Bramson AD; Pfanni: Julia Ziegler & Goetz Ulmer ADs; Olé:* Harald Winter AD; 1924 Underground: *Verney L. Danvers AD; Golf: Kjetill Nyboe AD; Bike Wheel: Tom Ewart AD* **96-97** *Noritsu: Yvonne Smith AD; Bailey's: Patrik Rohner & Tabea Guhl ADs; Nike: John Norman AD; Trombone: Yves Loffredo AD; Ants/Cake: Claudio Bortolotti AD; 1941 Air Corps Poster: Joseph Binder; Oreos: Dwee-Ling Ng & Thomas Yang ADs; Bee: Tiago Valadão AD; Matchbox: Joachim Silber AD* **98-99** *Vladimir A. Taburin: From the collection of Maria Shkolnik* **100-101** *Salon Platinum: Gordon Chislett AD; Globus petfood store: Christian Mommertz AD* **102-103** *Gulf: Roger Mader AD; Saab: Barry Vetere & Ron Arnold ADs* **104-105** *Stomach Pain: Kevin Dickerson AD; BMW from above: Bill Schwab AD; Shaver: FHK Henrion AD* **106-107** *BITE98: Why Not Associates; Miliken Carpets: Joel Nendel AD; Brasil Doorknobs: Giba Trindade AD; German Machinist: Graphicteam, AD* **108-109** *Ford: Rob Brünig & Martin Nigl ADs; Pay Car: C.P. Helck AD; Carolina Boots: Russ Shuler AD; Cigarette TVC: Marcelo Pires & Marcelo Nepomuceno ADs; Sawing man: Vladimir V. Lebedev: From the collection of Maria Shkolnick; Puma car: Cassio Moron AD; 1950 Cristal beer: Luis López AD* **110-111** *Samsonite: Arjan van Woensel & Ferry van Tongeren ADs; Barilla: G. Conti AD; Sudler & Hennessey: Herb Lubalin AD; Bianco: Sepo AD* **112-113** *Boker knives: Everett F. Boykin AD; 1955 WOR: Arnold Roston AD; 1955 AA: Suren Ermoyen* **114-115** *Lou Reed: Stefan Sagmeister AD; Bergdorf: Reba Sochis AD; Performer Magazine: Kevin Daley AD* **116-117** *Dangling Phone: Amee Shah AD; Pine Trees: H.J. Rau, AD; Demolition: Neil White AD; Windsor Canadian: Tom Lichtenheld AD* **118-119** *Ill-Hospitals: Peter Andress AD; Bardahl Oil: Raul Cruz Lima AD; Amnesty: Ralph Prins AD; Cancer: Jelly Helm AD; WLW: Lawrence Zink AD* **120-121** *1963 Alfieri & Lacroix: Franco Grignani AD; 1961 Cinzano: Pierre Monnerat AD; Special K: Marianne Besch AD; Bed: CP&B AD; Guiness: Huw Williams AD; Joyco: John McConnell* **122-123** *1977 Guggenheim: Ivan Chermayeff AD; Rapala: Frank Haggerty AD; Caviar: Andrei N. Logvin: From the collection of Maria Shkolnick; 1952 K: Richard Roth AD; Van Nelle coffee: Jacques Jongert AD; Village Voice: Nick Cohen AD* **124-125** *Flag: João Roque AD; Toyota Banner: Susan Dearn AD; Bisley: James cé Cruickshank AD; Bow Wow: James Hendry AD; Land Mines: William Hammond & Hylton Mann ADs; Red Cross/JW Robinson: Jeff Wilks AD; Olivetti MIAC: F. Bassi AD; Olivetti Graphika Typewriter: G. Pintori AD; Einstein: Stefan Sagmeister & Joel Cuyler ADs; Nike: Bill Karow & Jayanta Jenkins ADs* **126-127** *Milk Bones: Daniela Montanez AD; Doctores w/o Borders: Vanesa Sanz AD; VW Concert Hall: Tim Vaccarino AD; MS: Colin Jones AD* **130-131** *Cash: Rob Sweetman AD; Swedish Newspaper: Steffan Forsman AD; Silhouettes: Benny Jiang AD; Four Seasons: Karen Costello, AD; McDonald's: Brian Shembeda AD; Noxema: Darryl Vasilinda AD; Blood: R. Copping & M.-Z. Liyu ADs; Blick: Roland Scotoni AD; Bab-o: Paul Rand; Modern Marvels: Graham Clifford* **132-133** *Apple iPod: Susan Alinsangan AD on all; Target: Dave Peterson AD for all; John Hancock: Jamie Mambro AD; Northgate Mall: Paul Renner AD; 1954 Look Magazine: Allan Hurlburt AD* **134-135** *VW: Andrew Fraser AD; Children/Guns: Erich Pfeifer AD; Coldene: George Lois AD; Motel 6: Jim Baldwin AD; Brasil Phone: T. Figueiredo, F. Legname & H.T. Correa ADs; Vote: Al Christensen AD; Coffee Mug: Brian Harrod AD; Toyota: Flavio Kampah AD* **136-137** *Darfur: Shelly Bevilaqua, Gemma Mitchell, & Alice Ann Wilson ADs; Blind: PJ Pereira, E. Martins & E. Veelo ADs; Saturn: Milena Sadee AD; Mercedes Interactive: A. Scholz & M. Volkmer ADs* **138-139** *Highway Laundry: T. Granger & S. Barclay ADs; Target Lamps: Dave Peterson, AD; Soccer Shoes: Birgit Hogrefe AD* **142-143** *Hands: Photo by National Geographic: Carsten Peter; Zapotec: Photo by Professor Boris Beltrán* **156-157** *Cyrillic: I. Keleynikov; I. Gordon; K. Sirotin; I. Gordon; Y. Gordon* **158-159** *Fish: Laboratorivm; Elvis: Mike Sheen & John Heinsma ADs* **160-161** *Coffee: Ashley Caballes AD; Falling Letters: Albrecht Ad AD; Ccccold: Robert MaHarry AD* **162-163** *Flag/Snakes: Peter Bradford AD; 02 Pause: Coup, The Netherlands AD; Folk: Intro AD; Heart: Philippe Apeloig AD; Tonnage Don Eggensteiner AD; Basel: UNA, Amsterdam AD; Truth: Theo Dimson AD* **166-167** *Detailing photo: Roger C. Parker; See Britain: Eric Cumberbatch* **168-169** *Faucet: Vito Tassone, Keely Hackett, Simon Hakim ADs; Gorgeous Ampersand: Ed Benguiat AD; Scars: Paul Hirsch AD; Mobil: Alan Peckolick AD* **170-171** *Texaco: Anspach Grossman Portugal, Inc.; Trout Bum: Brian Deaver, AD; 1956 Addo-X: Ladislav Sutnar AD; Chupa Chups: Peter Hibberd AD; Infiniti: Craig Shibley AD; Elten Boots: Boris Aue AD* **172-173** *Atlas MTB: Tito AD; MoMA Oxford: Kit Hinrichs; Zurich: Laura Roble at Parsons School of Design; Bank of America: Bob Guidi & John Hubley ADs* **176-177** *L'Aiglon: Peter Hirsch AD; Pavesi: Erberto Carboni AD; Fishing Tackle: Scott Schmehl AD; Slaughter: Isabela Ferreira AD; Rotterdam & GISO: Willem Hendrik Gispen AD; Child abuse: John Fisher AD; Cell Phone: Jim Clark AD; Ironman Wetsuits: Mark Sorensen AD; Savin copier: Bob Glynn AD* **178-179** *Yellow Pages: Cassio Moron AD; Swift's Bacon: James Sherman AD; 1947 Woodcarver: Viktor B. Koretskii: From the collection of Maria Shkolnick; Apple: Lucie Pardo AD; Champagne: Marcello Serpa, AD; Studies: 1 Romy Cordero; 2 Haroon Baig; 3 Yusef Joseph; 4 Philip Sheridan; 5 Maria Karantzalis, all at City College of New York* **180-181** *Reddi-Wip: Mortimer Leach artist; Amtrak: Greg Braun AD; 1910 Odessa Poster: Y. Ponomarenko: From the collection of Maria Shkolnick.; 1965 Querschnitt: Hermann Otto AD; 1936 Tea: Edward McKnight Kauffe AD* **182-183** *Nike: Storm Tharp AD; Moonpie: Michael Cohen AD* **184-185** *New Yorker: Rich Silverstein AD; Cleavage: Ian Grais AD; Dunlop: Jay Furby AD; Time Magazine: Bob Barrie AD; Cheese: Phil Clarke AD; Apollo-Optik: Michael Steeger AD* **186-187** *DHL: David Mously AD; Global Alliance for Preserving The History of WWII in Asia: Eric Yeo AD; Louis Boston: Cheryl Heller AD* **188-189** *Oakland As: Stefan Copiz & Steve Yee ADs; Heineken Brazil: Danny Baarz AD; Citi: Harvey Marco AD* **190-191** *Finn: Guto Kono AD; Holiday Inn Express: Scott O'Leary AD; Western Union: Prasanna Sankhe AD; International Truck: Dan Bryant AD; VW billboard: K. Dailor, A. Ellis, & D. Shelford ADs; Land Rover: Andy Vasey AD* **192-193** *Fish art by Jan V. White; Library of Congress: Tim Ryan & Kerry Koritsas ADs; 1955 Achromycin: Leonard Ruben AD; SW Air: Bill Schwab AD; Swiss Army Knife: Stefan Leick AD* **194-195** *Absolut: Raj Kamble AD; Car Stereo: Barney Goldberg & Elke Ditschuneit ADs; Adidas: Dave Dye AD; Yamaha Motorcycle: Houman Pirdavari AD; Lotus: Derek Birdsall AD; Light Bulbs: Chris Lange AD; Lexus: Greg Wells AD* **196-197** *Suicide: Paulo Lemos AD; 3 Animals: Luigi Del Medico AD; Jet: John Boone AD; Pronto: Franco Grignani AD; Infiniti: Duncan Bruce AD* ***My thanks to every one of you***

Dear Lilian —
always remember the power of ART DIRECTION !
If ever anyone should have the temerity to question your ideas or
reject your solutions — or even just disagree — use this as a gentle reminder

An ad agency can be an intense, ego-driven environment. Like any business, it is not always fun. Seen on an art director's wall, this illustration – with a real feather – is, perhaps, a suggestion of where the talent resides at an ad agency. Or is it a reminder to be self-confident? Or encouragement to be a little forceful? Maybe its says only that some chickens are more equal than others? I suspect that it is meant as a little of each. Neither the art director nor the artist is saying.

Allworth Press books

 Allworth Press is an imprint of Allworth Communications, Inc. Selected titles are listed below.

Thinking in Type: The Practical Philosophy of Typography by Alex W. White
(paperback, 6 x 9, 224 pages, $24.95)

The Elements of Graphic Design: Space, Unity, Page Architecture, and Type by Alex W. White
(paperback, 6⅛ x 9¼, 160 pages, $24.95)

Emotional Branding: The New Paradigm for Connecting Brands to People by Marc Gobé
(hardcover, 6¼ x 9¼, 352 pages, $24.95)

The Graphic Design Business Book by Tad Crawford
(paperback, 6 x 9, 256 pages, $24.95)

American Type Design and Designers by David Consuegra (paperback, 9 x 11, 320 pages, $35.00)

Editing by Design, Third Edition by Jan V. White
(paperback, 8½ x 11, 256 pages, $29.95)

Graphic Idea Notebook: A Treasury of Solutions to Visual Problems, Third Edition by Jan V. White
(paperback, 8½ x 11, 176 pages, $24.95)

Designing Effective Communications: Clearing Contexts for Clarity and Meaning Edited by Jorge Frascara (paperback, 6 x 9, 304 pages, $24.95)

Communication Design: Principles, Methods, and Practice by Jorge Frascara
(paperback, 6 x 9, 240 pages, $24.95)

Careers by Design: A Business Guide for Graphic Designers, Third Edition by Roz Goldfarb
(paperback, 6 x 9, 240 pages, $19.95)

Inside the Business of Graphic Design: 60 Leaders Share Their Secrets of Success by Catharine Fishel (paperback, 6 x 9, 288 pages, $19.95)

Please write to request our free catalog. To order by credit card, call 1-800-491-2808 or send a check or money order to Allworth Press, 10 East 23rd Street, Suite 510, New York, NY 10010. Include $6 for shipping and handling for the first book ordered and $1 for each additional book. Eleven dollars plus $1 for each additional book if ordering from Canada. New York State residents must add sales tax.

To see our complete catalog on the World Wide Web, or to order online, you can find us at www.allworth.com.

ADVER TISING DESIGN AND TYPO GRAPHY

ALEX W. WHITE

Little People, **BIG DREAMS**

MARTIN LUTHER KING JR.

Written by
Maria Isabel Sánchez Vegara

Illustrated by
Mai Ly Degnan

Frances Lincoln
Children's Books

Little Martin was a spiritual boy from Atlanta who came from a long line of preachers. His dad was a preacher, his uncle was a preacher, his grandfather was a preacher... maybe he'd become a great preacher, too.

One day, a friend invited him over to play.
Martin was shocked when he was asked to
leave because he was black. That day, he
realized something terrible was going on.

This terrible thing was called segregation. It meant that public places—like restaurants and buses—had separate spaces for black and white people. Martin and his friend were sent to different schools.

Martin believed that one shouldn't remain silent or accept something if it's wrong. He promised himself that when he grew up, he'd fight injustice with the most powerful weapon of all: words.

Martin studied at universities in Georgia, Pennsylvania, and Massachusetts, where he read about Mahatma Gandhi—the man who had improved the lives of millions of Indians with peaceful methods of protest.

When he finished his studies, Martin moved to Alabama and became the pastor of a church in Montgomery. Every Sunday, from his pulpit, he encouraged his congregation to speak up about things that mattered.

One evening, a woman named Rosa was arrested for
refusing to give up her seat to a white man on a bus.
Martin asked the people in his community not
to take the bus again until the law was changed.

Many citizens were inspired by Rosa's story and Martin's words. Suddenly, buses were almost empty! They stayed empty for more than a year, until segregation on Montgomery's buses finally ended.

It was the first major civil rights action in America...but not the last. Martin encouraged people all over the country to stand up for their rights and join in with peaceful protest.

They were often attacked, and Martin was arrested twenty-nine times. But he and his followers never fought back with force.

He knew that hate can't drive out hate;
only love can.

Martin helped to organize a protest march on Washington where he gave a life-changing speech. It began with four simple yet powerful words: "I have a dream."

The next year, Martin became the youngest person to win the Nobel Peace Prize. His words of hope, peace, and justice called a nation to change its laws and make them equal for everyone.

And if you listen to your heart, you can still hear little Martin asking you to keep his dream alive.

A dream of a world where we are judged by our character, not by the color of our skin.

MARTIN LUTHER KING JR.

(Born 1929 • Died 1968)

1953

1956

Martin Luther King Jr. was born "Michael" in Atlanta, Georgia, but later changed his name to Martin. Growing up in a family of pastors, Martin quickly learned to tell the difference between right and wrong. His happy childhood gave him what he later called a "strong determination for justice," and an optimism that cut through the segregated world he was born into. When he was old enough to leave home to go to college, he combined studies of religion with the teachings of Gandhi—a leading activist who chose to protest with peaceful demonstration, not violence. Martin learned from this, and discovered that his writing—and speeches—were the best ways to change people's hearts and minds. One of his first opportunities to do

1963   1965

so was as pastor of the Dexter Avenue Baptist Church in Montgomery, Alabama. There, his passionate sermons inspired a new sense of hope. At the same time, he also became the leader of the first African American non-violent demonstration, started by Rosa Parks, known as the "bus boycott." The protest lasted 382 days, and following that time, the Supreme Court of the United States declared that both black and white Americans should ride the buses as equals. Over the next ten years, Martin traveled more than six million miles, catching the attention of the world with his dream where children would "not be judged by the color of their skin but by the content of their character." Martin's dream continues to inspire us to action today.

Want to find out more about **Martin Luther King Jr.?**
Read one of these great books:

I Have a Dream by Kadir Nelson
Martin's Big Words: The Life of Martin Luther King, Jr. by Doreen Rappaport

BOARD BOOKS

COCO CHANEL	MAYA ANGELOU	FRIDA KAHLO	AMELIA EARHART	MARIE CURIE	ADA LOVELACE	ROSA PARKS
ISBN: 978-1-78603-245-4	ISBN: 978-1-78603-249-2	ISBN: 978-1-78603-247-8	ISBN: 978-1-78603-252-2	ISBN: 978-1-78603-253-9	ISBN:978-1-78603-259-1	ISBN: 978-1-78603-263-8

EMMELINE PANKHURST	AUDREY HEPBURN	ELLA FITZGERALD
ISBN: 978-1-78603-261-4	ISBN: 978-1-78603-255-3	ISBN:978-1-78603-257-7

BOX SETS

WOMEN IN ART	WOMEN IN SCIENCE

ISBN: 978-1-78603-428-1	ISBN: 978-1-78603-429-8

BOOKS & PAPER DOLLS

EMMELINE PANKHURST
ISBN: 978-1-78603-400-7

MARIE CURIE
ISBN: 978-1-78603-401-4

Collect the
Little People, **BIG DREAMS** series:

FRIDA KAHLO	COCO CHANEL	MAYA ANGELOU
		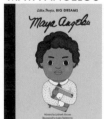
ISBN: 978-1-84780-783-0	ISBN: 978-1-84780-784-7	ISBN: 978-1-84780-889-9

AMELIA EARHART

ISBN: 978-1-84780-888-2

AGATHA CHRISTIE

ISBN: 978-1-84780-960-5

MARIE CURIE

ISBN: 978-1-84780-962-9

ROSA PARKS

ISBN: 978-1-78603-018-4

AUDREY HEPBURN

ISBN: 978-1-78603-053-5

EMMELINE PANKHURST
ISBN: 978-1-78603-020-7

ELLA FITZGERALD

ISBN: 978-1-70603-087-0

ADA LOVELACE

ISBN: 978-1-78603-076-4

JANE AUSTEN

ISBN: 978-1-78603-120-4

GEORGIA O'KEEFFE

ISBN: 978-1-78603-122-8

HARRIET TUBMAN

ISBN: 978-1-78603-227-0

ANNE FRANK
ISBN: 978-1-78603-229-4

MOTHER TERESA
ISBN: 978-1-78603-230-0

JOSEPHINE BAKER

ISBN: 978-1-78603-228-7

L. M. MONTGOMERY

ISBN: 978-1-78603-233-1

JANE GOODALL

ISBN: 978-1-78603-231-7

SIMONE DE BEAUVOIR

ISBN: 978-1-78603-232-4

MUHAMMAD ALI

ISBN: 978-1-78603-331-4

STEPHEN HAWKING

ISBN: 978-1-78603-333-8

MARIA MONTESSORI

ISBN: 978-1-78603-755-8

VIVIENNE WESTWOOD

ISBN: 978-1-78603-757-2

MAHATMA GANDHI

ISBN: 978-1-78603-787-9

DAVID BOWIE

ISBN: 978-1-78603-332-1

WILMA RUDOLPH

ISBN: 978-1-78603-751-0

DOLLY PARTON

ISBN: 978-1-78603-760-2

BRUCE LEE

ISBN: 978-0-7112-4629-4

RUDOLF NUREYEV

ISBN: 978-1-78603-791-6

ZAHA HADID

ISBN: 978-0-7112-4641-6

MARY SHELLEY

ISBN: 978-0-7112-4639-3

DAVID ATTENBOROUGH

ISBN: 978-0-7112-4564-8

Brimming with creative inspiration, how-to projects, and useful
information to enrich your everyday life, Quarto Knows is a favorite
destination for those pursuing their interests and passions. Visit our
site and dig deeper with our books into your area of interest:
Quarto Creates, Quarto Cooks, Quarto Homes, Quarto Lives,
Quarto Drives, Quarto Explores, Quarto Gifts, or Quarto Kids.

Text © 2020 Maria Isabel Sánchez Vegara. Illustrations © 2020 Mai Ly Degnan.

First Published in the USA in 2020 by Frances Lincoln Children's Books, an imprint of The Quarto Group.

400 First Avenue North, Suite 400, Minneapolis, MN 55401, USA.

T (612) 344-8100 F (612) 344-8692 www.QuartoKnows.com

First Published in Spain in 2019 under the title Pequeño & Grande Martin Luther King, Jr.

by Alba Editorial, s.l.u., Baixada de Sant Miquel, 1, 08002 Barcelona

www.albaeditorial.es

ISBN 978-0-7112-4567-9

Set in Futura BT.

Published by Katie Cotton • Designed by Karissa Santos

Edited by Rachel Williams and Katy Flint • Production by Nicolas Zeifman

Manufactured in Guangdong, China CC112019

9 7 5 3 1 2 4 6 8

Photographic acknowledgments (pages 28–29, from left to right) 1. Martin Luther King, 1953 © Michael Evans / Hulton Archive via
Getty Images 2. Martin Luther King mug shot, 1956 © Kypros via Getty 3. Martin Luther King, Jr. March on Washington, 1963 © Hulton
Deutsch via Getty 4. March from Selma to Alabama, 1965 © Stephen F. Somerstein via Getty

MIX
Paper from
responsible sources
FSC® C008047